Protestants and
American Business Methods

Studies in
American History and Culture, No. 7

Other Titles in This Series

Protestants and
American Business Methods

by
Ben Primer

RESEARCH PRESS

Text first published as a typescript facsimile in 1977

Library of Congress Cataloging in Publication Data

Primer, Ben, 1949-
    Protestants and American business methods.

    (Studies in American history and culture ; no. 7)
    Bibliography: p.
    Includes index.
    1. Protestant churches—United States—History.
2. United States—Church history. 3. Church management.
4. Bureaucracy. I. Title. II. Series.

BR517.P74 1978   280'.4'0973   78-20879
ISBN 0-8357-0982-5
ISBN 0-8357-0983-3 pbk.

FOR MOM AND DAD

PREFACE

One does not produce an opus such as this without acquiring some enormous intellectual and emotional debts. This work could not have been written without the assistance of a number of religious archives (and their staffs): the Disciples of Christ Historical Society (Marvin Williams); the Dargan-Carver Library of the Baptist Sunday School Board (Mrs. G. Kearnie Keegan); the Episcopal Archives (V. Nelle Bellamy and Elinor S. Hearn); the Lovely Lane Museum in Baltimore (Edwin Schell); the Commission on Archives and History of the United Methodist Church (William C. Beal, Jr.); and the Central Records Division of the Board of Global Ministries, United Methodist Church (Carolyn Pelletier). In addition, the able librarians at the Enoch Pratt in Baltimore, the Alderman at the University of Virginia, the Library of Congress and the Milton S. Eisenhower Library at Johns Hopkins (Interlibrary Loan Department in particular) have assisted me in acquiring various obscure religious journals and tracts.

My friends and colleagues in the Department of History at Johns Hopkins have made my years here ones of intellectual challenge and growth. I was especially sustained by the enjoyment I received from two years of service to the department as a teaching assistant. William L. Freehling in particular provided a model for my own understanding of how survey courses should be conducted. Timothy L. Smith and his students (especially Arunas Alisauskas, Tom Jacklin and Joel Carpenter) offered advice on the parts of this dissertation relating to American religious history. Professor Smith constantly (almost exasperatingly) suggested alternative ways of looking at this subject, thereby improving it. In addition, he provided encouragement to continue my work at the doctorate at a critical point in my first years at Hopkins. No seminar at Hopkins is more creative than that run by Louis Galambos. His students learn from the master the dedication to constructive criticism of each other's work. I am especially grateful to those in that seminar who suffered through early drafts of this work and by doing so made it better: Alan Anderson; Jim Duffy; Bob Collins; Steve Medley; Joe Pratt; Steve Sass; Bill Roberts; Bob Garnet; Naomi Lamoreaux; Terry Rockefeller; Andy Bartels; Chris Tomlins.

A number of friends have sustained me in times of personal crisis in these years. My three roommates—John Caldwell, Steve Medley and Wayne Shandera—have suffered through dining tables piled high with books. The fellowship of Woodbrook Baptist Church and of the Baptist Student Union of Maryland (especially its choir) have made life more enjoyable. Mike Alliston, John Roberts and Bob Horner have listened long hours in times of depression. Terry Thomas, my next roommate, has inspired me to complete this work and helped me with its typing. For her love I am grateful.

Finally, I could not begin to thank Louis Galambos for the many hours he has sweated over my turgid prose in order to produce a work that would be understandable to the reader. He is a marvelous teacher—always available and intellectually stimulating. He has been generous in his praise and enjoyable for his ready wit.

CONTENTS

CHAPTER 1

INTRODUCTION

In 1876 the Disciples of Christ supported three independent missionary societies. Each was located in a different city, and only one had a full-time administrator. Together they spent less than $20,000 annually to maintain a small number of missionaries at home and abroad. A half-century later startling changes had occurred in both the dimension and the meaning of this enterprise. This American Church had created a United Christian Missionary Society. Work was now organized into four divisions which were further divided into various departments. More than one hundred "experts" and "office workers" were needed to direct the expenditure of a two million dollar budget. The total number of missionaries was larger than ever, but the Society's program now included such new functions as Christian education, social service and promotion.

This metamorphosis in the Disciple's organization was in turn part of a broader process evident in all mainline Protesant denominations in the United States during these same years—a process I have termed the bureaucratization of the Church. In this book I explore two major questions relating to these organizational developments. First, I examine the causes and nature of bureaucratization in American Protestantism. As a study of the process of organizational change, this work is tied closely to what one historian has called "The Emerging Organizational Synthesis in Modern American History."[1] A second line of inquiry focuses on the effects of these bureaucratic innovations upon the role of the Church in the twentieth century. By linking these two aspects of the story of American Protestantism, I hope to suggest a new context and explanation—one largely overlooked by most students of American religious history—for some of the most important aspects in the changing pattern of modern religion.

Nearly sixty years ago Max Weber first advanced an explicit *Theory of Social and Economic Organization*[2] which defined the bureaucratic structure of authority. Weber described a variety of characteristics exhibited by bureaucratic organizations, but all of these characteristics can be grouped into four basic areas.[3] Above all, bureaucratic organizations are distinguished by their "belief in the 'legality' of patterns of normative rules."[4] Administrative decisions and rules are rationally formulated and then recorded in writing. "Systematic division of labour"[5] and its concomitant specialization constitute a second dimension of bureaucracy. Expertise is important, and the individual's office normally constitutes a professional career. Weber delineates as a third quality of this type of organiation "the principle of hierarchy"[6] or chain of command. The organization is departmentalized, with lower divisions under the control and supervision of higher ones. Bureaucracy tends to promote centralization; power is centered at the top of the hierarchy. Finally, as a result of the first three elements, a "spirit of formalistic impersonality"[7] pervades bureaucratic organization. The system of rules and hierarchical authority that prevents arbitrariness also promotes formality of relationships.

Since World War II sociologists and economists have used these elements of Weber's theoretical framework, with certain adjustments, to describe many contemporary organizations and their problems.[8] More recently historians have begun to study the roots of these organizational developments as a way of grasping the essential meaning of America's twentieth-century experience. Basically, these organizational historians argue that the scope and scale of organization changed dramatically in the years after about 1880. The most significant economic, political and professional organizations of the new century were larger in size than their nineteenth-century predecessors. These modern organizations focused primarily on national rather than local or regional concerns. They developed all the characteristics of bureaucratic authority that Weber had delineated. In addition, these large national organizations increasingly came to define the problems of society and then to determine the solutions through their control of available resources and expertise. Bureaucratization was as much a process as a result, and as organizations sought to control their internal and external environments, they continually influenced other institutions and the lives of millions of Americans.

The historian's recognition of the importance of bureaucracy in modern America was first apparent in studies written in the 1950s which detailed the fascination of Progressive reformers with organization. Richard Hofstadter devoted a chapter of his *Age of Reform*[9] to organization-building by the Progressives, although much of his analysis described the ambivalence many reformers felt toward their own creations. For Samuel P. Hays, Jr., organization, at least in the economic sphere, became a precondition for existence in the modern world. Business corporations, merchandisers, farmers and laborers all discoverd that they must "Organize or Perish."[10] Studies of the various aspects of Progressivism written since these early syntheses have stressed the shift from personal relationships among individuals to formal, well-organized relationships in groups—a shift resulting from the struggle for power.[11]

Robert Wiebe's *The Search for Order, 1877-1920*[12] was the first major attempt to understand the entire course of American history around the turn of the century in terms of a revolutionary shift in American values from those of the small town to those of an urban, bureaucratically-minded middle-class. During these years, Wiebe argues, the impersonal forces generated by industrialization and urbanization resulted in a "distended society." Small-town customs and values and community-oriented institutions could no longer cope with the expanding world around them; dislocation and bewilderment resulted. For a time movements ranging from Populism to Prohibition sought to turn back the clock in an effort to preserve the old order of community control. At the same time, however, another set of Americans, a middle-class with professional aspirations and special skills, began to view the new conditions as avenues for advancement. Professional organizations extending beyond the local level proliferated and an optimistic middle-class began to advocate new bureaucratic values. Scientific and technological images dominated the new ideology. Efficiency and system, businesslike methods, scientific management and supposedly far-seeing experts defined a new world order that stressed man's ability to understand his universe empirically. Progressivism, in Wiebe's terms, may be seen as an attempt through political bureaucracies to impose order and system on America, first at the local and then at the state and national levels.

More recently Wiebe has qualified his earlier work in certain ways.[13] Concentrating on the "enduring qualities of American society," he sees a continuing history of segmentation in American life. In the nineteenth century, Americans had been compartmentalized along geographical and cultural lines; in the twentieth century Americans were largely segmented into a network defined by economic function (occupation). Wiebe seems less certain, however, about the pace and timing of the transition between the two networks. The rise of bureaucratic values is a tendency, not the revolution he had earlier described. Wiebe is also more aware of the divisions within the new order due to functional segmentation. Moreover, he argues for the persistence of the older geographical network, although in a weakened state, in influencing the lives of many Americans.

What historians such as Wiebe have been saying about the United States at the turn of the century seems to be bolstered by my study of Church organization. As we shall see, bureaucratization of the sort suggested by Weber's typology was very much a part of mainline Protestant development in these years. A word of caution is needed at this point, however. One must realize that religious organizations are not exactly comparable to business enterprises, government agencies or labor unions. We must be careful to distinguish, as Amitai Etzioni has counseled, between normative and utilitarian organizations.[14] The normative organization (the Church, for instance) relies on moral commitment and manipulation of symbolic rewards and punishments for maintenance of its structures and values. Utilitarian organizations (business and to an extent labor) rely on calculative commitments and material rewards. Churches simply do not—indeed cannot—function exactly as business corporations do. The voluntary nature of American religion[15] places certain constraints on religious bureaucracies, constraints that Churches share with many other voluntary bureaucracies.

Because the Church differs from economic organizations it offers a particularly fruitful subject for research—one which should provide some refinements for the organizational synthesis. As a traditional institution, the Church should indicate the degree of persistence of the older geographical network. Wiebe's suggestion that bureaucratic values were adopted because they helped to restore order also merits attention. Religious leaders seem to have pursued bureaucracy for its "modernity" as much as for its ability to provide coordination and control. Religious leaders were quite fearful of falling behind the times. There are, I think, elements of what Hofstadter termed "status anxiety" in the motivations of the religious organizers. The Church bureaucrats sought reassurance by doing that which was current. Whether they actually imbibed the bureaucratic ethos and goals, or simply acted out of a sense of conformity to the cult of efficiency, is uncertain. But it is evident that they had clear doubts—probably stronger than those of business leaders—about the effects of organization on the future of the Protestant Church. Religious leaders nevertheless overcame those doubts and sought to strengthen the Church through reorganization.

If, as I have been contending, the adoption of bureaucratic means and values was one of the most important trends in American religion at the turn of the century, why then have students of religious history largely ignored this development? Admittedly certain historians have expressed an awareness of the Church's fascination with organization. Denominational historians, usually insiders, have regularly described in considerable detail the growth of their own bureaucratic structures in these years. Unfortunately their denominational focus has caused them to overlook the existence of this pattern throughout Protestantism. Among professionally trained historians, William Warren Sweet, the father of American religious history, long ago noted the rising "emphasis on efficiency, system and organization" within the Church between the Civil War and World War I.[16] A "steady secularization" of the Church which "borrowed the techniques of big business" was apparent to Henry Steele Commager.[17] None of these histories provide a clear picture of the course or timing of these trends, however. A few authors inspired by the sociology of religion[18] or by business history[19] have speculated on the nature of bureaucratic organization in the Church. One impressive monograph by Paul M. Harrison has thoroughly investigated the bureaucratic system of the American Baptist Convention.[20]　At best, however, these studies have merely been suggestive and have had primarily a contemporary (not an historical) orientation. The focus of American religious history has been directed elsewhere.

The question that has served as the organizing framework for most religious historians has been how the Church responded to certain intellectual and social developments around the turn of the century. Arthur M. Schlesinger, Sr., fleshed out the details of the answer to this question more than forty years ago in his seminal essay on "A Critical Period in American Protestantism, 1875-1900."[21] Schlesinger argues that late nineteenth-century religion faced serious challenges from a rapidly changing social and intellectual environment. The bedrock of Biblical authority was weathered by the blasts of modern science, particularly biology and geology. Old understandings of Scripture were undermined by "higher criticism" and the "new theology." The study of comparative religion challenged the uniqueness of the Christian message. Explorations into the sociology and psychology of religion raised doubts about transcendence. To these intellectual problems were added more concrete ones. The nation's cities seemed to be imperiled by moral decline, governmental corruption, alien illiteracy and papist propaganda. Industrial unrest threatened to divide Americans into two different classes.

The response of the Church to the problems of the "critical period" was varied. In general, however, historians have categorized the responses into what Martin E. Marty has called "The Two-Party System."[22] The crisis of the late nineteenth century, Marty argues, divided American Protestantism into two camps. One party, which Marty labels "Private Protestantism," is generally characterized as evangelical. These Protestants continued to emphasize individual salvation and personal morality. Most of the adherents subscribed to what may be termed orthodox theology. The Christian's duty was to convert others because the fulfillment of God's kingdom was in the life everlasting; most aspects of the reform-oriented Social Gospel were rejected by these Churchmen and women. Historically this party has been the more appealing to middle-class Protestants in that it usually has accepted the given social order. Its main solution to the perplexities of the "critical period" was to ignore them on the grounds that they were irrelevant to the central task of reconciling men to God. Other manifestations of Private Protestantism included Fundamentalism, Prohibitionism, and a continued stress on revivalism.[23]

The other party Marty calls "Public Protestantism." This sector of the Church accentuated the social dimensions of the Christian gospel. Many of its members accepted the tenets of the "new theology."[24] Strongholds of Public Protestantism have usually been the seminaries and certain urban Churches. Its partisans realized that there were institutional as well as individual reasons for mankind's plight. Christians were to work to bring the Kingdom of God to earth through the efforts for political reform, church union and pacifism that comprised the Social Gospel.

This historical framework has served to organize most of the surveys of American Protestantism dealing with this period. Its strengths are simplicity and generalization. There are, however, some obvious weaknesses in this approach. One has been the tendency of scholars working in this context to concentrate almost wholly on the Social Gospel and the new theology. Perhaps this bias stems from the fact that religious historians themselves often have had strong links to Public Protestantism. They thus find the movements associated with Public Protestantism interesting and are desirous of showing the progressive elements in our religious heritage. They have felt that religion somehow must be linked to liberal or useful causes. Henry F. May, for instance, argues for the relevance of religion by saying that "Christian doctrine had given American progressivism authority, power and a link with tradition."[25] The net effect of the emphasis on Public Protestantism has been a bias toward intellectual and political history. Perhaps the very nature of religion, with its explicit ideological elements, has forced such an approach. After all, the Social Gospel was largely a creation of the mind; May is aware of its "neglect of machinery."[26] It is thus understandable that in studying the Social Gospel and the new theology, historians have largely ignored institutions. More disconcerting, however, is the fact that this framework has caused them to slight the greater body of American religion; as Marty observes, the Social Gospel movement "remained a minority voice in the denominations."[27]

Most religious historians seem nevertheless to be wedded to a progressive interpretation of American history. Marty's division of the Church into two camps is indicative of the continuing power of the progressive framework. One tendency of this approach has been to picture the significant elements of our religious heritage as those which are in tension with the surrounding culture. Whenever religion exhibits elements of conformity to the culture around it, the religious historian of this ilk promptly deduces another era of "complacency."[28]

Yet to respond to a changing culture in ways other than those of Public Protestantism is not to give in to complacency. The twentieth-century Church was, as Stow Persons has written, more than "a religious community at bay before a secular culture with which it was unwilling or unable to come to grips."[29] There is a real need for religious history to discover those elements which American Protestants had in common—both with themselves and with the culture around them. Religious leaders, irrespective of polity or theology, geography or constituency, sought through bureaucratic values to remain a part of contemporary culture. They attempted to solve real problems through new forms of organization. All mainline Churches faced problems resulting from numerical, financial and programatic expansion. Bureaucracy was thus often a specific and new means to achieve general and traditional goals.

The traditional synthesis has not focused on these changes and has, as a result, been unable to explain many important long-term trends in the development of American Protestantism. The nature of the mid-twentieth-century Church is not to be found in Social Gospel ideology. Martin E. Marty frankly admits the weaknesses of the traditional approach:

> Were the common people, those who did not get elected to attend church conventions and those who did not read theological journals, all lining up on one side or the other of liberal-conservative party lines?
>
> To pose the question is to imply the answer. No, much religious activity goes on, as it were, in a private place, a personal sphere, far removed from the public realms which interest historians.[30]

Somehow we must find ways to identify those forces that did affect the average Churchman. The organizational context seems an especially fruitful means to that end.

To argue that the ideological focus of much of religious history has been misplaced is not to argue, however, against the role of ideas. Those who reshaped the institutional framework of the denominations were simply intellectuals of another sort. The key to understanding their importance is an awareness of the central place organizations have played in shaping the lives of modern Americans. Institutions are created by men and women with specific goals in mind, but the organizations in turn mould ideas and values; modern institutions reach Marty's "common people" in ways that complex ideologies alone never could. The fact that "independent," local Southern Baptist churches all promote the same stewardship emphasis on the same Sunday using the theme music, posters, bulletins, pledge cards and literature provided by the central organization is, I think, indicative of the need to study the origins of religious bureaucracy.

The merits of the "organizational synthesis" as another way of understanding the changes in the Church from 1876 to 1929 have been demonstrated in the sociological analysis of Peter L. Berger.[31] Berger's work focuses on the secularization of contemporary religion, but it has historical applications. Berger defines secularization as the progressive lessening of the place of religious institutions, symbols and theodicies in defining the various sectors of society and culture. The roots of this process, according to Berger, lay in the rise of modern industrial capitalism to its place of dominance in Western culture. Religious legitimation became unnecessary for governing, for educating, and for many other social activities.

Berger maintains that Churches have succeeded in preserving their importance in our society "only by becoming highly secularized themselves."[32] Secularization is manifested at two basic levels: "structural," defined as the "establishment of highly rational bureaucracies;" and "ideological," seen as the "maintenance of legitimations that are adequate for such bureaucracies."[33] In my own study, I will look primarily at secularization on the structural level, a development which seems to precede the sort of legitimation Berger describes. In part, my emphasis stems from my own lack of formal theological training, but it also is a product of my resesarch; in the period I have studied I found few links betwen the reigning theological ideas and the new institutions that were being erected. Only when severely challenged did the religious bureaucrats seek explicitly theological legitimation, a fact which may in itself indicate the extent of secularization. More often the tendency was simply to follow business in citing the economy and efficiency which the new methods afforded. Thus theology plays a minor role in my dissertation; following Berger, I would argue that the decisive variable in contemporary American religion is not a Church's polity or theology, but rather its degree of bureaucratization.[34]

By taking this position I do not mean to suggest that religion has ceased to play a major role in the lives of many individuals. As a corollary of secularizaton, Berger sees an increasing individualized or privatized religion, distinct from the institutionalized one that sought to define reality for the whole of society. In his terms, "religion manifests itself as public rhetoric and private virtue. In other words, insofar as religion is common it lacks 'reality,' and insofar as it is 'real,' it lacks commonality."[35] This seems to me an accurate statement of the current situation, and I hope to achieve a better understanding of one important reason why this has happened.

Berger did not search for the roots of the "religious establishment" that he described. In this book I hope to show how modern religious organization became what it is. In Chapters 2 and 3 I look at the nature of Church organization before 1876. I trace developments in the period from 1876 to 1910—crucial changes which impelled the Church toward bureaucracy—in the next two chapters (4 and 5). In the final chapters (6-8) I consider the nature and the effect of the resulting changes in Church structure in the years from 1910 to 1929. A short Epilog suggests conclusions related to issues raised in this introduction.

NOTES

[1]Louis Galambos, *Business History Review*, 44 (Autumn 1970), 279-90. Galambos prefers the term "organizational" to "bureaucratic" because the latter has pejorative connotations. Perhaps for the same reason I have elected to use bureaucratization. At best I view bureaucratization as a necessary evil, at worst the most evident symptom of the secularization that has destroyed the Church's power to provide meaning and purpose in our world. There are several other formulations of the "organizational synthesis." See Robert Cuff, "American Historians and the 'Organizational Factor'," *Canadian Review of American Studies*, 4 (Spring 1973), 19-31; Samuel P. Hays, "Introduction: The New Organizational Society," *Building the Organizational Society: Essays on Associational Activities in Modern America*, ed. Jerry Israel (New York: Free Press, 1972); and Tom G. Hall, "Agricultural History and the 'Organizational Synthesis': A Review Essay," *Agricultural History*, 48 (April 1974), 313-25.

[2](New York: Oxford University Press, 1947).

[3]Peter M. Blau, *Bureaucracy in Modern Society* (New York: Random House, 1956), pp. 27-43.

[4]Weber, *Theory of Social and Economic Organization*, p. 328.

[5]*Ibid.*, p. 330.

[6]*Ibid.*, p. 331.

[7]*Ibid.*, p. 340.

[8]For example see Blau, *Bureaucracy in Modern Society;* Peter M. Blau and William G. Scott, *Formal Organizations: A Comparative Approach* (San Francisco: Chandler, 1962); William H. Whyte, Jr., *The Organization Man* (Garden City, N.Y.: Doubleday, 1956); C. Wright Mills, *White Collar: The American Middle Classes* (New York: Oxford University Press, 1956); and John Kenneth Galbraith, *American Capitalism: The Concept of Countervailing Power* (Boston: Houghton-Mifflin, 1952).

[9](New York: Vintage, 1955), pp. 215-71.

[10]*The Response to Industrialism, 1885-1914* (Chicago: University of Chicago Press, 1957), Chapter 3, pp. 48-70.

[11]For example see Samuel P. Hays, Jr., *Conservation and the Gospel of Efficiency: The Progressive Conservation Movement, 1890-1920* (Cambridge: Harvard University Press, 1959); Samuel Haber, *Efficiency and Uplift: Scientific Management in the Progressive Era, 1890-1920* (Chicago: University of Chicago Press, 1964); Gerald N. Grob, *Workers and Utopia: A Study of the Ideological Conflicts in the American Labor Movement, 1865-1900* (Evanston, Illinois: Northwestern University Press, 1961); Roy Lubove, *The Professional Altruist: The Emergence of Social Work as a Career, 1880-1930* (Cambridge: Harvard Univesity Press, 1965); and Robert M. Wiebe, *Businessmen and Reform: A Study of the Progressive Movement* (Cambridge: Harvard University Press, 1962). Two impressive collections of essays have also stressed this theme. See

also *Building the Organizational Society*, ed. Israel and *The Emergent American Society: Large-Scale Organization*, ed. W. Lloyd Warner (New Haven: Yale University Press, 1967).

[12](New York: Hill and Wang, 1967).

[13]*The Segmented Society: An Introduction to the Meaning of America* (New York: Oxford University Press, 1975), especially pp. 64-65, 116-23, 130-37 and 179-82. A very similar analysis is suggested by John Higham, "Hanging Together: Divergent Unities in American History," *Journal of American History*, 61 (June 1974), 5-28.

[14]*A Comparative Analysis of Complex Organizations* (New York: The Free Press, 1961), pp. 3-67. See also Chester I. Barnard, *The Functions of the Executive* (Cambridge: Harvard University Press, 1938), pp. 139-60.

[15]See Winthrop Hudson, *The Great Tradition of the American Churches* (New York: Harper and Row, 1953), pp. 27-41 and Sidney Mead, *The Lively Experiment: The Shaping of Christianity in America* (New York: Harper and Row, 1963), pp. 113-15.

[16]*The Story of Religion in America* (New York: Harper, 1939), p. 500.

[17]*The American Mind: An Interpretation of American Thought and Character Since the 1880s* (New Haven: Yale University Press, 1954), p. 167. See also Hudson, *Great Tradition*, pp. 195-225; Clifton E. Olmstead, *History of Religion in the United States* (Englewood Cliffs, N.J.: Prentice Hall, 1960), p. 479; and Martin E. Marty, *Righteous Empire: The Protestant Experience in America* (New York: Dial Press, 1970), p. 175.

[18]Gibson Winter, "Religious Organizations," *The Emergent American Society*, ed. Warner, pp. 408-91 and Robert Lee, "The Organizational Dilemma in American Protestantism," *Ethics and Bigness: Scientific, Academic, Religious, Political, and Military*, ed. Harlan Cleveland and Harold D. Lasswell (New York: Conference on Science, Philosophy and Religion in their Relation to the Democratic Way of Life, 1962), pp. 187-211.

[19]William T. Doherty, "The Impact of Business on Protestantism, 1900-1929," *Business History Review*, 28 (June 1954), 141-153.

[20]*Authority and Power in the Free Church Tradition: A Social Case Study of the American Baptist Convention* (Princeton, N.J.: Princeton University Press, 1959).

[21]*Massachusetts Historical Society Proceedings*, 64 (June 1932), 523-47. Schlesinger's influence may be seen in Mead, *Lively Experiment*, p. 157; in Winthrop S. Hudson, *Religion in America: An Historical Account of the Development of American Religious Life* (New York: Scribners, 1955), p. 262; and in Sidney E. Ahlstrom, *A Religious History of the American People* (New Haven: Yale University Press, 1972), p. 736.

[22]*Righteous Empire*, pp. 177-87.

[23]See Ernest R. Sandeen, *The Roots of Fundamentalism: British and American Millenarianism, 1800-1930* (Chicago: University of Chicago Press, 1970); Norman F. Furniss, *The Fundamentalist Controversy, 1918-1931* (New Haven: Yale University Press, 1954); Joseph Gusfield, *Symbolic Crusade: Social Politics and the American Temperance Movement* (Urbana: University of Illinois Press, 1963); James H.

Timberlake, *Prohibition and the Progressive Movement, 1900-1920* (Cambridge: Harvard University Press, 1963); William G. McLoughlin, *Modern Revivalism: Charles Gradison Finney to Billy Graham* (New York: Ronald Press, 1959).

[24]Marty wisely cautions that not all proponents of the new theology accepted social Christianity, nor did all Social Gospelers favor giving up the traditional tenets of transcendental religion. Those on the side of Private Protestantism did, however, tend to lump the two groups together, pp. 190-91.

[25]*Protestant Churches and Industrial America* (New York: Harper and Row, 1967), p. 231.

[26]*Ibid.*

[27]*Righteous Empire*, p. 205; see also May, p. 234.

[28]The term is originally May's, pp. 37-87, but also note its use by Hudson, *Religion*, p. 302; Mead, *Lively Experiment*, p. 142; and Olmstead, *History of Religion*, p. 447.

[29]"Religion and Modernity, 1865-1914," *The Shaping of American Religion*, eds. James Ward Smith and A. Leland Jamison (Princeton: Princeton University Press, 1961), p. 369.

[30]*Righteous Empire*, p. 167. Marty rejects the logical consequences of this statement by observing that "theological changes in seminaries trickle down" to the masses through the ministers trained in those institutions.

[31]*The Sacred Canopy: Elements of a Sociological Theory of Religion* (Garden City, N.Y.: Doubleday, 1967), especially pp. 105-71, and *The Noise of Solemn Assemblies: Christian Commitment and the Religious Establishment in America* (Garden City: Doubleday, 1961).

[32]*Sacred Canopy*, p. 108.

[33]*Ibid.*, p. 131.

[34]*Noise of Solemn Assemblies*, pp. 163-64.

[35]*Sacred Canopy*, p. 133.

CHAPTER 2

THE ORIGINS OF THE AGENCY STRUCTURE

There were no missionary societies in colonial America. Nor did Bible and tract-carrying colporteurs scour the countryside in search of a lost soul or a ready sale. The Sunday school had yet to be invented. The locus of American religion, in sum, was at the community level. Churches functioned as they had for generations: proclaiming the Gospel; calling sinners to repentence; administering the sacraments; serving as centers of social cohesion. Some denominations—for example the Methodist and the Episcopalian—did operate through an episcopal hierarchy, and others, like the Presbyterians, relied on a form of collective decision-making by synods and assemblies. After the Revolution most denominations also established national legislative bodies. In no sense, however, was this "pastoral structure"[1] comparable to modern, bureaucratic organization. In 1800 organization beyond the local level was quite simple. Bishops were generalists who worked alone. Only one step removed from the pastorate, and limited by poor communications, they continued to be locally oriented. National assemblies met only intermittently, and no national executive or staff existed to manage affairs in accord with the whims of the delegates. Above all, organization beyond the local level was designed to support the priestly and pastoral functions of the local minister, not to manage them.

During the nineteenth century, however, there grew up alongside this traditional pastoral structure a new creation which may be termed agency bureaucracy. Most of these agencies remained small and regionally-oriented until after the Civil War, although there were sporadic and incremental steps in the direction of large-scale, national organization during the first half of the century.[2] In addition, the most successful of these antebellum agencies were interdenominational in character. Not until the latter half of the century did these organizations begin to play major roles in the individual denominations and the Church thus enter its modern phase of bureaucratic development.

The antebellum agencies were nonetheless important antecedents of the agency structure that came to dominate the modern Church. A number of historians have explored the genesis of organized missionary and benevolent activites by American Protestants.[3] In the search for causes these historians have tended to jumble together what should more likely be called preconditions for development with what were the actual sources. Three influences seem to have been necessary but not sufficient ingredients in the development of the agency structure. One was the rise of religious voluntaryism following the Revolutionary War that forced Churches to depend on themselves rather than the state. In addition, American religious leaders were significantly influenced by English ideas and models for the benevolences. Finally, the newly powerful natural rights philosophy combined with an Arminian theology to make benevolence more appealing. The two specific elements which seem in an immediate way to have sparked the creation of the agency structure, however, were the sense of social disorder and the nationalistic tendencies that pervaded early nineteenth-century America.

The American Revolution had a profound effect on American religion, especially in New England.[4] The victory over the British did, of course, seem to confirm the special destiny of the nation and its religious forces. But it also meant that the Churches would now have to expand their horizons beyond the local level if they were to continue to have a hand in the direction of society. In addition, the fruits of the Revolution—especially the principle of religious toleration, the official disestablishment of religion in many colonies and the adoption of the First Amendment to the Constitution—necessitated changes in religious practices. Churches were now forced to depend on their own resources. If they merely were to survive, Churches would have to attract followers on a purely voluntary basis. Beyond survival, if Churches were to produce a moral society, they could no longer rely on governments, but must instead direct their energies to converting the hearts and minds of a significant segment of the community.

This voluntary principle, Sidney Mead argues, has meant that American Churches conceived of themselves as movements to be promoted. Where "success depends upon persuasion" and achievement helps to attract additional followers, the religious agency structure was a logical development. As Mead contends, early nineteenth-century conditions obliged missionary and benevolent societies to form on a voluntary basis.[5] But while the voluntary principle can inform us about the constitution of the new agencies, it cannot by itself provide an answer to the question of causation. After all, American religion had been shifting away from coercion from the time of John Winthrop, but this change had taken place without the development of specialized agencies. Nor was success-oriented religion a sudden development around 1800. Voluntaryism fails to tell us why men began to look beyond the local church for answers, especially in New England where the official disestablishment of religion did not come until after the creation of the agencies.

If voluntaryism is not a sufficient explanation for the agency structure in American Protestantism, neither is the influence of English ideas and institutions spawned by a religious movement one historian has termed the "Evangelical United Front" (E. U. F.). To some degree the E. U. F. seems to have been the product of a growing fear among conservative Englishmen that the ideas of the French Revolution and the Enlightenment, as enunciated by Tom Paine and Joel Barlow, would destroy English institutions. To calm their troubled social waters and to promote the glories of the English way of life, these evangelical Christians united to create new benevolent and educational institutions.[6] The E. U. F. was not, however, without sincere concern for the poor. It called for sacrificial giving by those materially blessed by God. The E. U. F. established Sunday schools to bring education to those who were illiterate. E. U. F. leaders were moved to action more by the conscious desire to share the gospel more effectively than by latent impulses to stamp out radical conspiracies.[7]

There is no doubt that these trends in English religious circles reached an American audience. For instance, William Wilberforce's treatise on the merits of persuasion over coercion in religious affairs, *A Practical View of the Prevailing Religious System*, went through twenty-five American printings.[8] In addition, the British development of the voluntary national society, beginning with the London Missionary Society in 1794, greatly influenced later American organizations. These societies were carefully organized by able clergy and businessmen, operated by salaried agents who developed local auxiliaries, and popularized through effective propaganda, often using contemporary commercial techniques. The success of the E. U. F. in Britain led its leaders to extend the movement both to the Continent and to America. Beginning in 1809 Bibles and tracts were sent to America. A year later the British and Foreign Bible Society urged American Churchmen to form a national society in this country. The organizers of American agencies could not help but be influenced by these British ideas and models. But even the foremost student of the "transmission of British ideas to the United States" has emphasized that the "British example was not in itself a sufficient incentive" for the establishment of American agencies.[9] Moreover, state benevolent agencies in the United States antedate these British developments.

A final precondition necessary to the development of national religious agencies in America was a particular theological and philosophical setting. Natural rights philosophy, especially the Jeffersonian version of inalienable rights, had caught the fancy of many in the Revolutionary generation. According to the Jeffersonians, the worth of each man was measured in terms of ability, not in terms of status in society. Such ideas comported poorly with the older Calvinist notion of man's total depravity. Both the Unitarian insistence on the worth of all men and the Methodist gospel of God's love for all were signs of the change in theology that these ideas necessitated. Arminian notions of God's free offer of salvation to all men who would repent and be saved abounded in sermons. Among leading thinkers, some like Nathaniel W. Taylor of Yale sharply modified the older Calvinism, stressing man's free will and personal role in his salvation. Others such as Samuel Hopkins clung to the idea of man's depravity and his passive role in regeneration, but sought to define active tasks for regenerate men that were consistent with this idea. Hopkins argued that all sin consisted in self-love; to attend to the externals of religion in an unregenerate state was without reward. Since men could not know their future condition, Hopkins reasoned that they should act benevolently without regard for their own interests and without seeking any sign of God's love. Good works were not a response to God's love, as the Wesleyans believed, but rather a reflection of man's utter helplessness. As Hopkins asked: "Are you willing to be damned for the glory of God, and for the greatest good of the whole?"[10]

Out of both this disinterested benevolence theology and the growing Arminianism came a desire to "labor in heroic and unselfish service."[11] Clearly a theology that emphasized the duty of the Christian to serve his fellow man through disinterested benevolence was more conducive to the formation of religious agencies than was traditional Calvinism which stressed the foreordination of mankind's condition. Arminians naturally felt considerable compulsion as well to carry the Gospel to all men who might freely believe.

These theological changes, however, seem insufficient alone to have generated the new benevolent agencies. In many ways Daniel Boorstin's emphasis on the pragmatic nature of American life without regard for ideology is paticularly true for American religion.[12] The limits of linking theology to religious practice have often been noted by students of American religious history.[13] In the case of benevolent agency development, Whitney R. Cross even suggests that the evangelistic excitement and benevolent activity around 1800 actually demanded the changes in theology that Taylor and Hopkins helped to achieve.[14] Indeed, many of the early organizers seem to have been Calvinists untouched by Taylor's new theology. The whole question is moot, however, as the important point is that religious ideas helped to undergird the agency structure, not to produce it.

Given a theology that proved compatible with mission activity, a social system that compelled Churches to recruit constituents on a voluntary basis, and an oranizational model that could easily be adapted to the American environment, the creation of American missionary and benevolent agencies only awaited some peculiarly American precipitating conditions. The social disorder resulting from political strife during the early years of nationhood and from the rapid movement of settlers to the West provided those conditions. Christian leaders united to organize benevolent agencies to deal with the new problems. These organizers, mostly from Presbyterian or Congregational (Presbygational) backgrounds, were deeply concerned about the future of the nation as well as the souls of men.

Part of what disturbed these men was the freethinking and infidelity that seemed rife in the new nation. Such leading skeptics as Paine, Ethan Allan and Joel Barlow attracted wide audiences, and even powerful political leaders like Jefferson openly espoused rationalistic beliefs. Attendance at worship services fell off in these years, and Protestants jeremiads reflected alarm at the evidences of increasing immorality in the nation. Deism, and its later refinements, Unitarianism and Universalism, seemed to challenge the foundations of revealed religion. In some quarters existing Churches were viewed as enemies of progress. As the French Revolution proceeded, American Protestants saw the frightening results of what they believed was rationalism carried to its fullest degree. If political anarchy and irreligious despotism were to be the results of these trends, then Christians everywhere had new cause to organize in an effort to change the course of their society's development.[15]

An even more important source of the social disorder that disturbed Protestants in the East was the settlement of the West. As people moved into western New York and the Ohio Valley, Protestants began to fear that "barbarism" would be the natural consequence of withdrawal from the civilizing and Christianizing influences of the East. Harsh frontier conditions and the savagery of nature, they thought, would stimulate men's animal instincts.[16] Visitors to the West frequently commented on the filthiness, drunkenness and vulgarity of the pioneers. The Reverend Timothy Dwight, president of Yale, after several trips to northern New England and upstate New York, observed that men there were "impatient of the restraints of law, religion and morality."[17] Others echoed his charge. Throughout the first half of the nineteenth century, the writings of such leading Protestants as Lyman Beecher (*A Plea for the West*) and Horace Bushnell (*Barbarism, The First Danger*) reflected the concern of many Christians about the nation's future religious life. Nothing aroused Eastern Churches more than the widely published accounts of mission tours of the West by Samuel J. Mills between 1812 and 1815. Mills described the area west of the Alleghenies as the "Valley of the Shadow of Death."[18] In his reports, the twin threats of

Deism and barbarism were carefully surveyed in each area of the West; Mills gave his readers a studied appraisal of the religious forces, or lack thereof, in each county or settlement.

As Eastern Churchmen became cognizant of the sad state of religion in the West, they were moved to form missionary societies that would, they hoped, create Christian order on the frontier and carry the faith to all who would believe. Even given this rationale for organization, however, one still might wonder why nationally-oriented agencies were necessary. In colonial times, for instance, the response of religious leaders to challenges to faith and seasons of immorality had been to preach repentence, prayer and fasting. The Great Awakening occurred in an earlier period of religious crisis but did not prompt the creation of religious agencies. Historian John B. Boles has described how Southern Churches responded to the perceived problems of social disorder and infidelity in these years not by creating benevolent agencies but by preaching a Great Revival at hundreds of emotionally-charged camp meetings.[19] In the light of the Baptist and Methodist records of growth in the West, one can probably conclude that this sort of revivalism, with its emphasis on personal conversion, proved a far more effective means of bringing religion to the frontier than all of the national agencies spawned in the first half of the nineteenth century. But other Christian denominations saw just the opposite lesson in this experience; the emotional excesses of frontier revivalism actually encouraged their leaders to follow a conservative course of organizational change.

Established denominations such as the Presbyterians and Congregationalists turned to national agencies in part because of the revulsion which many of their leaders felt toward the emotionalism of the revival. Mills' reports from his tours of the West abound with his disdain for the illiterate Baptist and Methodist preachers he found there. Eastern clergymen, accustomed to what they felt were the ways of civilization, were generally not prepared to go to the frontier on their own, as Baptist farmer-preachers and Methodist circuit riders had. But still these Eastern clergymen were concerned. Mills' assignment to survey the West reflects their anxiety, as well as the sense of national responsibility that was growing in the established churches. The latter attitude was especially obvious after the successful conclusion of the War of 1812. Nationalistic impulses encouraged Eastern Churches to act in some concerted way to care for the souls of the frontiersmen.

America's search for national identity during the first half of the nineteenth century is a theme that has long engaged the attention of historians.[20] Frederick Jackson Turner depicted the development of a nationalistic "New West" that turned its back upon European developments. Henry Clay's American System, John C. Calhoun's national plans for internal improvements, and the Monroe Doctrine of 1823 were all products of this new spirit. The sense of national identity was strengthened during these years by the "transportation revolution" that produced first regional and then finally national markets. National turnpikes like the Cumberland Road (1806), canals like the Erie (1825) and railroads in the 1830s and 40s made Americans increasingly aware of the interdependence of all parts of the country—and especially the East and West.[21]

As some religious historians have pointed out, "nationalistic tendencies" and "patriotic interest" at this time encouraged the formation of national agencies.[22] During the previous century missionary activity had been confined to the local level. Often a church, a synod, or an association would support a mission tour by a minister. Spending a day or two in each settlement along the way, the missionary would preach, administer the ordinances, encourge the faithful, and attempt to establish a permanent church. In the newly enlarged nation, however, such capricious and spasmodic local efforts were insufficient. Even the state societies that had proliferated in the years following 1796 (when the first such society was created in New York) were no longer adequate to the task. In the climate of opinion that existed following the War of 1812, the creation of nation-wide organizations seemed to be the only appropriate response to a variety of Eastern Churchmen. Nationally oriented merchants, bankers and lawyers predominated among the founders. The leading force behind the creation of the first national agency, the American Bible Society (1816), was Elias Boudinot, a New Jersey lawyer and a director of the Bank of the United States. Relying on his business experience, Boudinot recommended that local and state Bible societies unite to coordinate their efforts, to eliminate duplication of work, to assure greater stability, to increase available funds, and to attract more attention to their efforts by virtue of increased size and wealth. Other prominent businessmen served as managers, including Arthur and Lewis Tappan, Jasper Corning, and Anson G. Phelps. Additional agencies soon arose on a variety of fronts: the American Education Society (1816); the American Colonization Society (1817); the American Tract Society (1823); the American Sunday-School Union (1826); the American Home Missionary Society (1826); the American Peace Society (1828); and the American Anti-Slavery Society (1833). Some denominations also established religious agencies in these years, but most of these remained small by comparison with the united front societies. Of the fourteen national societies in 1827, only four of the smallest were under denominational direction.[23]

Several characteristics of the E. U. F. organizations made for their immediate success. They were formed by a wealthy and dedicated group of individuals, mostly laymen. The managers of the societies stressed the need for "systematic" operations: effective central staffs numbering as many as ten; national advertising and promotion through magazines; voluminous annual reports; anniversary meetings; an energetic group of field agents to speak at every sort of ecclesiastical assembly and to organize local auxiliaries. Above all, they had secure financial foundations based upon nation-wide sales of uniformly-priced and packaged merchandise, upon regular financial drives, and upon the Dudley method of collection that organized responsibility through neighborhood teams.

The societies also proved effective at first because they were not, in a formal sense, structurally related to the Churches. They were designed for quick, concerted action without the need for approval by various denominational assemblies. Open to all Christians, they were organized so as to avoid the sectarian differences that were so common in these years; they united individuals, not ecclesiastical bodies. Because these societies were oriented toward single, specific objectives, they were able to avoid theological differences for the most part, and to attract relatively broad support.

The years immediately following the election of Andrew Jackson were the heyday of these early missionary organizations. The annual income of the societies grew from $362,000 in 1827 to $1,014,000 in 1836.[24] The American Bible Society vowed to place a Bible in every American home in 1829, and the other societies quickly followed with pledges to do equally well in their own areas of endeavor. By 1837 the Bible Society had published more than two million Testaments; the Temperance Union had convinced millions to sign the pledge; the Sunday-School Union was educating 120,000 scholars; the Tract Society had already distributed some 35,000,000 pamphlets and books.[25]

The year of 1837 was a crucial point in the development of these early national organizations. The depression of that year forced cutbacks in operations due to declining sales and contributions. More significant, however, were the internal strains that began to be evident in the movement. Methodists and Baptists, who earlier had been willing to take minor roles in the united front, began to chafe under the Presbygational dominance and to assert their denominational independence. Their members increasingly resented the continuing disparagement of social conditions in the West by E. U. F. organizations. The creation of the American Home Missionary Society in 1826 provided a further source of unrest since unlike the earlier Bible, tract and Sunday school organizations, this new society had the distinctly sectarian goal of establishing Presbygational congregations in the West. The success of E. U. F. operations also threatened fledgling denominational enterprises;

united front societies slashed prices on Bibles, tracts, and Sunday school materials in what seemed an effort to destroy their denominational competitors.

The resulting tensions encouraged those who were looking for reasons to undermine the E. U. F.   Some feared the loss of denominational identity.   Baptists were particularly aroused in the 1830s when the American Bible Society first refused to translate the word "baptizo" as "immerse" and then withdrew support from all Baptist translators.   The Methodist Book Concern denounced the "'national' combinations which, in our opinion, threatened for a while to swallow up, and absolutely to annihilate, every other plan of operation in our country."[26]   Some   opponents—Alexander   Campbell,   for instance—identified the united front with the power and arrogance of Eastern upper classes.   The movement, said Campbell, was just another form of Eastern speculation in the West.

Another reason for the breakdown of the E. U. F. was simply the apparent end of those conditions that had inspired its creation. As Charles I. Foster suggests, the West was becoming more settled and it appeared that the movement was actually taming this region, stamping out infidelity and thereby destroying the urgent need for a Protestant alliance. Denominations could now stand on their own.[27] A measure of growing denominational independence was the increase in the percentage donated to denominational benevolences from nine percent of the total in 1828 to thirty-five percent in 1836.[28] Moreover, the sense of nationalism that had sustained the E. U. F. was also becoming less powerful among Protestants. Each of the major denominations was faced with internal dissensions. Those who favored the united front with its pragmatic methods, lay leadership, and new social organization were opposed by those who saw these developments as a sign of corruption of traditional values. The conflict between High and Low Episcopalians, the struggles between Old and New School parties among Presbyterians and Baptists, and the schism of the Methodist Protestant Church in 1830 were all manifestations of the sharp division over new ideas and methods that was taking place within the denominations. In addition, the E. U. F.—a movement built around the formation of local auxiliaries in urban areas—had never had much success in the South, and that too weakened the movement. Increasing involvement in such political concerns as abolitionism contributed to the schism along geographical lines that took place in the 1840s in most American Churches.

Despite the collapse of the E. U. F., however, the missionary and benevolent work begun by the united front organizations was carried on—although in a somewhat weakened state—by denominational agencies.[29] The basic structure of national agencies remained intact and would be re-energized when new problems replaced the earlier concerns with infidelity and frontier barbarism. Meanwhile, the denominations had to struggle to ensure that the existing agencies would obtain enough resources to survive and to continue their work.

NOTES

[1]Winter, "Religious Oganizations," p. 439. The pastoral structure includes of course those hierarchical elements described above which facilitated the ongoing work of the local pastor.

[2]Kenneth E. Boulding, *The Organizational Revolution: A Study in the Ethics of Economic Organization* (Chicago: Quadrangle Books, 1953), p. 3, discusses the failure of certain early nineteenth-century organizational efforts.

[3]For example see Oliver Wendell Elsbree, *The Rise of the Missionary Spirit in America, 1790-1815* (Williamsport, Pennsylvania: Williamsport Printing and Binding Co., 1928); Colin Brummitt Goodykoontz, *Home Missions on the American Frontier, With Particular Reference to the American Home Missionary Society* (Caldwell, Idaho: Caxton Printers, 1939); William Warren Sweet, *Religion on the American Frontier* (4 vols.; New York: Harper, 1931-1946) and *Religion in the Development of American Culture, 1765-1840* (Gloucester, Massachusetts: Peter, Smith, 1963); Charles I. Foster, *An Errand of Mercy: The Evangelical United Front, 1790-1837* (Chapel Hill: University of North Carolina Press, 1960); Clifford S. Griffin, *Their Brothers' Keepers: Moral Stewardship in the United States, 1800-1865* (New Brunswick, New Jersey: Rutgers University Press, 1960); Edwin Wilbur Rice, *The Sunday-School Movement and the American Sunday-School Union* (Philadelphia: American Sunday-School Union, 1917); and Timothy L. Smith, *Revivalism and Social Reform: American Protestantism on the Eve of the Civil War* (New York: Abingdon, 1957).

[4]This paragraph is based largely on Winthrop Hudson, *American Protestantism*, pp. 65-71. See also Mead, *Lively Experiment*, pp. 103-33; Ahlstrom, *Religious History*, pp. 360-84; and Olmstead, *History of Religion*, pp. 211-18.

[5]Mead, *Lively Experiment*, pp. 66-67. Winter, "Religious Organizations," p. 409, mistakenly equates Mead's voluntary principle with the creation of agencies. In truth, Mead merely argues that "religious groups become voluntary associations;" the agency structure was not a direct result. Mead sees voluntaryism as a "corollary of religious freedom." Voluntary consent had to replace coercion if religious equality were to exist.

[6]The term is Foster's *Errand of Mercy*, especially pp. 37-38, 99-100. See also in a similar vein Edward P. Thompson, *The Making of the English Working Classes* (New York: Pantheon Books, 1964), pp. 37-54, 350-400; and Eric J. Hobsbawm, *Labouring Men: Studies in the History of Labour* (New York: Basic Books, 1964), pp. 23-33.

[7]See Bernard Semmel, *The Methodist Revolution* (New York: Basic Books, 1973) and David Spring on "The Clapham Sect: Some Social and Political Aspects," *Victorian Studies*, 5 (September 1961), 35-48 and on "Aristocracy, Religion and Social Structure in Early Victorian England," *Victorian Studies*, 6 (March 1963), 263-80.

[8]Hudson, *American Protestantism*, pp. 66-67.

[9]Foster, *Errand of Mercy*, pp. vii, 156.

[10]On these theological ideas see Sweet, *Religion in the Development*, pp. 234-36; Griffin, *Their Brothers' Keepers*, pp. 5-6; Rev. Charles Buck, *A Theological Dictionary* . . (Philadelphia: William W. Woodward, 1825), pp. 221-23; Ahlstrom, *Religious History*, pp. 405-09; and Elsbree, *Rise of the Missionary Spirit*, pp. 146-52.

[11]Elsbree, p. 152.

[12]See *The Genius of American Politics* (Chicago: University of Chicago Press, 1953), pp. 1-35 and *The Americans* (3 vols.; New York: Random House, 1958-1973).

[13]See Mead, *Lively Experiment*, p. 114.

[14]*The Burned-Over District: The Social and Intellectual History of Enthusiastic Religion in Western New York, 1800-1850* (New York: Harper and Row, 1950), p. 28. Hudson, *Great Tradition*, pp. 63-79, stresses the "practical rather than theological considerations" that compelled Lyman Beecher's conversion to voluntaryism.

[15]On Protestant fears of rationalistic religion see Foster, Chapter 2 ("Conservative Terrors"), pp. 11-27; Griffin, pp. 15-16; Hudson, *Religion in America*, pp. 131-32. On *Republican Religion: The American Revolution and the Cult of Reason*, read G. Adolph Koch (New York: Henry Holt, 1933).

[16]On barbarism in the West see Griffin, pp. 16-18; Foster, pp. 179-207; Hudson, *Religion*, pp. 132-34; Ahlstrom, pp. 429-54; and John B. Boles, *The Great Revival, 1787-1805: The Origins of the Southern Evangelical Mind* (Lexington: University Press of Kentucky, 1972), pp. 12-24.

[17]Quoted in Griffin, p. 17.

[18]On Mills' missionary tours see Griffin, pp. 26-27; Foster, pp. 110-11; John F. Schermerhorn and Samuel J. Mills, *A Correct View of That Part of the United States Which Lies West of the Allegany Mountains with Regard to Religion and Morals* (Hartford, 1814); and Mills and Daniel Smith, *Report of a Missionary Tour Through That Part of the United States which Lies West of the Allegany Mountains; Performed under the Direction of the Massachusetts Missionary Society* (Andover, Massachusetts, 1815).

[19]*The Great Revival*, pp. 51-89.

[20]For instance see Frederick Jackson Turner, *The Rise of the New West, 1819-1827* (New York: Collier, 1962) and George Dangerfield, *The Awakening of American Nationalism, 1815-1828* (New York: Harper, 1965).

[21]George Rogers Taylor, *The Transportation Revolution, 1815-1860* (New York: Rinehart, 1951); Douglass C. North, *The Economic Growth of the United States,*

1790-1860 (Englewood Cliffs, N.J.: Prentice Hall, 1961); and Stuart Bruchey, *The Roots of American Economic Growth, 1607-1861: An Essay in Social Causation* (New York: Harper & Row, 1965), pp. 74-215.

[22]Goodykoontz, *Home Missions*, p. 214.

[23]Foster, pp. 121-22.

[24]*Ibid.*, pp. 121, 250.

[25]Griffin, pp. 114-15.

[26]"Address of the Managers of the Methodist Episcopal Book Concern" (1828), quoted in Foster, p. 238.

[27]pp. 250-51.   I suspect also that such denominations as the Methodist, Baptist and Campbellite had learned that their success came through the revival, not the E.U.F.

[28]*Ibid.*, p. 250.

[29]Elwyn A. Smith, "The Formation of a Modern American Denomination," *Church History*, 31 (March 1962), 74-79.

CHAPTER 3

AGENCY STRUCTURE AND THE DENOMINATIONS

In response to the same conditions that led to the formation of the E. U. F. agencies, and no doubt somewhat envious of their early successes, most Protestant denominations began to establish their own national missionary, publishing, and benevolent enterprises during the first half of the nineteenth century. Most of these denominational agencies remained small, however, until the final third of the century. They were located on the periphery of denominational power structures that were still largely decentralized. Agency executive and administrative functions were limited to oversight of their specific areas of interest. Their primary task was to serve as clearinghouses for handling money.

These agencies were nevertheless the foundation stones of the modern Church bureaucracy, and they deserve our careful attention. But since it would be impossible to study in detail the organizational development of every major Protestant denomination in nineteenth-century America, I have selected four Churches—the Methodist Episcopal Church, the Protestant Episcopal Church, the Southern Baptist Convention, and the Christian Church (Disciples of Christ)—that I think are representative of the religious diversity of the American experience. Furthermore, an examination of the secondary literature related to other denominations suggests that they too underwent changes similar to those which will be described here.[1]   In each case, however, the particular denomination was unique in some regards, and in looking at our four denominations, it will be necessary to understand something of the history of each in America. The variety of experiences and the social and theological differences of these Churches were significant, especially in determining the timing and extent of the organizational developments which are of interest here.

Of the four Churches, only the Protestant Episcopal (PEC) was prominent in colonial America.[2] The origins of the Episcopal Church in America can be traced back to the first settlers at Jamestown in 1607. English settlers, especially in the South, brought their Anglican faith with them and by the time of the Revolution, the Church of England was the established Church in the five Southern colonies. In addition, the PEC had gained a foothold in New England among "old lights" who were converted by agents of the Society for the Propagation of the Gospel (SPG). After the Revolution, an American episcopacy was established in 1784, and the first General Convention met in 1789 to adopt a constitution, a set of canons, and a liturgy (the Book of Common Prayer).

The constitution created a triennial General Convention, divided into a House of Bishops and a House of Deputies, as the supreme governing body of the Church.

The PEC was a very weak denomination in the early national period. No longer was it able to depend on support from the state or the SPG. The early bishops seem to have been virtually devoid of any leadership ability, especially the sort of aggressiveness that was needed in an expanding society. Most Episcopalians continued to think of their denomination as a loose confederation of independent dioceses (states), and General Conventions were sparsely attended. Episcopalians fared poorly on the frontier, partly because of their social standing—the frontier was not very attractive to the average Episcopalian who was accustomed to the amenities of wealth and culture—and partly because the Church's ecclesiology, which assumed an already settled society, made no provision for expansion to or government of unsettled regions. Not until 1835 did the Church begin to adjust, creating "missionary bishops" to provide leadership in frontier areas.

The adjustment process was not any easier when Episcopalians initiated an "agency structure" in the early years of the century. Cooperation among Episcopalians began not at the behest of the General Convention, but rather at the local and diocesan levels in response to specific situations. The need for missionaries was first answered by the formation of New York's Committee for the Propagation of the Gospel. In 1820, however, concern over reports that Episcopalian pioneers were falling into the hands of "dissenting denominations" finally led the General Convention to create the Domestic and Foreign Missionary Society (D&FMS). At first this Society imitated the E. U. F. pattern of raising money through private support from local individuals and auxiliaries that were independent of local churches. All persons or groups who contributed three or more dollars annually to the Society were entitled to vote at the Society's meetings and to select the twenty-four directors who managed the day-to-day affairs of the D&FMS. As a result of this "society" type of organization, there was little sense of local church obligation to or national church direction of the Society. Little enthusiasm for missions seems to have been generated in the early years of the Society's existence, and in 1832 the General Convention abandoned "society" organization in favor of "denominational" organization in which all local churches would provide direct support and government through the General Convention. A Board of Missions, consisting of thirty members elected by the Convention and of all bishops, now administered the organization though two committees—one for domestic and one for foreign missions.

The one clear advantage that denominational agencies had over the "united front" organizations was their ability to exploit the local churches directly. As the Convention reported, "the Society shall be considered as comprehending all persons who are members of this Church." It would be a long time before this condition would in fact exist, if ever, but from the beginning the denominational agencies had great potential resources at the local level.

In the years after 1832, the Episcopal Church began to adjust more successfully to the problem of expansion. The General Convention and its missions organization provided a degree of organization and direction for the Church. The number of communicants grew from only 32,000 to nearly 300,000 by 1876. Financial support of the D&FMS, upon whose organization we shall focus, increased dramatically following the Civil War; its income averaged over $300,000 annually during these years.

Unlike the PEC, the Methodists were from the first well-suited to coping with the problems of a rapidly growing society. Schism within eighteenth-century Anglicanism had led to the creation of the Methodist Episcopal Church (MEC).[3] The story of Methodism in America begins with John Wesley's commissioning of two young preachers to minister to brethren in New York in 1769. Following the Revolutionary War, Francis Asbury was ordained as the first bishop of an independent Methodist Episcopal Church, created at the Christmas Conference of 1784. The structure of the new Church was defined in *The Discipline*, a body of laws written at the first General Conference and subsequently revised and expanded greatly.

American Methodism soon developed an elaborate local, district and national organization comparable to that of their Episcopal forebears—at least on paper. Methodism succeeded on the frontier, however, in large part because of the adoption of the itinerant system. Early Methodist preachers were appointed to circuits, spread over wide areas, instead of to a single church. Preaching was done from village to village and house to house by circuit riders. Nor did early Methodist bishops have established territorial areas under their jurisdiction. As time passed the camp meeting became the primary means of Methodist evangelism. Only gradually did the Methodists begin to erect church buildings.

While the General Conference, which met quadrenially, provided guidelines for the early Methodist Church, the basic administrative units were the Annual Conferences, first devised in 1792 as regional associations of clergymen. Among the duties of these Conferences were determination of ministerial qualifications within their jurisdictions, interpretation and execution of the instructions of the General Conference, creation of committees to deal with local problems, and selection of delegates to convey Conference opinion to the General Conference. The Episcopacy, consisting of the Church's bishops, was more or less the executive arm of the Church at this level. Each bishop presided over several Annual Conferences, stationing pastors within the Conference through the itinerant system and selecting the presiding elder of the Conference to oversee local affairs in his absence.

When such nation-wide and enduring problems as mission aid developed, the Methodists began to form permanent organizations. The Missionary Society of the Methodist Episcopal Church (1819) provides a good example of agency development in these early years. The first Methodist missionaries were dependent on committees of friends at home for their salaries and supplies. This system proved unreliable, but attempts to create a national missionary organization were at first stymied by the Methodist structure of scattered bishops and infrequent national meetings. As a result, concerned Methodists decided to unite outside the official framework in order to answer the missionaries' call for aid. The resulting Missionary Society, although soon endorsed by the General Conference of 1820, did not officially become an arm of the Church until 1872 when its organization was changed from the society to the denominational type. Beginning in that year, membership was by churches rather than individuals, and the General Conference elected the Society's Board of Managers.

By 1876 the Missionary Society was financially the most successful agency of all those created by the Protestant Churches; this was true despite the fact that the Church had experienced two schisms: the Methodist Protestants in 1830 and the Methodist Episcopal Church, South, in 1844. Nevertheless, Methodism grew faster than any other denomination in America in the early years of the nineteenth century, and by 1876 it was the largest of America's Churches, with some 1.5 million members.

Like the MEC, Southern Baptists traced their lineage back to the religious toleration that eighteenth-century America afforded. Baptists, however, organized independent local churches without any ecclesiastical hierarchy. In the early eighteenth century Baptist congregations were established in Charleston and the piedmont areas of North Carolina and Virginia by groups from General Baptist churches in England and from "new light" sects in New England.[4] By mid-century Baptists had organized associations like the ones in Charleston and Sandy Creek, N. C., that allowed for fellowship and discussion of mutual problems facing the local churches. In the years following the Revolution there were calls for a national meeting and for national union, but it was 1813 before any action along these lines was taken. The precipitant was the sudden conversion in that year of two Congregational missionaries to Baptist views. Mission funds were urgently needed and Baptists in Boston provided most of the leadership in the establishment of the General

Missionary Convention of the Baptist Denomination in the United States of America for Foreign Missions.

The founders, strong adherents to the principle of local church autonomy, opted for the society type of structure rather than the denominational organization favored by many Baptist leaders in the South. Membership in the Convention was based on contributions from individuals or auxiliaries. The General Missionary Convention, probably influenced by the united front organizations, adopted a very narrow view of its work and was unwilling to diversify its operations. This made it necessary to form independent organizations to perform other functions—for example the American and Foreign Bible Society and the American Baptist Publication Society, each with its own convention.

Baptists in the South, dissatisfied with the society framework of the national organization from the beginning, became even more perturbed when the national societies seemed to ignore the need for home missionaries in the South. Later, when the Board of the General Missionary Society announced that it would no longer appoint slaveholders as missionaries, Southern churches terminated their connection with their Northern brethren. Delegates from eleven Southern states met in Augusta, Georgia, in May of 1845, to form the Southern Baptist Convention (SBC). The resulting structure was a compromise between society and denominational organization in that membership in the convention still had a financial basis, but the constitution also spoke of "churches composing the Convention" which suggested a church rather than an individual composition. The single Convention, moreover, governed all boards, such as the Foreign Mission and Domestic Mission Boards.

The two mission boards of the Convention fared poorly during the Civil War. Most of the work of the Domestic Board was abandoned as missionaries entered the service of the Confederacy and funds became scarce. The work of the Foreign Board was kept alive by generous support from Baptists in border states. At war's end there were some who doubted that the SBC should continue to exist, but Southern anger at Northern "meddling" during Reconstruction, particularly that of the agents of the American Baptist Home Missionary Society among Southern Negroes, dashed any hopes of a reunion of the two denominations.

By the time of the nation's Centennial, Southern Baptists had an annual denominational convention consisting of messengers from the local churches, and two national mission boards, which provided a degree of South-wide leadership. Each local church remained autonomous, affiliating with the SBC on an entirely voluntary basis. Each of the mission boards was relatively weak; the Home Board in 1880 had but one paid administrator and a budget of $21,000 with which to support thirty-five missionaries.   At this time, too, Baptists did not yet have an agency to handle Sunday school administration and it was 1890 before they established their Baptist Sunday School Board (BSSB).   In general, then, the agency structure in the SBC played a minor role in the years prior to 1876.

The last of the four Churches we are examining was distinctly an American creation.   The Christian Church (Disciples of Christ)[5] originated in the midst of the "Great Western Revival," a period of religious turbulence at the beginning of the nineteenth century.   If any Church bore a resemblence to William Warren Sweet's model of frontier-oriented religion, it was the Disciples.   Unlike the other three denominations, the Disciples had no European antecedants.   They were in effect the product of two separate schisms in frontier Presbyterianism. In 1803 five Presbyterian ministers, greatly influenced by the success of the Cane Ridge camp meeting of 1801, withdrew from the Synod of Kentucky.   Several months later, led by Barton Stone, they organized what they called the "Christian church."   Several beliefs influenced their decision to secede.   These included their rejection of the strict Calvinism of the Presbyterians in favor of a gospel that preached Christ's atoning death for all who would believe; their denial of the validity of man-made creeds (such as the Presbyterian Westminster Confession) and reliance instead on Scripture for faith and practice; their repudiation of the right of any "man-made" institution (such as a presbytery) to exercise control over the independent local congregation; and their renunciation of the sectarianism of the existing Churches with a pledge to restore the unity of the first-century Church as the body of Christ.

The second root of what became the Christian Church was the withdrawal of Thomas Campbell, later joined by his more famous son Alexander, from the Seceder Presbyterians of Pennsylvania.   Campbell left after being disciplined by his presbytery.   The reasons for his withdrawal were stated in his "Declaration and Address of the Christian Association of Washington" (1809).   Like Barton Stone, Campbell condemned division among Christians in light of the essential unity of the church of Christ, called for sole reliance on Scripture for faith and practice (rejecting so-called man-made doctrines), and proposed to admit to the church all who made professions of faith in Christ and demonstrated obedience to his commands.   The Campbells soon formed a rather loose connection with the Baptists of western Pennsylvania and Ohio, a tie which lasted until 1830.

The early years of the movement that became the Christian Church have been aptly characterized by David E. Harrell, Jr., as "schizoid."[6]   The strong reliance on Scripture as a guide for all of one's personal life and for the Church's organization and practice produced a very rationalistic and legalistic religion. Yet these early Disciples also adopted the religious enthusiasm so common in the frontier Church. The legalistic reliance on Scripture led to countless disagreements on the meaning of the Word, creating strains that would characterize the movement for the rest of the century. There was, after all, little to unite the isolated clusters of automonous Christian churches in these early years. Even the union of the Stoneite and Campbellite strands of the movement in 1832 was little more than a recognition among the leaders that they had common beliefs and interests; they created no denominational organization.

The movement nonetheless grew, and grew rapidly. The early leaders either possessed or developed skills that were successful on the frontier. Few had formal education and most were lay preachers. They were accomplished in the art of debating the religious issues of the day at mass meetings. Especially effective was Walter Scott's formulation of a simple five-finger plan of salvation that allowed the Disciples to establish the distinctiveness of their faith in the midst of the religious variety of the frontier. This common experience and similar beliefs held the early Disciples together, as did the newspapers of the movement which exercised great power over local church members. Alexander Campbell's *Christian Baptist* and later *Millenial Harbinger* and Stone's *Christian Messenger* were the most successful of several journalistic ventures by the early leaders.

Two central ideas of the movement deserve particular attention because they had long-term effects on the type of organization the Disciples would adopt. That these two ideas were not entirely compatible was less apparent to the early Disciples than it would be to their descendents. First, the Disciples, as we have noted already, rejected the sectarian divisions of the day. They believed in the essential oneness of the Church and the reunion of all Christians. The goal was not to create yet another denomination, but rather to spread those principles that they believed would lead to the restoration of a united Church. Second, the Disciples understood the cause of sectarianism to be the creeds, the clericalism, the ecclesiastical hierarchies of existing denominations. If somehow the principles of first-century Christianity could be recovered, they felt, Church divisions would end. The way to do this was to depend on Scripture as a guide in the restructuring of the restored Church.

After the union of the two streams of the early Church, certain kinds of cooperation among local churches were inaugurated, but always with the strictest assurance of the independence of each congregation. Ministers ("elders") met at informal regional conferences for mutual encouragement and edification. Eventually county and statewide meetings were held in the late 1830s and 40s. Finally, in 1849 the first national convention met in Cincinnati, resulting in the formation of the American Christian Missionary Society (ACMS). None of these voluntary organizations claimed any power over the local churches. Membership in the missionary society was on an individual basis; financial support of the organization entitled one to vote at the national convention which exercized final authority over the Society. Day-to-day operations were in the hands of a Board of Managers.

The creation of the ACMS was the first attempt of the Disciples to form a national organization, but the early years of its operation produced little income and few missionaries. Most evangelical work remained in the hands of individuals who took the Word to the West, sometimes with the financial aid of a home congregation. The Disciples were clearly hesitant about the ACMS and its role in their Church. The chief reason for the weakness of the ACMS was a widespread belief that mission societies were unscriptural, since in Campbell's words, Scripture was silent on the question. In all things the Church must become like its New Testament forebear, and the first-century Church had not included a missionary society, as such.

The Civil War—and the internal conflicts it created among Disciples—saw mission funds dwindle to less than ten thousand dollars. Something had to be done if the organization were to survive and the Disciples responded with the Louisville Plan of 1869. In retrospect we can see that this program was hardly a wise choice, given the basic ideology of the denomination. The Louisville Plan created an elaborate network of district and state boards governed by church "messengers" to conventions. At the national level a General Christian Missionary Society was to be established and governed by a Convention consisting of "messengers" from the state conventions. In reality the plan was soon discontinued, although it was not officially abandoned until 1895. In the meantime it undermined the financial base (individual subscription) of the old society, replacing it with direct appeals to local churches by district treasurers. As a result, receipts fell even further and only by returning to the society structure did the organization survive.

In the midst of the chaos created by the Louisville Plan, those Disciples interested in benevolent work concluded that the ACMS was an inadequate vehicle for their concern. They created new independent organizations along society lines—the Christian Woman's Board of Missions (1874) and the Foreign Christian Missionary Society (1875)—to raise funds to send missionaries. The Disciples, as a result, had three autonomous societies which held separate, although consecutive, annual conventions in the same city.

The Disciples thus had the weakest agency structure of the four Churches we have examined. Dedicated, as they were, to local autonomy, and determined to cleanse the Church of modern corruptions, the Disciples were unable to form strong national agencies. Unlike most American Churches which had adopted denominational structures by 1876, the Christian Church clung to the old society type of organization, perhaps because, as in the case of the E. U. F., such a structure allowed divergent interests to achieve a degree of harmony.

By 1876, then, the agency structure that had been developed by the E. U. F. had largely passed into denominational hands. There were differences as a result of this shift, but they had little effect at first. Representatives of the Churches, for instance, now governed the agency structure which under united front auspices had been run by wealthy, non-sectarian patrons. Despite this change, however, the internal operations of the agencies were basically static; they adminstered larger budgets and sent out more missionaries over time, but their existing modes of management seemed adequate. The agencies also continued the E. U. F. pattern of having limited, single objectives, and as a result, the number of agencies in each denomination proliferated.

The typical Church agency in 1876 was under the direction and supervision of a national convention. Each society or board presented a long printed report of its work in the period since the last convention. The report was considered by a standing committee of the convention. This committee could make suggestions to the floor for changes (usually prompted by the advice of the report itself) in the operation of the agency. Usually the committee presented a glowing account of the successes of the organization. The Convention elected the officers and selected a large group of individuals to serve on the permanent board of the agency. A constitutional provision often stipulated a certain mixture of lay, clerical and, where appropriate, episcopal members. In addition some attempt was frequently made to achieve a good geographical mix. Once elected, a member of the board generally served for life, although all faced reelection at each convention. Vacancies occurring between meetings of the conventions were filled by the boards, the effect being to make the boards virtually self-perpetuating.

The entire board normally met once a year. Actual oversight was vested in the hands of a smaller group of managers chosen from among the board's members. Managers usually lived near the board's headquarters, making it easy for them to attend the regular monthly meetings as well as any special sessions. The managers further divided their work through standing committees for both internal (e.g., office expenses, trust funds, ways and means, candidates) and external affairs (e.g., China and Japan, Africa, Home Field).

The managers of the various agencies were well-informed about the organization's workings in these early years. Attendance at meetings was almost unanimous, especially among those laymen who, through their dollars and their role in the creation of the agencies, felt a special responsibility for their success. At committee meetings the managers heard about conditions in the field, the qualifications of missionary candidates, and the financial status of the organization. Every item of correspondence was carefully evaluated by the appropriate committee and any necessary action referred to the managers as a whole. No item was too small for consideration, whether it be the authorization for the ACMS to purchase a typewriter or approval for the Alaskan mission of the Methodist Missionary Society to accept several reindeer from the United States government.

Day-to-day adminstration was left in the hands of the corresponding secretaries,[7] who were the chief executives for the agencies. Because of the size of the Methodist operation, that Church had two secretaries in the 1870's, but normally a single one sufficed. Compared to the executive officers in twentieth-century Church organizations, the corresponding secretaries of 1876 were in a relatively subservient role. This was the result, in part, of the keen interest of the managers in the boards' affairs. In addition, the corresponding secretary was a jack-of-all-trades, but master of none. He was always an ordained clergyman in these years, selected often as much for his abilities in the pulpit as for his adminstrative talents. Almost every Sunday he was out promoting the cause of his agency in a local church. The Annual Conferences of the Methodist Church, the diocesan conventions of the PEC and the state conventions of the Baptists and the Disciples also demanded his presence as often as possible. The corresponding secretary served as a recruiter for the mission field and as a salesman for board literature. Sometimes he acted as treasurer for the agency, although that duty often fell to one of the managers who had accounting experience. The corresponding secretary answered all the board's mail and sent out the managers' instructions to the various fields.

The agencies received their financial support from three main sources.[8] The largest part of the income came from appeals to local churches. One Sunday every year—the ACMS for instance designated the first Sunday in May—the churches were asked to take up a collection for the work of the agency. The denominational press publicized the annual event, citing the hard work and dedication of the missionaries. A second source of funds was the individual patron who gave designated gifts for specific purposes; these offering were known as "specials." Legacies from the estates of long-time supporters of the work provided a final type of funding. By the 1870s the boards were beginning to tap this source by the more secure means of establishing annuity funds for individuals who turned over some portion of their wealth during their remaining years in return for a fixed-interest payment annually until death.

The goals of the agencies were as clear and simple as their organizations. A Methodist preacher wrote in 1877 that the true test of any Church's strength and influence was "its success in extending the kingdom of God."[9] The primary task of all of these organizations was that of evangelism—spreading the good news of Jesus Christ. The Methodist Board declared in 1881 that "the principal business of the Missionary Society is to bring the knowledge of Christ within the reach of those who have not received that knowledge."[10]

All of the agencies were thus similar in certain regards, but there were differences between the denominations that help to explain the organizational changes that would take place in the years after 1876. Diversity in terms of size, geographical location, social and economic status, polity and theology had effects on the nature of each Church's agency structure.

The oldest of the Churches, the Protestant Episcopal, was also the smallest of the four in 1876. Most of its 300,000 communicants lived in the small towns and cities of the industrial Northeast. The slightly larger Disciples (some 400,000 members) were clustered primarily in rural areas of the Old Northwest and in the border states of Kentucky, Tennessee, and Missouri. Southern Baptists, found of course primarily in the South, claimed slightly fewer than one million members in 1880. Largest of all was the Methodist Episcopal Church with an estimated 1.5 million followers. Although Methodism was strong throughout the North and West, its center of strength was in New York, Pennsylvania, and the Ohio Valley.

Of the four Churches, the Episcopalian was the only one that was liturgical. Most of its members were in the middle or upper income brackets and were generally well-educated. Almost all Episcopalian clergymen had received professional training at the denomination's theological seminaries. In the late nineteenth century, Methodism had become a middle-class denomination, with an increasingly urban and educated constituency. Both Methodists and Episcopalians had substantial numbers of businessmen in their congregations. The Disciples and the Baptists, however, remained largely rural denominations led by country preachers called to deliver that "old-time religion" to the faithful. The typical member of these two Churches was likely a small farmer or sharecropper. In both these denominations the educated minister was looked upon with some suspicion. Disciples did not even have formal "ministerial training" (never theological education) until the 1890s.

In terms of Church polity, the MEC and PEC had a great deal in common. Both had episcopal oversight through the bishop and highly developed local, district, and national organs that governed their

Churches. In both denominations the local church was accustomed to some amount of direction from the religious hierarchy. Baptists and Disciples, on the other had, believed in the autonomy of the local church, although both had allowed the creation of independent connectional bodies that some saw as a challenge to the primacy of the congregation.

The different ways in which these denominations organized their agencies were related to these basic characteristics. Those denominations with more urban, better educated, and middle income memberships—the Methodists and the Episcopalians—were generally favorable to the agency structure from the start. Accustomed to episcopal hierarchies, they readily adopted national agencies. There were, at first, some unresolved questions about the relationship of the early societies to the episcopacy and the existing national conventions, but both Churches soon answered them by eliminating society organization and replacing it with denominational boards selected at national conventions. Bishops would sit on these boards, but would be no more powerful than clergy or laity.

The Baptist and Disciples, on the other hand, found that the agency structure sharply conflicted with their traditions of local autonomy. Southern Baptists no doubt saw clear links between their theory of church polity and the prevailing notion throughout the South of state sovereignty. The rural members of these two Churches were unlikely to look to business for models of how religious organizations should operate. The Baptists did, however, adopt the denominational agency structure, although the Convention itself was not based on a strictly democratic representation of local churches at first. Perhaps since the SBC was only a regional denomination, its members felt less threatened by Church-wide organization. Its members had become accustomed to missionary work as well in the years before the schism of 1845. In addition, the large size of the Convention may have made its members more amenable to the agency structure. None of these conditions existed in the Christian Church, however, and it alone maintained the society form of organization throughout the nineteenth century. Its national conventions had no legal relationship to the autonomous local churches.

These differing denominational approaches to the development of agency structure seem to have been more important in the years prior to 1876. Disciples and Baptists would continue to be plagued with the problem of how to justify the evolving national structures, but the pattern of agency development in the years after the nation's centennial was remarkable for its similarity in the face of these denominational differences.

By 1876 most of the missionary and benevolent work originally begun by the "united front" had thus passed into denominational hands.

Most of the denominational agencies were small, with limited incomes and objectives. The agency structure was weak vis-a-vis the traditional pastoral structure. On the horizon, however, were events that would give these organizations larger and more powerful roles in the work of the Churches in America.

NOTES

[1]For example see Abdel Ross Wentz, *A Basic History of Lutheranism in North America* (Philadelphia: Fortress Press, 1955), pp. 292-309; Ernest Trice Thompson, *Presbyterians in the South* (3 vols.; Richmond: John Knox Press, 1973), III, 365-83; Gaius Jackson Slosser, ed., *They Seek a Country: The American Presbyterians* (New York: Macmillan, 1955), pp. 258-59. My research in Roman Catholic sources leads me to believe a case could be made for that Church as well. See also Philip Gleason, *The Conservative Reformers: German-American Catholics and the Social Order* (Notre Dame: University of Notre Dame Press, 1968), pp. 216-25, 316-17; Thomas T. McAvoy, *A History of the Catholic Church in the United States* (Notre Dame: University of Notre Dame Press, 1969), pp. 353-401; and John Tracy Ellis, *American Catholicism* (Chicago: University of Chicago Press, 1969), pp. 124-62.

[2]There are several useful histories of the PEC. See James Thayer Addison, *The Episcopal Church in the United States* (New York: Scribners, 1951); Raymond W. Allbright, *A History of the Protestant Episcopal Church* (New York: Macmillan, 1964); George E. DeMille, *The Episcopal Church Since 1900* (New York: Morehouse-Gorham, 1955); Powell Mills Dawley, *The Episcopal Church and its Work* (Greenwich, Connecticut: Seabury Press, 1955); William Wilson Manross, *A History of the American Episcopal Church* (New York: Morehouse-Gorham, 1950); and Charles Comfort Tiffany, *A History of the Protestant Episcopal Church in the United States of America* (New York: The Church Literature Company, 1895).

[3]My understanding of Methodist history is aided by Wade C. Barclay and J. Tremayne Copplestone, *A History of Methodist Missions* (4 vols.; New York: Board of Global Ministries of the United Methodist Church, 1949-1973); J. M. Buckley, *A History of Methodists in the United States* (New York: Church Literature Company, 1896); Richard M. Cameron, *Methodism and Society in Historical Perspective* (New York: Abingdon, 1961); Robert E. Chiles, *Theological Transition in American Methodism, 1790-1935* (New York: Abingdon, 1965); Nolan B. Harmon, *The Organization of the Methodist Church* (Nashville: Methodist Publishing House, 1962) and *Understanding the Methodist Church* (Nashville: Methodist Publishing House, 1955); Emory S. Bucke, et. al., eds., *A History of American Methodism* (3 vols.; New York: Abingdon, 1964); Halford E. Luccock and Paul Hutchinson, *The Story of American Methodism* (New York: Methodist Book Concern, 1926); Walter G. Muelder, *Methodism and Society in the Twentieth Century* (New York: Abingdon, 1961); and William Warren Sweet, *Methodism in American History* (New York: Abingdon, 1954).

[4]This discussion of Baptist developments in the South is informed by Robert A. Baker, *The Southern Baptist Convention and its People, 1607-1972* (Nashville: Broadman Press, 1974), *The Story of the Sunday School Board* (Nashville: Convention Press, 1966) and ed., *A Baptist Source Book* (Nashville: Broadman Press, 1966); William Wright Barnes, *The Southern Baptist Convention, 1845-1953* (Nashville: Broadman Press, 1954); *The Encyclopedia of Southern Baptists* (Nashville: Broadman Press, 1958); Robert G. Torbet, *A History of the Baptists* (Valley Forge: Judson Press, 1963); and William Warren Sweet, *Religion on the Frontier: The Baptists* (New York: Henry Holt and Company, 1931).

[5]On the history of the Disciples see Louis and Bess White Cochran, *Captives of the Word* (Garden City, N.Y.: Doubleday, 1969); Winfred Ernest Garrison and Alfred T.

DeGroot, *The Disciples of Christ: A History* (St. Louis: Bethany Press, 1958); David Edwin Harrell, Jr., *A Social History of the Disciples of Christ* (2 vols.; Nashville: Disciples of Christ Historical Society, 1966-1973); Loren E. Lair, *The Christian Churches and Their Work* (St. Louis: Bethany Press, 1963); Grant K. Lewis, *The American Christian Missionary Society and the Disciples of Christ* (St. Louis: Christian Board of Publication, 1937); and Archibald McLean, *The History of the Foreign Christian Missionary Society* (New York: Fleming H. Revell, 1919).

[6] *A Social History of the Disciples of Christ,* I, 34-39.

[7] The D&FMS called him the General Secretary.

[8] The Baptist Sunday School Board (BSSB) was later an exception to this pattern; its income was totally derived from sales of Sunday school literature.

[9] Rev. John Atkinson, "Methodism in the Cities of the United States," *Methodist Review,* 59 (July 1877), 503.

[10] "Minutes of the Board of Managers of the Missionary Society of the Methodist Episcopal Church," June 21, 1881, p. 303.   These minutes are located in the central records division of the Board of Global Ministries of the United Methodist Church in New York City.   Hereafter "Board, MEC."

CHAPTER 4

EARLY STRUCTURAL DILEMMAS, 1876-1910

The years following the Civil War and Reconstruction witnessed the fruition of numerous trends that had started, but had not yet been obvious to most American citizens, in the antebellum era. Native agrarians left the plow and joined a flood of European immigrants that were peopling vast new cities. While roughly one-eighth of all Americans lived in urban areas (over 8,000 in population) in 1850, by 1890 city dwellers were about one-third of the population. The completion of a national transportation and communication system following the war enabled business combinations to operate effectively on a national level. Industry came to dominate the American economy. In 1870 agricultural income had surpassed that of factories by $500 million, but by 1900 farm income stood at only $4.7 billion, a far cry from industry's $13 billion.[1]

The story of how the Church dealt with this changing environment is a complicated one. As we have seen, students of American religious history have described these years as a "critical period" during which Christians struggled to come to grips with the twin challenges of new ideas (primarily Darwinism and theological liberalism) and new social conditions (labor unrest and urban chaos, for example). To the extent that this analysis stresses the increasing sense of crisis within the Church between 1876 and the First World War, I believe it is valid. The Church saw itself plagued by a variety of what Josiah Strong called "perils." In a world that appeared to be vexed by rum and Romanism and by socialism and Mormonism, many inside and outside the Church began to wonder about its future. Social Gospel historians have shown us how religious forces struggled to halt the Church's abandonment of urban areas, to overcome the rejection of labor and intellectuals, and to restore the fallen status of the clergy.

Unfortunately this depiction of the Church in crisis does not correspond precisely to the situation faced by the denominational agency structure in the years from 1876 to 1910. While Social Gospelers were bemoaning the Church's loss of the city, the suburbs were in fact becoming the life blood of Protestantism. The Methodist Church Extension Society reported building more than one church a day in these years. The religious press may have lamented membership statistics,[2] but Protestant increases continued to exceed total population growth. Churches were larger and wealthier than ever before; total expenditures by the national agencies of the Churches reached all time highs. Reports of the Church's demise did not correlate with rapidly expanding missionary staffs at home and abroad.

Not that the agencies were without their problems, but the problems were more the result of the Church's successes than its failures. Brought on by increasing size and complexity of the Churches, these difficulties proved more practical and immediate than those faced by the Social Gospelers. They did not captivate the denominational press, but they did occupy the time of a growing circle of denominational executives. These men also felt the Church was threatened, but they were concerned about structures more than ideas. They were convinced that the nineteenth-century pastoral structure could no longer serve a modern, nationally-oriented Church. They also thought that the existing agency structure was plagued by problems of its own, difficulties that checked its ability to provide the direction and organization that the Church needed.

These religious leaders served Churches that experienced sudden growth and greater complexity of activity at the national level after about 1876.   The job of bringing men to Christ was becoming increasingly involved. Between 1880 and 1900 each of the four Churches we have examined enjoyed phenomenal growth.   The Disciples mushroomed from 473,000 members to 1,025,000.[3] The Episcopalians and the Methodists roughly doubled in numbers of communicants, reaching a total of 700,000 and 2,900,000 members respectively.[4] Southern Baptists lagged behind somewhat, but they too grew from 960,000 to 1,658,000 constituents.[5] The membership of all four of the denominations was growing faster than the population of the United States as a whole.   Indeed the period from 1890 to 1920 saw a major jump in total Church membership after a period of relative stability.[6] Churches that kept statistics on total contributions showed a doubling or trebling of total Church receipts, and an even greater increase in the value of Church property.[7] Seymour Martin Lipset may have been correct when he argued that there was "little change in the strength of institutionalized religion"[8] in these years, but he failed to understand that growth in size (whatever an institution's relative strength was) forced significant adjustments in structure. The existing Church structure could neither handle the problems resulting from a larger Church nor take advantage of the opportunities opened up by added strength and wealth.

The agencies surveyed in this study grew at a pace similar to or exceeding that of the denominations as a whole. The General Missionary Society of the Methodist Church saw its contributions increase from approximately $630,000 in 1880 to $1.3 million in 1900. The number of foreign missionaries supported went from 156 to over 600 in the same period.[9] The ACMS, able to collect only $5,000 in 1875, had by 1902 raised its annual receipts to over $100,000, a sum which went to support some 225 missionaries. The total raised by the three Disciples missionary societies amounted to over $465,000 in 1900—and that was after only 25 years of existence. Instead of one corresponding secretary, the ACMS now had three full-time secretaries, a bookkeeper, and four stenographer/clerks to handle its business.[10] The Baptist Sunday School Board (BSSB), only organized in 1891, increased its annual business from $20,000 to $232,000 in its first fifteen years of operation. Total missionary gifts to the Foreign and Home Mission Boards of the SBC expanded from $71,000 to $391,000 in the final two decades of the nineteenth century, and the number of home and foreign missionaries went from sixty to over 800 in those same years.[11] Receipts of the Episcopal Domestic and Foreign Missionary Society (D&FMS) more than doubled between 1880 and 1900, reaching $843,000 in the latter year. The staff in New York City had in 1880 included only a corresponding secretary, his assistant, an assistant treasurer, and three office workers; by 1900 it numbered four executives, two treasurers, two editorial assistants, twenty office workers and ten maintenance employees for the Church Mission House.[12]

New agencies and auxiliaries proliferated. At the beginning of this period, women in all four denominations established home and foreign missionary unions. These organizations usually coordinated their efforts with existing missionary societies while maintaining a semi-autonomous operation. Boards of church extension were created after the Civil War by Methodists, Disciples and Episcopalians to provide financial assistance to erect church buildings throughout the nation. Except for Southern Baptists, all of the Churches organized work among Black Americans: The Methodist Freedman's Aid Society was launched in 1866; the Episcopal Commission for Work Among the Colored People in 1891; and the Disciple Board of Negro Evangelization and Education in 1891. In order to coordinate the effort of the various educational institutions supported by Church funds, boards of education were formed (the Methodists in 1872, the Episcopalians in 1890, the Disciples in 1894 and the Baptists in 1915). Some sort of organization for religious education and Sunday school promotion developed in each Church (the Sunday School Union of the MEC in 1872, the Episcopal American Church Sunday School Insitute in 1884, the Baptist Sunday School Board in 1891, and the National Bible School Association of the Disciples in 1903). Other new agencies included national benevolence associations to coordinate the work of local orphanages, rest homes and hospitals; boards of ministerial relief to care for retired clergymen and their dependents; young people's societies to develop a missionary spirit and Christian virtues in the youth of the Church; and boards of temperance, whose roles eventually were broadened in the hands of the Social Gospelers to include a wide spectrum of social services. The Episcopal *Church Almanac and Yearbook* of 1904 illustrated the proliferation of Church agencies. Besides the various diocesan charities, the *Almanac* listed six societies officially endorsed by the General Convention, twenty-two educational institutions, twenty-one guilds, fourteen missionary organizations, four devotional fraternities, three financial endowments, thirty-five religious orders for men and women, and ten miscellaneous organizations.[13]

As the national denominational enterprise grew in size and scope, the financial methods that had served during most of the nineteenth century proved increasingly inadequate.[14] Reliance on a few rich benefactors, the vestige of the earlier society organization, had gradually been replaced by the more "democratic" and potentially more fruitful appeal to the local churches. All major denominational benevolences reported substantial increases in income between 1880 and 1900. Unfortunately, income did not always match the expansion in expenditures, particularly during periods of financial depression like the 1890's. Concern about the debts and "the interest charges resulting therefrom," as well as a desire for "a much more liberal supply of money," was frequently expressed in the minutes of the boards of managers.[15] More than once were agencies compelled to turn to one of their wealthy lay managers to bail them out until the financial picture improved.[16]

The periods of insufficient income and indebtedness concerned the Boards for two basic reasons. First, such periods forced cutbacks in the work of the Church. In 1896, the D&FMS had to make a "readjustment" in the salaries and stipends of its missionaries.[17] Lack of funds sometimes compelled the Boards to discourage missionary candidates.[18] Methodist cutbacks in 1911 threatened the "recall of missionaries, the dismissal of native preachers and workers, and the abandonment of many undertakings."[19] Opportunities for potential service had to be passed by. "If the Church is to embrace the opportunities which are before it, much more money must be contributed. The alternative is to curtail the work, refuse the call of Divine Providence, and be content with a contracted and contracting sphere instead of possessing an enlarged and enlarging domain."[20] Complaints from the mission fields about the effects of capricious financing were common. The Episcopal Bishop of Shanghai wrote:

> All I can say is that we cannot go on the plan of a growing work one year and a contracting work the next . . . . Nothing cuts the sinews of work in full course that is really prospering as quickly as this uncertainty from year to year as to whether it can be supported

or not. . . . What the lack of confidence is in business enterprise,
that is what this everlasting uncertainty about appropriations is to
us.[21]

Periods of inadequate income also proved embarrassing to the
boards' staffs and managers. The Methodist Board issued an appeal to
its members in 1911: "In this crisis, when a bold advance is plainly
demanded, we find ourselves embarrassed by the inadequacy of our
resources. The contributions of the Churches to foreign missions
declined during the past year sufficiently to necessitate a 'cut' of three
per cent in the appropriations for 1912."[22] Much of the agencies'
mortification stemmed from the additional ammunition that such
financial defects provided for their critics. Throughout the nineteenth
century the boards had been accused of spending as much as half their
incomes on administration. Times of financial insolvency seemed to
many opponents to be the product of agency prodigality. In defense, the
annual reports of the boards described in detail the economy of their
management. An outside accountant was sometimes asked to certify the
parsimony of the denominational servants.[23] Increases in the size of the
central staff had to be justified by both the expanding work and the
"exceptionally small" expense of administration.[24] More substantial
incomes might have silenced the agencies' critics, but in these years the
best the executives could do was to abscribe their financial troubles to
such external causes as the general state of the economy, the failure of
pastors to communicate the needs of the boards to their communicants,
and the lack of a real concern for missions among the members. The
Methodist Board chalked up its debt of $220,000 in 1896 to "the growth
of the work beyond the income of the Missionary Society and not of
extravagant or careless administration."[25]

There was, of course, some validity to the charge that certain
local churches failed to support the mission effort adequately, despite the
fact that total agency income was rising. Throughout the 1890s the
Episcopal Board reported that roughly half of the Church's parishes gave
nothing to the cause of missions.[26] In its 1904 report the Episcopal
Board noted "that among the chief obstacles to the progress of the
Church's Mission are diocesanism and parochialism. . . . The weak point
in our missionary giving has been the parochial congregation."[27] The
Disciples publication *The Christian Standard* called the failure of three-
quarters of the churches to contribute "a fact so humiliating that we
could wish to hide it from knowledge if it were not that it should
provide a spur to greater exertion."[28] Often local churches seemed more
interested in erecting beautiful edifices than in spreading the Gospel.
"Many of our parishes would be more sure of God's blessing if they

accepted greater simplicity and let their offerings flow out more abundantly to those who lack everything."[29]   Other churches, while raising money, rejected the Boards' suggested procedure in favor of an "omnibus" collection.   Instead of having a separate appeal for each benevolence, many pastors simply held one annual offering for all and divided the total contributions among the various agencies.   This perturbed the boards, especially the older established ones, because their causes did not receive what they felt was their just exposure.[30]   In addition, the division of funds did not seem to reflect any sense of the relative importance of the various benevolences (at least in the eyes of the querulous board).[31]

The solution to these problems of local dereliction of duty seemed to agency executives to be some means to intensify the existing annual offering.   Most mission secretaries were convinced that "more stress upon the value of personal presentation of the work of missions" would somehow solve their problems.[32]   Pastors were reminded of their duty to preach a missions sermon and offered materials to help in the preparation of such sermons.[33]   Seminaries were urged to offer instruction on the importance of missions as an addition to their regular curricula.[34]   When the single annual offering proved insufficient, denominational leaders added a Sunday School Children's Day for mission study and offerings. The local women's and young people's societies were also enlisted in the appeal for funds.[35]   One fruitful innovation to intensify the existing system was the "Apportionment Plan."   Under this arrangement, the agencies assigned a quota, either directly or through the local legislative or executive arms, to each church in the denomination.   Given a goal, more local churches responded and income generally increased.   In 1904, for instance, 4,190 Episcopal congregations contributed to missions as compared to the 2,226 which had done so in 1900, before the adoption of the plan.[36]

From the perspective of the local church, however, the agencies' solution was, ironically, the problem.   Local congregations seldom were totally disinterested in benevolences or absorbed in local affairs, as the financial growth of the agencies indicates.   They were, nonetheless, frequently perturbed about the proliferation of denominational collections.   By the 1890s some four to eight national organizations in each Church expected local pastors to spend at least one Sunday annually promoting their work.   In addition there were various state, diocesan and local offerings to be taken.   At the first lay congress of the Disciples of Christ, one member noted "that the churches are beginning to wince under the multiplicity of appeals."[37]   The Methodist bishops told the General Conference of 1904 that there was a "growing sentiment that we have too many benevolent collections."[38]   A poll of Methodist pastors in 1912 found that 1,475 of 1,910 clergymen responding (77%) felt that multiple collections hindered "the religious zeal of the Church."[39] A letter to *The Christian Standard* summed up the situation: "It is one thing for our Acting Boards to send out frequent and earnest appeals to our churches and Sunday-schools for missions money, and it is a different thing for pastors and superintendents of those churches and schools to go into them and collect the required amounts of money."[40] There is little wonder local churches often opted for the "omnibus" collection.

As the Boards became aware that they were alienating the local churches with their multiple appeals, animosity between competing agencies in each denomination tended to increase. In 1902 the ACMS criticized the rival Foreign Christian Missionary Society for interfering with its missionary offering "by sending out appeals during the month of April."[41] The *Christian Advocate* felt compelled to refute the contention "that what are called the minor collections would be likely to suffer from the extraordinary efforts now making to raise $1,250,000 for Missions by collections only."[42] Proposals for the creation of new competitors for the religious dollar also rankled the established boards. The ACMS opposed the proposed National Board of Evangelism: "They must necessarily be rivals to a greater or less [sic] extent, and must create division in the minds, the plans, and the efforts of the brotherhood. . . . The income naturally belonging to the ACMS would be divided."[43] The head of the Baptist Foreign Mission Board expressed both envy and resentment toward the new Sunday School Board because its publishing income made it financially independent.[44]

The dangers of alienating local churches and competing agencies by attempts to intensify the existing financial program—in addition to the uncertain income and periods of debt which the agencies faced—ultimately led certain individuals to ask bluntly whether the financial methods in use were not antiquated. As early as 1882, Methodist pastor J. W. Young (who later developed the Methodist Board's Apportionment Plan) wrote:

> We have hitherto acted upon the masses by means calculated to move only a few. . . . Our talented and zealous Secretaries, our anxious Boards of Management, our Bishops and other prominent men, lay and clerical, have been making the most powerful appeals. . . . We can gain little by more vigorously working present plans.[45]

Calling the existing method "impulsive," the Rev. Alfred Yeomans commented that it was "inevitably limited in its expansiveness and fitful and unsteady in its operation." Yeomans went on to say that "the old system is worn out. Publishing and begging agencies whip up languid and unsteady zeal. Sermons on missions, eloquent appeals to pity, vivid pictures of pagan woes, all are unavailing to keep the stream of beneficence enlarging."[46] A Baptist pastor echoed these sentiments: "We have pitched out church finances upon the inspirational and spasmodic appeals so long it has become a habit of character with us."[47]

The system itself added an additional "hazard of enthusiasm." Reliance on a single annual offering meant that mission boards frequently lost thousands of dollars due to "the simple incident of rain on a given Sunday."[48] Furthermore, due to the single annual offering, most boards received the bulk of their income in a short span of time. The money had to be spread out, however, over an entire year. With income varying from year to year, budgeting was extremely difficult. Often the agencies were forced to borrow to pay expenses until the offering was taken, necessitating costly interest payments. Many local churches waited until the end of the fiscal year to send in their offerings, leaving the boards puzzling until the last minute whether or not they would run in the black.[49]

The erratic nature of the system of annual offerings had an undesirable effect on the other major source of funds, the specials. Specials allowed an individual or church to contribute to a specific project, such as the construction of a mission school or hospital. These projects were conceived as supplements to the regular income of the agency and had the advantage of giving churches and individuals a sense of personal involvement in a particular mission enterprise. The enormous growth of mission work during these years was financed increasingly by means of specials. Between 1895 and 1901, for instance, Episcopal regular offerings for missions increased $13,000, while specials increased $106,000. In 1900 the members gave eight times as much in regular offerings as in 1850, but they donated sixteen times as much in specials. Methodist "special gifts" increased from $22,000 in 1890 to $438,000 in 1911.[50]

Like the annual offering, specials relied heavily on impulse and emotion. The individual missionary had to approach the local church, either by mail or more commonly on a fund-raising tour, to obtain support for his project. Such a system naturally disturbed those less willing or less able to campaign for funds. In 1893 the Episcopal Board considered complaints from bishops who were too busy to spend time as fund-raisers.[51] The result of specials, according to the Methodist Board, "has been that the missionaries have been overworked on the fields in the attempt to keep up the line of correspondence with the home church. Missionaries at home on furlough have been raising money when they should have been resting."[52] Bishop Graves of China prayed for an "emancipation from the present constraints and the obligation to beg."[53]

The major disadvantage of the specials was the manner in which they undermined the planning and superintendence of the national boards. The agencies had little control over the frequency or magnitude of the appeals by the fundraisers, nor were they certain that the totals raised were accurately reported to the home office.[54] As a result, mission stations could carry on an almost independent existence. Bishop Graves of China, for instance, informed the D&FMS that it "would be astonished to realize that the Mission has largely been built up without direct aid from them."[55] Charismatic missionaries could obtain large contributions regardless of the boards' evaluation of the worth of their projects. The D&FMS warned that "it often happens that work of lesser importance, represented by effective speakers, secures a much larger response than can be awakened by speakers of less preeminent gifts."[56] Bishop J. S. Johnston bemoaned the fact that "the success of each missionary bishop at home is made to depend upon his begging ability, regardless of the importance of his work."[57] A Methodist manager reported after a tour of the mission field that the most popular missionaries were those who raised the most money for their mission while they were home on furlough.[58]

The agencies' fragile relationships with local churches were also strained by the specials. Arthur R. Gray, Educational Secretary of the Episcopal Board, observed that "it very frequently happens that what the Church [meaning the Board] thinks should be done is quite different from what this or that parish or individual prefers to do."[59] The agencies felt they were "in a position to take a broad view of the whole field," and should establish some sort of control over a system that had gotten out of hand.[60] General Secretary Arthur S. Lloyd of the D&FMS wrote in 1907 that "the system is intolerable and must be brought to an end."[61] Some local churches, no doubt annoyed by frequent solicitations, pressed for board authorization of all special appeals.[62] Rules requiring a missionary to obtain authorization for such apeals from the board and his bishop and to funnel all of the money raised through the treasury of the board were, however, regularly ignored.[63]

By 1910 the major Protestant denominations were thus all aware that the scheme of benevolent finance had significant shortcomings in the light of the increased size of agency operations. Their understanding of the problem was as yet incomplete, however, and their approach to reform was far from systematic. Each board tended to view its difficulties in isolation rather than as a condition facing other agencies both in and outside its denomination. Criticism of the financial structure, moreover, tended to be haphazard, and few had carefully thought out solutions to the problems. As we have already seen, the most common recommendation is this period was to streamline and invigorate the existing mechanism. The "Apportionment Plan" was the most successful innovation along these lines, but even with it, the problems of multiple and impulsive appeals that the annual offering and specials produced still remained.

From those who had concluded that "something more is needed than a fresh stimulus infused into old methods"[64] came little more than vague generalizations about the urgency of a "permanent plan for providing for the income necessary for the work of the Board,"[65] the "importance of devising some plan,"[66] the desire for "a method so organized,"[67] or "the need of some radical change in the process by which the consecration of Christian wealth is to be secured."[68] Workable solutions to the problems of finance were not immediately forthcoming. The old system persisted long after its problems had been clearly identified.

Moreover, the agencies' financial problems were matched by their administrative difficulties, and these too proved hard to solve. The most common complaint from the corresponding secretaries was that of overwork. Requests for additional stenographic or clerical help and for new labor-saving machinery dotted the minutes of the managers in the 1890s. At the Disciples' General Convention of 1891, a committee reported:

> The work now laid upon the Corresponding Secretary is too large and multiform for one man. He is expected to lay and execute all plans for raising money; to receive all funds and acknowledge the same; conduct all correspondence touching all departments of the work; to ascertain all facts relating to mission stations and the men to fill them, and report, with recommendations to the Board; and to take a general supervision of all the missionary work, and counsel with reference to difficulties, external and internal, that may arise at mission stations; and to furnish manuscript regularly for the official paper.[69]

Ten years later the corresponding secretary of the same society said, "The day has come when we must make larger plans for home missions. One man can do about so much and then he reaches his limitation."[70]

In part the problem stemmed from the fact that the work of the individual agencies was expanding and becoming more diversified. The original function of the home mission boards, for instance, had been to support missionaries in frontier settlements. After the Civil War, however, the boards broadened their efforts to include church extension, evangelism, immigrant work, military chaplains, city ministries, rural churches, mountain schools, territorial aid (Cuba, Panama, Puerto Rico, Hawaii and Alaska), and missions to special groups like Indians, Orientals, Negroes and Jews. Foreign mission boards extended their mission fields, especially after the Spanish-American War, to all of the continents. More work and more complex administrative problems arose as a result of agency expansion along these lines.

Another symptom of the growth of these organizations was the frequent complaints about cramped quarters. The Baptist Sunday School Board moved three times in the 1890s in search of more commodious quarters for its expanding business. The Corresponding Secretary of the ACMS and his assistant were compelled to share a single office in the YMCA in Cincinnati, while eight other employees were squeezed into another room.[71] The Episcopal Board built what seemed a spacious Church Mission House in 1893, but by 1912 the executive officers were complaining of the building's inadequacies.[72]

The pressure of day-to-day operations allowed Church leaders little time for the long-term planning or central oversight that might have generated solutions to these problems. Bishop Graves, the Episcopal leader in Shanghai, complained constantly to the D&FMS that it never made contingency plans. The loss of two of his medical missionaries in 1904 prompted him to write; "No management or wit of ours can prevent such things, but the consequences would be less serious if I could have a reserve. Some day I am going to strike! To work under this system is to roll stones up hill and see them roll down again."[73] Harvey Beauchamp, looking back on a dozen years of service with the Baptist Sunday School Board, wrote to Corresponding Secretary J. M. Frost: "I think you know that my only complaint at you has been that you would not often tell us what to do. I have felt often that I would like to have a clearer view of how you would like the Field Work done."[74] A letter to the Episcopal weekly, *The Churchman*, also lamented the fact that "our Church has no watchful eye or set of eyes, to spy out her faults, and no wisely scheming practical brain authorized to devise ways and means to do the Gospel work properly and fully; . . . it lacks an administrative and executive head."[75]

The need for central direction was felt most acutely when the multiplication of denominational agencies produced heated rivalries. The most common cause of friction, as we have seen, was financial competition, but overlapping authorities also created problems. Since jurisdictional disputes threatened the public images of the boards, denominational executives like Archibald McLean of the FCMS tried to minimize the extent of the competition. "True, there is a generous rivalry between the different organizations," he said, but each, he added, "seeks to provoke the others to love and good works."[76] In reality, the rivalries provoked more animosity than love, more conflict than good works. The distribution of time allotted to the national conventions of the ACMS and FCMS produced a serious rupture between those two societies in 1897.[77] Fearful that competing organizations were using its national convention to further their own causes, the ACMS banned them from the agenda to deny them the "prestige of the ACMS program,"[78] a move which seems unlikely to have generated either "love" or "good works." The Methodist Board of Missions and the Methodist Sunday School Board angrily debated the question of who should organize religious education on the mission field.[79] Nor was the Board of Missions willing to surrender its educational work to the Epworth League when that organization tried to launch its own program of missionary training.[80] Corresponding secretaries were especially wary of any attempt to compel their organizations to support some fledgling operation. The frequent requests that the ACMS aid in the support of a National Superintendent of Christian Endeavor met with stony silence at board meetings.[81] The Corresponding Secretary of the BSSB was forever concerned that the Convention would try to expend his contingency fund in support of the good works of some other agency of the Convention.[82]

The proliferation of agencies and the overlapping of authorities also perturbed many Church members. The fruits of such proliferation, they believed, were dissension, disorder and waste. As early as 1877, an unsigned letter to *The Churchman* compained, "We have too many societies, too many wheels within a wheel, to be able to accomplish all the good that the Church should."[83] Thirty-five years later the editor of the same paper described with greater insight the same condition: "The creation of too many departments of the work and the multiplication of organizations, which the growth and activity of the Church have made necessary, have resulted in serious confusion, and duplication and waste."[84] The Methodist *Christian Advocate* said,

> Every additional piece of machinery not actually necessary is an impediment. It diverts power from necessary channels; it is an occasion of friction; it produces a false form of activity, hallucinating those who are working the machinery into the belief that they are accomplishing something for *Christ* and the Church. . . .
>
> Methodism has been adding new machinery for many years. . . . Machinery should be regarded like medicine, as an evil in itself, only to be tolerated when it removes a greater evil.[85]

Southern Baptist Landmarkers, who were the strongest defenders of local church autonomy in that denomination, were especially concerned that "the ever increasing multiplication of extra-church agencies and consequent expenses prolonged and intensified the strife" within the Church.[86]

In the first decades of the twentieth century, denominational executives began to discuss these problems of administration more frequently. The problems of the Church seemed larger than ever in the eyes of its executives. As J. M. Frost closed out his twenty-five years as first Corresponding Secretary of the BSSB, he wrote: "We have grown so big we don't know what to do with ourselves."[87]   A similar observation appears in the *Journal of the Methodist Board of Foreign Missions* in which the corresponding secretaries stated: "The very magnitude of our denominational enterprise constitutes our chief problem.   As Dr. Leonard [Corresponding Secretary from 1888 to 1912] used to say, our success is our chief embarrassment. We have grown too big—the cost of reaching our constituency is enormous."[88]

In the years from 1876 to 1910, however, few fully understood the administrative problems faced by the boards. The internal structure of the agencies had changed little as the volume of work grew. The normal pattern of adjustment was as follows: the corresponding secretary first added stenographic help to handle his growing corespondence; he hired a clerical assistant to do odd-jobs around the office. An assistant corresponding secretary—or as in the Methodist Episcopal Church three co-equal secretaries—might be employed, but little differentiation in the work resulted from such a change. The staff of all these agencies was larger in 1900, but there was little evidence of the sort of specialization or departmentalization that might have achieved a higher degree of efficiency.

The boards occasionally formed committees to study the administrative efficiency or bookkeeping practices, but there appear to have been no major organizational changes in any of the agencies before 1900. The most immediate effect of the expansion of the agencies' work was the construction of large headquarters buildings. The Methodists erected their own building in 1889, the Episcopalians in 1893, the ACMS in 1910, and the Baptists in 1914. In addition, the agencies acquired such laborsaving machinery as typewriters, telephones and calculators.

Proposals for streamlining the overall organizational structure of each Church were advanced but few changes resulted. The ACMS Board called for "unification" of all Disciples agencies at least three times in the 1890s. A committee representing the three major Disciple boards met in 1899, but rejected any form of agency consolidation. A Baptist Joint Committee of Cooperation was established in 1899 to plan a united appeal for missions in celebration of the new century; a year later, however, the Convention refused to establish a permanent Committee of Cooperation to harmonize the work of the national Boards and to coordinate state and national efforts. The Methodist General Conference of 1884 established a Commission on the Consolidation, Unification and

Reorganization of Church Benevolences, but then rejected the Commission's proposals in 1888 and 1892.

The reasons for this failure of Church leadership to come to grips with the financial and administrative problems brought on by growth are not hard to find. As yet, the problems were ill-defined and hazy in the minds of most leaders. Few agency executives thought in systematic ways about what changes were needed. The advantages of a centralized bureaucracy were not yet apparent to religious leaders. Furthermore, denominational leadership was conservative—not unlike the leadership in most large organizations. Despite all their problems, agency executives frequently were unwilling to rock the boat. The system had, after all, worked well for over half a century. Existing organizations were, some insisted, meeting the needs of the Church. As one executive put it, they were "well-nigh perfect."[89] General Secretary Langford of the D&FMS refused to consider plans to replace the Board's missions magazine with a more "popular" one since the current periodical ably satisfied the need for communication with clergy and laity.[90]

Denominational conservatism also stemmed from fear as well as from satisfaction. To consolidate or reorganize existing organizations would mean that certain leaders would be faced with losses of status, influence and independence. J. M. Frost of the BSSB, for instance, feared that the SBC was going to "make hash" of his work by consolidating the Convention's boards. Frost called the proposed unification an "untried experiment, . . . visionary and speculative, . . . utterly unbusinesslike and even reckless."[91] In addition, Baptist and Disciples executives were well aware that any structural changes that hinted of increased central size and power would generate cries of "episcopacy" and "papacy" from their local churches. ACMS leaders, remembering the ill-fated Louisville Plan for consolidation that had almost destroyed the Society in the 1870s, were wary of anything that smacked of centralization. In 1900, Archibald McLean, Corresponding Secretary of the Foreign Christian Missionary Society and later an architect of Disciple agency consolidation, argued that "our people are very sly of any one master mind and a Board with supreme authority. . . . I am convinced that a general Board over all the others would be as useless as a fifth wheel to a wagon."[92]

As a result of this overall mood of conservatism among agency leaders, the bureaucracies of these agencies were still small in the early years of the twentieth century. Even the largest board, The Methodist Missionary Society, had a central staff of only fourteen in 1900, although its annual income totaled more than $1.2 million. None of the agencies had yet created specialized departments. Nor was there a central executive authority in any Church empowered to make decisions between meetings of the national conventions.

After 1910, however, these conditions changed. The boards sought to resolve the problems of chaotic finances, inefficient administrations, and conflicting authorities in order to facilitate the accomplishment of their traditional goals. This process of change, however, involved more than a history of adjustment to structural dilemmas. A more positive rationale for change began to influence the leaders in the Churches; they were touched by the Progressive fascination with organization, efficiency and system. As a result, the agencies of the Churches became central figures in the Church's adjustment to the twentieth century. They became in effect symbols of Protestant modernity.

NOTES

[1]Marty, *Righteous Empire*, p. 156.

[2]See for example, Charles Graves, "Are the Churches Declining?," *World's Work*, 4 (May 1902), 2076-80.

[3]"Minutes of the Annual Convention of the American Christian Missionary Society," (1906), pp. 394ff. Hereafter "Convention, ACMS." Copies of these minutes are available on microfilm at the Disciples of Christ Historical Society, Nashville, Tennessee.

[4]*The Methodist Yearbook* (New York, 1902), p. 36; *The Church Almanac and Yearbook* (New York, 1880 and 1900).

[5]Barnes, *The Southern Baptist Convention*, pp. 306-07.

[6]United States Bureau of the Census, *Religious Bodies: 1906* (Washington: Government Printing Office, 1910). The sudden spurt in total Church membership as a percentage of population is seen in the following figures based on Benson Y. Landis, *Yearbook of the American Churches* (New York: National Council of Churches, 1961):

1850 - 17%	1870 - 18%	1900 - 27%	1910 - 42%
1860 - 23%	1880 - 21%	1900 - 36%	1920 - 42%

See, however, Landis' article on the problems of religious statistics: "Trends in Church Membership in the United States," *Annals of the American Academy of Political and Social Science*, 332 (November 1960), 1-8.

[7]Between 1884 and 1900, for example, total Baptist offerings grew from $1.5 to $3.5 million and the value of Church property increased from $4.7 to $20 million. *Encyclopedia of Southern Baptists*, p. 1256. See also the *Episcopal Almanac and Yearbook* (New York, 1880-1900).

[8]*The First New Nation: The United States in Historical and Comparative Perspective* (New York: Basic Books, 1963), p. 148.

[9]*The Methodist Yearbook* (New York, 1880 and 1900).

[10]Garrison and DeGroot, *The Disciples*, p. 366; Lewis, *The American Christian Missionary Society*, Appendix; "Convention, ACMS," (1900).

[11]See the "Annual Reports" of the Home and Foreign Boards in the *Proceedings of the Southern Baptist Convention*, (1880-1900), later known as the *Annual.* Hereafter, *Proceedings (Annual), SBC.*

[12]See the monthly Treasurer's Reports, 1880-1900, and lists of staff members, 1880-1902, in the "Minutes of the Board of Managers of the Domestic and Foreign Missionary Society of the Protestant Episcopal Church." Hereafter "Board, PEC." These minutes may be found in the Episcopal Archives, Austin, Texas.

[13](New York, 1904), pp. 57-70.

[14]This was not the case, of course, for the BSSB, which was able to finance its operations out of its publishing income. The BSSB made no local collections.

[15]"Board, MEC," June 16, 1896, p. 165; "Board, PEC," December 8, 1891, and June 13, 1893; and "Annual Report, Foreign Mission Board" in *Proceedings, SBC* (1897).

[16]"Board, PEC," December 8, 1891. Both Cornelius Vanderbilt and J. P. Morgan lent money to the D&FMS.

[17]"Board, PEC," May 12, 1896, p. 217.

[18]"Board, PEC," January 13, 1891; "Minutes of the Board of Managers of the American Christian Missionary Society," December 15, 1895. Hereafter, "Board, ACMS." These Minutes are on microfilm at the Disciples of Christ Historical Society, Nashville.

[19]"Board, MEC," November 28, 1911, p. 216. See also the same minutes for September 17, 1912, p. 461.

[20]"Board, PEC," January 13, 1893, p. 271.

[21]Bishop Graves, "Board, PEC," September 15, 1903, p. 35.

[22]"Board, MEC," November 28, 1911, p. 216.

[23]See the "Annual Report" of the Foreign Mission Board in *Proceedings, SBC* (1893), p. x; "Report of the General Missions Committee," in the *Handbook of the General Conference of the Methodist Episcopal Church* (New York, 1908), hereafter *Handbook, MEC; Annual Report of the Board of Managers of the Domestic and Foreign Missionary Society of the Protestant Episcopal Church* (New York, 1901), p. 20, hereafter, *Annual Report, PEC; The Churchman,* 36 (June 7, 1877), 3-4; and "Board, ACMS," October 30, 1908, p. 499.

[24]*Annual Report, PEC* (New York, 1898), p. 23.

[25]"Board, MEC," June 16, 1896, p. 166.

[26]*Annual Report, PEC* (New York, 1897), pp. 20-21. In 1896 there was even a decrease of 258 in the number of contributing parishes.

[27]*Ibid.,* (New York, 1904), p. 26.

[28]31 (January 19, 1895), 96.

[29]*Annual Report, PEC* (New York, 1899), p. 20.

[30]"Board, MEC," December 17, 1901, p. 250 and *Handbook, MEC* (New York, 1912), p. 193.

[31]Rev. J. W. Young, "The Problem of Our Church Benevolences," *Methodist Review,* 64 (January, 1882), 55.

[32]The boards frequently stated that "the chief obstacle to interest in the missionary operations of the Church is ignorance." See "Board, PEC," November 10, 1904, p. 25 and November 14, 1899, p. 111; Rev. Young, "The Problem of Church Benevolences," pp. 60-65; "Convention, ACMS," (1904), p. 311.

[33]The Methodist Board, for instance, discussed sending such literature regularly. See "Board, MEC," June 21, 1881, p. 314; September 20, 1887, p. 212; January 15, 1895, pp. 361-62; and March 1, 1898, pp. 130-31. Note also "Board, PEC," November 14, 1899, p. 111.

[34]"Board, PEC," November 14, 1899, p. 111; *Annual Report, PEC* (New York, 1893). The BSSB provided funds to establish a Chair of Sunday School Pedagogy at the Southern Baptist Theologial Seminary in 1906. See "Minutes of the Sunday School Board of the Southern Baptist Convention," April 12, 1906. Hereafter, "Board, SBC."

[35]An excellent description of this accretion of annual offerings among the Disciples may be found in Lair, *The Christian Churches and their Work, p. 148.*

[36]*Annual Report, PEC* (New York, 1904), p. 25. Results were somewhat less spectacular in other denominations, however. The Plan, developed in the 1880's, was adopted by the Methodist Board in 1891, the SBC's Foreign Mission Board in 1892, the ACMS in 1893, and the D&FMS in 1900.

[37]J. H. Garrison, ed., *Our First Congress* (St. Louis: 1900), p. 207. See also "Board, ACMS," May 26, 1905, p. 609.

[38]"Episcopal Address," *Journal of the General Conference of the Methodist Episcopal Church* (New York, 1904), p. 133. Hereafter *Journal, MEC.*

[39]*Journal, MEC* (New York, 1912), p. 198.

[40]J. F. Floyd, 33 (November 27, 1897).

[41]"Board, ACMS," May 16, 1902, pp. 415-16.

[42]Rev. R. W. Van Schoick, "All Other Benevolences Debtors to Missions," 66 (March 19, 1891), 187.

[43]"Board, ACMS," December 28, 1903, p. 501. See also the "Report of the Board of Church Extension" in *Journal, MEC* (New York, 1900), pp. 732-33.

[44]See the letters of H. H. Harris of the FMB to J. M. Frost, Corresponding Secretary of the BSSB, March 29, 1893 and April 3, 1893 in the manuscript records of the administration of J. M. Frost, Box 1, located in the Dargan-Carver Library of the BSSB, Nashville, Tennessee. Hereafter Frost MSS.

[45]"The Problem of our Church Benevolences," p. 58. A letter from E. R. in the Methodist *Christian Advocate* called "the loose voluntary plan of contributing" the "bane" of the MEC, 67 (February 25, 1892), 117.

[46]"Reorganization of Church Giving," *Presbyterian Review*, 7 (April 1886), 270-72.

[47]Selsus E. Tull, et. al., *Church Organization and Methods: A Manual for Baptist Churches* (Nashville: Baptist Sunday School Board, 1917), pp. 9-10.

[48]*Ibid.*; see also *Annual Report, PEC* (New York, 1897), p. 49.

[49]"Annual Report," Foreign Mission Board, *Proceedings, SBC* (1890), p. xxv; "Board, MEC," March 15, 1881, p. 286.

[50]"Board, PEC," December 13, 1904, p. 295; "Board, MEC," July 16, 1917, p. 418 and September 17, 1892, p. 458.

[51]"Board, PEC," June 13, 1893, p. 198.

[52]"Board, MEC," September 17, 1912, p. 458.

[53]"Board, PEC," September 17, 1901, p. 33.

[54]"Board, MEC," June 20, 1911; "Board, PEC," November 13, 1906, p. 204.

[55]"Board, PEC," November 13, 1906, pp. 192-93.

[56]"The Board of Missions and Special Gifts," Leaflet #914, D&FMS, June, 1915, found in two boxes of miscellaneous pamphlets issued by the D&FMS in the early years of this century at the Episcopal Archives, Austin, Texas.   Hereafter, Pamphlet Boxes.

[57]Letter to *The Churchman*, 80 (September 2, 1899), 264.

[58]"Board, MEC," September 16, 1913, p. 378.

[59]"Information," leaflet in Pamphlet Boxes.

[60]*Annual Report, PEC* (New York, 1899), p. 20.

[61]Letter to John Wood, Corresponding Secretary of the D&FMS, May 1, 1907, in a meagre collection of letters relating to Board affairs; most came primarily during Lloyd's mission tour of 1906-1907 and are located in one box at the Episcopal Archives in Austin. Hereafter Lloyd MSS.

[62]"Board, PEC," June 11, 1907, p. 799.

[63]*Ibid.*, April 14, 1896, p. 205.

[64]Yeomans, "Reorganization of Church Giving," p. 270.

[65]"Board, PEC," December 8, 1891.

[66]*Ibid.*, September 17, 1895, pp. 43-44.   See similar statements in Garrison, ed., *Our First Congress*, p. 200.

[67] *Annual Report, PEC* (New York, 1896), p. 10.

[68] Yeomans, p. 270.

[69] "Convention, ACMS," (1891), p. 13.

[70] "Board, ACMS," May 17, 1901, p. 362.

[71] "Board, ACMS," January 16, 1903, January 15, 1904.

[72] "Board, PEC," May 8, 1912, p. 109.

[73] "Board, PEC," September 20, 1904.

[74] Letter of July 30, 1916, in Frost MSS., Box 32.

[75] 79 (April 8, 1899), 518.

[76] "The Consolidation," *The Christian Standard,* 36 (May 12, 1900), 581.

[77] "Board, ACMS," June 25, 1897, p. 213.

[78] *Ibid.,* December 17, 1909.

[79] For example see letters of Corresponding Secretary Frank Mason North to S. Earl Taylor, April 8, 1914, and June 19, 1914 in the Taylor file in the manuscript records of the Methodist Missionary Society located at the Methodist Archives, Lake Junaluska, N. C. Hereafter Methodist MSS. See also *Handbook, MEC* (New York, 1916), pp. 187, 416; Commission on Finance File, 1912-1914 in Methodist MSS.; and "Board, MEC," July 15, 1913, pp. 328-32.

[80] "Board, MEC," June 6, 1905, pp. 349-50.

[81] "Board, ACMS," December 17, 1909.

[82] "Board, SBC," January 9, 1902 and December 14, 1916; letter of W. B. Crumpton to Frost, July 19, 1916, in Frost MSS., Box 32.

[83] 35 (Februry 10, 1877), 152. See also *Journal of the General Convention of the Protestant Episcopal Church* (New York, 1907), p. 453. Hereafter *Journal, PEC.*

[84] "The Convention's Opportunity," 108 (September 27, 1913), 406.

[85] "Church Machinery," 67 (May 5, 1892), 291.

[86] J. A. Scarboro, *The Bible, The Baptists and The Board System: An Appeal for Biblical Missions* (Chicago, 1904), p. 61.

[87] Frost to T. P. Bell, June 8, 1916 in Frost MSS., Box 32.

[88](New York, 1916), p. 81. The *Journal* was an annual report to the Society's Board of Managers.   Hereafter, *Journal, MBFM.*

[89]"Shall the Missionary Machinery Be Changed?," *Spirit of Missions* (the D&FMS house organ), 66 (September 1901), 596.   See also W. E. Dodge in Evangelical Alliance, *National Needs and Remedies* (New York: Baker and Taylor, 1890), p. 3.

[90]"Board, PEC," January 14, 1896, pp. 132-33.

[91]"From a Business Viewpoint," a draft of an article written by Frost, c. 1915, Frost MSS., Box 33.

[92]"The Consolidation," *The Christian Standard,* 36 (May 12, 1900), 604.   See also in the same journal, 33 (November 27, 1897); 35 (August 26, 1899), 1082-83; 35 (September 9, 1899), 1141; and 41 (October 13, 1906).

CHAPTER 5

IDEOLOGY OF ORGANIZATION

The Churchmen who restructured American Protestantism during the early decades of this century drew heavily on a set of ideas that were linked to the Progressive Movement and to a number of related changes taking place in American society. A new vocabulary was used to express the set of values associated with these developments; scientific method, efficiency, order, and organization were major themes. These ideas, expressions of a new bureaucratic ideology, developed outside the sphere of religion. It was business that played the leading role in the adoption of bureaucratic means in the final decades of the nineteenth century.[1] Other groups ranging from government to agriculture later followed in the footsteps of business. Churches too were caught up in the spirit of the new age.

Religious historians have rarely viewed the twentieth-century Church in this light. They have not looked on the Progressive Movement, for instance, as an organizational phenomenon. Instead they have accepted a more traditional framework based largely on the reformers' own account of events; thus they have described the period as a social and political revolt of the people, led by middle-class reformers, against corporate interests, political machines and social injustice.[2] Progressivism, accordingly, sought a more moral and democratic society in the face of the menaces of industrialism. Included among the reformers were the Social Gospelers.

This viewpoint is not entirely inaccurate. There were strong moral elements in Progressivism; there was an ardent desire for a better and more democratic society. Progressives were concerned about vested interests and social injustice. They sought means to preserve the small-town, individualistic values of the nineteenth century. They believed they were "only modernizing, not destroying democracy" as Robert H. Wiebe has said.[3] Unfortunately, the Progressives' idealistic notions of expanded democracy and social consensus never quite meshed with the bureaucratic systems being perfected in these years by educated elites—Progressives included.

Most of the research done by American historians since the 1950's suggests that the notion of Progressivism as a dualistic struggle between reformers and corporate interests is inadequate. Corporate interests, it was discovered, supported the passage of certain "Progressive" reform measures;[4] middle-class leaders were not as public spirited as had earlier been imagined.[5] As a result of such findings, many historians found themselves unable to define Progressivism in terms of support for a certain set of reforms.

In searching for a better means of understanding Progressivism, historians have developed sociological profiles of the leaders of the movement. Most of the leaders were young, middle-class urbanites, generally from older Anglo-Saxon, Protestant families.[6] They tended to be well-educated. Occupationally, they could be fitted into two broad categories: those with "strong professional aspirations" and those who were "specialists in business, in labor and in agriculture." Members of both groups were conscious of their distinctiveness and had close ties to people in similar occupations.[7] They were newcomers to reform; few had joined the Populist revolt of the 1890s. In their approach to social change, they tended on the whole to be elitist.

The essential nature of Progressivism, however, was less a question of social background than one of spirit. Progressives believed that they had discovered the means to achieve order and social harmony in an age of chaos. This spirit—whether one calls it bureaucratic, organizational or technological—is essential to an understanding of modern America.[8] Progressives were, in John Morton Blum's words, "seeking ways to accommodate American social, political and economic institutions to advancing industrialism, with all that it implied. They were not seeking to uproot those institutions."[9]

One key element in this new set of values was a belief in systematic planning based on scientific and technological principles. To a degree this faith was a new form of rationalism.[10] To the Progressive mind, the solution to problems issued from the application of science. Hence when Progressives spoke of "science," they usually meant "scientific method," or more accurately some kind of "system."[11] This new approach to problem-solving yielded several novel ideas. "Science" was utilitarian, and Progressives who thought in these terms stressed results as a new measure of success.[12] Specifically the new measure of success was efficiency, used not in the old sense of individual initiative and personal effectiveness, but rather in a social sense. As Samuel Haber has said, "Efficiency meant social harmony and the leadership of the 'competent'."[13] When applied properly, "science" would enable these leaders to engage in conscious planning for the future. Above all else, Progressives wanted to achieve order,[14] and the technological spirit was believed to provide the guideline for accomplishing that end. Planning and organization were essential if efficiency were to be achieved.[15] The "scientific" spirit also nurtured an intense optimism among Progressives; they were certain that "what was new and superior would drive out what was old and inferior."[16]

As a result of their fascination with "scientific" method, Progressives placed an enormous trust in specialists and experts. Large-scale organizations encouraged specialization and the development of expertise. Reformers felt that similar persons of skill, highly educated professionals, were needed to provide "scientific" solutions to contemporary problems. While Herbert Croly was praising specialization throughout American society for its promise of "greater practical efficiency,"[17] businesses were turning to Taylor's scientific management in order in achieve the same goal.[18] Government leaders like Theodore Roosevelt increasingly relied on the opinions of experts, appointing well-qualified administrators and establishing new fact-finding commissions.[19] Progressives were fascinated by statistics. Careful quantitative analyses, done on a continuing basis, would provide the data needed in a "scientific" approach to problem-solving.[20] Thus an exhibit of disease and poverty maps prepared by Lawrence Veiller had a profound impact on Roosevelt while he was governor of New York;[21] other Progressive leaders shared T. R.'s enthusiasm for statistical analyses.

Another by-product of the new organizational ideology was a belief in the value of education and publicity. The expertise demanded by the new systems naturally favored an interest in education. As J. B. Taylor wrote in a 1900 issue of the *Educational Review*: "The whole drift of present educational thinking is to produce the efficient man, the man related by forceful needs to the world without."[22] In addition to producing the specialists needed to man the new social organization, education would provide the means to restructure society as a whole. Progressives professed faith in the "infinite educability" of the people.[23] If men were made aware of the facts, they would act to correct any injustices that might exist. Publicity, whether by muckrakers or government investigators, would provide the moral suasion necessary to change society.[24] The Progressives did not explicitly link education and publicity to social engineering, but the two were increasingly intertwined in their minds.[25]

The organizational spirit also influenced changes in the Progressives' understanding of how institutions should function. The reformers tended to transfer decision-making authority out of legislative and into executive hands. The legislative process, they believed, was both "intermittent and inexpert." Impartial, trained technicians employed on a full-time basis were needed to design an efficient society.[26] An example of this process in action is provided by Harold T. Pinkett's description of Roosevelt's use of the Keep Commission to wrest control of administrative reform from Congressional committees more concerned with economy than with efficiency.[27] Progressives also tended to shift decision-making from the grass-roots and the state and regional

levels to the national center of society.   Orderly development, they
believed, was best accomplished on a national scale.   Roosevelt declared:
"This is an era of federation and combination."[28]   The strength of
Progressivism was in its ability to organize interests on a national level
much as business had organized in the closing decades of the nineteenth
century.[29]

Progressives tended to accept a common set of values about how
society should be governed.   Most believed that technology, and in
particular the "scientific" method, could be used to plan an ordered
world.   As a result of this technological bent, Progressives placed an
enormous trust in expertise.   The new order depended heavily on the
gathering of statistics, and the acquisition and dissemination of
specialized forms of knowledge.   Expertise, in turn, demanded shifting
decision-making from legislative to executive hands and from the grass-
roots to the center.   These combined elements are what I have termed
the "ideology of organization."

Bureaucratic values of this sort appealed to a growing number of
Churchmen in the years after 1890.   If any group within the Church fit
the Progressive profile, it was the denominational executives who
administered the agencies we have been studying.   Compared with other
men of the cloth, almost all these leaders were well educated, usually
having attended college and received advanced degrees at seminaries.
Denominational executives were more cosmopolitan than their
contemporaries, having traveled a great deal during their lives and
usually having authored at least one book. They clearly were better paid
than most in the ministry.   While pastors' salaries averaged less than
$800 in the early years of the century, denominational executives were
paid three or four times as much.   In 1904 the thirteen Methodist
administrators averaged over $3000 and their six Episcopalian
counterparts earned an average of $4500 in 1910.   The less wealthy
Baptists paid board secretaries an average of $2400, and sketchy figures
suggest the Disciples' mean was slightly higher.[30]

By the early years of the century, these denominational
executives were exhibiting an increasing degree of professional
consciousness.   Professionalization is normally the result of the types of
training and special skills necessary to perform a particular task.   The
professional operates in a world defined by a set of standards and ethics
usually established by a voluntary association of his peers.   His status is
achieved primarily by his performance in accordance with those
standards.   Decision-making by the professional is ideally based on an
objective assessment of fact without regard for self-interest.   The
professional normally has a sense of calling to his field and of obligation
to the public he serves.[31]   Weber did not distinguish between

professionals and bureaucrats in his typology, but more recent studies of business organizations have suggested that professionals are different from bureaucrats in that their primary loyalty is to the peer group rather than to the organization. Professionals are said to resist such elements of bureaucracy as impersonality, hierarchy and procedural specification.[32] There seems, however, to be less need to distinguish between these two types in our agencies. There is no inherent conflict between professionalization and bureaucracy. Religious professionals, unlike their business counterparts, moreover, have only limited ability to move from one job to another due to denominational barriers. The option of returning to the pastorate is often not very appealing. In addition, religious organizations tend to develop loyalties among their members, including leaders, that are not present in economic organizations. Indeed, one study of religious leaders suggests they tend to be "job bureaucrats," professionally trained but also entirely dedicated to a career within the bureaucracy.[33]

One indication of the rise of professionalism among religious executives was their increasing belief in the preeminence of their work in the life of the Church; they felt a keen sense of mission for the agencies they served. Frost's first Baptist Sunday School Board report in 1892 noted that "the Board now promises to be a unifying element in our denominational life and enterprises." Four years later he exhilaratedly declared that the Board was "the very life of the Convention."[34]

Denominational executives also began to have more frequent contacts among themselves. Beginning in 1893, leaders from the foreign mission boards, including the Southern Baptists, met each January to exchange ideas about their work. They formed the Foreign Missions Conference of North America which issued annual reports and published books on the latest mission strategy. Mission boards collaborated in dividing the mission fields between themselves. The Sunday School Council of Evangelical Denominations (1910), the Home Mission Council (1908), and the Council of Church Boards of Education (1911) were created to allow executives from those fields to share their knowledge about the best methods currently in use. A sense of the professionalization engendered by these interdenominational contacts may be seen in an Episcopal Board report for 1911:

> All the Boards [in other Communions] have like aims, and the problems which they have to meet and solve are strikingly similar. The experience of each Board in dealing with any particular class of subjects is of value to every other Board. If after consideration the same policy with reference to any given subject matter commends itself to all the Boards or to a large number of them, there is a maximum certainty that the policy is sound.[35]

The executives' concern for professionalism may also be sensed in their changing titles. "Corresponding Secretary" no longer seemed prestigious enough. The Disciples and Episcopalians began to call their top administrative officers "presidents" around 1910. The Episcopal Board believed "that the office ought to be enlarged in both its title and its powers. . . . Give the General Secretary a new name and make him what he certainly ought to be, the great inspiring presence and power of our entire Mission work."[36] Even lesser staff members began to feel the need for new titles. The Methodist Board, for instance, had for some time named one of its lay members as Treasurer, while leaving the actual work to a full-time Assistant Treasurer. This man reported: "It is humiliating to be in Conference with treasurers of other Boards and to have to be ranked as an assistant treasurer. It is an injustice to a competent man to expect him to do the work and not receive the credit."[37]

Another measure of the growing professional consciousness of denominational leaders was their interest in the development of pension systems that would provide security, order and independence both for themselves and for the ministry as a whole. Until this time, either the local church or the board had provided for retired clergy and their dependents. There were a number of small charitable organizations which also gave funds on a limited basis, but they did not offer insurance programs as such. To deal with this problem the Episcopal Board brought its employees under the Church Pension Fund when it was established in 1916. The Baptist Sunday School Board did even better, offering $100,000 to the Convention if it would adopt a program of ministerial relief.[38]

As denominational leaders became more professionally oriented, they sensed the need for further improvements in their organizations and methods of control. In describing the kind of Church they wanted, these executives appropriated the Progressive faith in rationally-conceived organization. They used the terms system, organization, and method almost interchangeably when they pictured the Church they hoped to create. These terms were applied both to the local church and the national agency, to both administrative and financial affairs. Bishop Huntington of the Episcopal Board remarked that some might find organization and administration "things far removed from the well-being of the human soul. But organization and administration, dear friends, are to be to the fishers of men what their nets were to the plain fisher-folk who plied their craft upon the waters of Galilee."[39] *The Churchman* called for "Army Tactics in Mission Work" saying, "like our volunteer army, which has done such splendid fighting in Cuba, the mission agencies of the Church need to be thoroughly organized and equipped in every department."[40]

System needed to be brought to administrative practices. *The Churchman* called for "radical adjustment of our administrative methods. Not theory or sentiment, but efficiency and economy demand it. . . . The time has come when our unrelated forces must be carefully coordinated and systematized."[41]   Inspired by a tour of the Anglican missionary societies in London, Arthur Lloyd predicted that: "After a while we shall go to work and develope [sic] the American Church intelligently and systematically, and then the Board will have to manage or the Church will have something to say."[42]

Financial operations in particular were in need of new, more systematic methods, the executives believed. The Disciples' journal, the *Christian Standard,* maintained that "the only Scriptural, and therefore the only businesslike method of church support is generous, systematic giving."[43]   The desire for regularity was strong.   In 1912 the Methodist Board reported "if a well-systematized financial plan can be presented to the local church, we have entire confidence that the church will respond in abundant measure."[44]   The Methodist bishops reiterated the point, saying:

> To educate the Church in the principles of Christian stewardship and systematic giving is a tremendous task, but it must be undertaken. And the first step toward it is to find a rational, Scriptural, systematic basis for asking. As the head of a family anticipates and provides for the incoming year, as a business man estimates the capital required for his contemplated improvements as well as conducting present enterprises, so should the Church forecast her estimates for all connectional demands.[45]

The Episcopal Church, Bishop Brewer wrote, "must have system and method if the whole Church is to be reached."[46]

The new systems of control were also needed at the local level. Religious leaders were told that there was a "vast unorganized religious force" which was ineffective because it was "not working through organizations." The problem was one of "efficiency," how to "get the human church into the churches."[47] A Baptist Sunday School Board manual on *Church Organization and Methods* noted the failure of local churches "to develop workable, successful and uniform methods." The result, said the author, was the "top-heavy, unwieldy, and unsystematic procedure which prevails in our churches." Especially of concern to denominational leaders were the "far-reaching limitations and incalculable waste both in local affairs and in their support of the enterprises of the denomination."[48] W. R. Stirling, a lay member of the Episcopal Board called for "business system and method" to be introduced at the local level by lay leaders.[49]

Organization and system became the panacea for all the Church's problems. All of society seemingly was in the midst of organizational change, and the Churches sought to be a part of "the genius for organization which characterizes the age."[50] Denominational leaders proclaimed modern, large-scale organization the symbol of the twentieth century. One Methodist pastor wrote that "the tendency of to-day is organization with central control,"[51] and another added, "Big system, big combinations—industrial and commercial—big expositions, big conventions are the order of the day."[52] "A spirit of organization, a principle of combination" was celebrated by the editor of *The Churchman.*[53] "Organization is the order of the day."[54] Shailer Mathews called for *Scientific Management in the Churches*: "The Christian spirit must be institutionalized if it is to prevail in an age of institutions."[55]

If any had doubts about the need for organization, the executives could point to contemporary developments that they felt showed the way for the Church. Business and government had both outdistanced the Church in the development of large-scale organization. A Disciples spokesman observed that "in politics the day of organization has come. The single man counts for little. In business, concentration is the rule. In education it is the same way."[56] The Rev. Clyde Elbert Ordway criticized "the unsystematic and unbusinesslike methods of administration in the great majority of the churches. And this in an age of the greatest business keenness and mastery of detail." Ordway added that "it is not an overstatement to say that no other enterprise could live a decade in our age managed as the average church is managed today."[57] *The Churchman* also noted that "the industrial development of the country since the Civil War has transformed the business world. A man who attempted to work on mercantile methods approved forty or fifty years ago would find himself hopelessly outdistanced." The editor applied this experience to the Church: "What brings success in industrial life will bring success in missions. The Church will have to learn that slowness and caution are out of place."[58] A member of the Methodist Board, George P. Mains of Brooklyn, analyzed how business had readjusted to new social conditions:

> Keenest ability, concentration of capital, most efficient organization of forces, vigilant and aggressive push—these are now the conditions

of business success as never before. But the changed conditions of life demand the spirit of adaptation on the part of the Church not less than in the business community.[59]

   In all these statements one senses a real fear among Church leaders that Protestantism might fall behind, or indeed already was behind, the most powerful forces in society—largely because it had not organized properly. There were increasing indications of what Richard Hofstadter has called "status anxiety" among Protestant leaders.[60] If this uneasiness seems a bit illogical given Protestantism's numerical and financial growth, it was nonetheless a very real phenomenon. One source of this anxiety was doubtless Protestantism's failure to reach the masses in the industrial cities.[61] Urban areas were increasingly important, Protestants realized, but downtown congregations simply abandoned the inner city and fled to the suburbs. Churches were not growing in urban areas, but crime, immorality and irreligion were. Labor unrest, socialism and corporate monopolies threatened to destroy the social order. Immigrants brought un-American culture and religion. The intellectual pressures from modern science and other secular trends may also have left Churchmen basically uneasy.

   Protestant leaders' anxiety about their lack of influence in the world around them was matched by what seemed a waning of influence over their own members. Many believed there had been a fall in church membership and attendance.[62] Fewer young men were willing to enter the ministry. Local churches expected an educated pastor, but often paid him no more than the average mechanic. Brighter minds were entering "other professions or business."[63] churches were no longer the dominant institutions in society many believed.[64]

   In the midst of these feelings of anxiety and inferiority, organization provided what seemed to the leaders a means to restore the Church's preeminence. Allan B. Philputt, for instance, told the Disciples' Congress that the Church had "surrendered" matters of education and charity to "the State and to large private munificence. . . . Foreign missionaries," he added, "are discredited by some who claim that the forces of commerce, war and government are the real factors in the uplifting of degraded peoples." Philputt's solution to the waning of the Church as a "citadel of power" was as follows:

> This is a century of progress, of steam and electricity, of wireless telegraphy and the motor cycle. The church should not use the methods of fifty years ago. Her plans and forces should be modernized. Her enterprises are, in a measure, discredited because

she is facing modern problems with antiquated methods. . . . It is through organization that large purposes are carried out.[65]

Others followed Philputt's logic; if local churches could no longer develop by themselves the leadership and plans necessary for an "up to date" church, a more centralized Church might. If laymen were disillusioned by an inefficient, poorly-organized Church, and were turning to secular organizations for solutions, a more modern religious enterprise might recapture their loyalties. If only the Church could be like business—unified, scientific, efficient—it could provide leadership in the new century. As the *Methodist Review* said, "The Church of to-day needs to awake to the fact that she must compete for the souls of men. . . . If by entering into competition we can hold the masses true to the Church is it not plainly our duty to do so?"[66]

In effect Church leaders looked to organization in order to reassure themselves and their members that they were modern in their approach to life. One example of this equation of organization with modernity is found in the Rev. Samuel W. Dike's article on "The Church's Need of the Efficiency Engineer." Dike argued that the Church should increase "its efficiency by scientific methods;" it would lose "its touch with society and its power over society if its spiritual power [was] not expressed in the thought and language of society itself as these appear in social laws and methods of work."[67] A modern Church would have to be organized and efficient. The Rev. John Haynes Holmes called for "a church so well organized and efficiently officered that it could once again assume its formerly exclusive prerogatives."[68] The report on the unification of Disciples' benevolences emphasized that "more systematic and economical administration of all our organized work. . .would strongly appeal to the sympathy and support of our active and consecrated business men."[69] A Disciple executive quoted the Rev. Charles Stelzle, Social Gospeler and Presbyterian organizer, in support of larger organization: "The national agency of the church which will set up so comprehensive and so constructive a program will be commended for its leadership, supported by intelligent contributions, and will gain the respect of the man outside of the church who has always believed that the church and its agencies are unscientific and unbusinesslike."[70]

When agency officials described the type of organization the Church needed, they often slipped into the Progressive rhetoric of bureaucratic action. Organization was to be scientific, utilitarian, and above all, efficient. A survey of Methodist accounting procedures found that "the present plan is a sort of patchwork and not a complete scientific system."[71] The Rev. George Craig Stewart called for "the application to our parochial affairs of the principles of scientific management."[72] The

Episcopal Board hoped to devise a "more scientific plan for securing volunteers for the mission field"[73] and a centrally-run financial system to "see to it that the whole work is economically and scientifically managed."[74] The Church, according to Shailer Mathews, ought to submit itself to the "era of 'scientific management'."[75]

Organization was also to be practical and useful. A member of the Methodist Board, the Rev. John F. Goucher, told the General Conference of the Methodist Episcopal Church, South, that "the age in which we live, more than any preceeding one, emphasizes the divine principle of utility. This manifests itself in specialization as to work, economy of material and time, and excellence of product. Trusts, syndicates, and divisions of industries are seeking to prevent the waste of competition. . . . The churches have been slow to adopt these business principles."[76] William T. Ellis, Secretary of the Commission on Publicity of the Men and Religion Forward Movement observed: "Christian work must, in the new age of scientific activity created by this [movement], meet the test of practical efficiency."[77]

Denominational executives sought "efficiency" in a host of activities in the years after 1910. The BSSB hoped to organize the "efficient Sunday school" at the local level. Mission societies began to call their staff members "efficiency experts." Methodist fundraisers organized "Area Efficiency Conferences." Meredith Nicholson, an Episcopalian layman and novelist, answered the question "Should Smith Go to Church?" by remarking, "The word we encounter oftenest in the business world nowadays is efficiency; the thing of which Smith must first be convinced is that the church may be made efficient."[78] Henry Cope added, "We read of efficiency in business management; we are told that the ultimate aim of general education is 'social efficiency;' that the test, like an acid to be applied to all our public and civic operations, is their social or civic efficiency. Now, there is a moral, even a spiritual obligation resting on us to apply to all activities and organizations of religion like tests."[79] In 1900 an Episcopalian Committee urged consolidation of benevolences in order to achieve "unity, simplicity, economy and efficiency." In 1916, a similar committee urged a "progressive plan of unification for efficiency."[80] Joshua Levering wanted to make Baptist work "more efficient" when he proposed a study of the methods of the Baptist Boards.[81] Coordinated activities in the mission field promised a "forward efficiency movement for our work abroad," reported the D&FMS.[82]

In the years immediately after the publication of Frederick W. Taylor's *The Principles of Scientific Management* in 1911, the Church was touched by what Samuel Haber has called the efficiency craze.[83] Books and articles on the subject rolled off the religious presses.[84] The

Efficiency Society, organized in New York City in 1912, heard addresses by Charles S. Macfarland, Secretary-General of the Federal Council of Churches, and by Charles Stelzle, both of whom spoke on the need for church efficiency. The Society organized a Church Efficiency Committee, which included Stelzle and Macfarland. In 1913, the Society's journal included three articles on efficiency in Church work.

The search for efficiency led denominational leaders, like others caught up in the Progressive spirit, to place a new emphasis on the need for expertise in the direction of religious affairs. The modern Church was a "business in itself." Like the railway and the factory it required "unusual business aptitude, technical skill, and financial and executive ability."[85]   In 1893, Frank Mason North, later Corresponding Secretary of the Methodist Board, urged that "the Church, in its press, its administrative offices, its schools" must "influence its best men and women to prepare themselves for this new day. Specialized service means a specialized ministry."[86] No longer, it seems, would the religious leader minister to the "whole man" as in earlier days. Denominational boards increasingly felt themselves incompetent to handle complex details of accounting and office management. As a result, they urged denominational executives to hire outside consultants—"business brains" and "efficiency experts"—to inspect the agencies' methods.[87]   In addition, the boards seemed convinced of the need to acquire their own staff of experts. Robert M. Hopkins, a Disciples' administrator told his board, "There can be no possible doubt that the same good business sense which prompts business enterprises to employ staff men for the carrying out of special programs will apply to the erection of bureaus and departments of our National work with experts at their head." Hopkins added that "a single secretary with a stenographer can no more administer the affairs of a national Bible-school organization these days than can an old-fashioned superintendent with his foreman run a big machine shop."[88] The Methodist Sunday School Board reached a similar conclusion: "This is the day of the Efficiency Expert. Giant corporations are employing men to advise and assist them in increasing the efficiency of their plants. Production is increased, cost reduced, margins greatly stimulated, and many a business revolutionized by the Efficiency Expert. The opportunity for such a work is quite as great in the field of religion as in the field of industry."[89]

Religious leaders also believed that expertise would have to play a larger role in the selection of missionaries.[90]   A Committee of the Methodist Board reported with alarm that many of its missionaries were "square pegs in round holes," ignorant of the English Bible and Church doctrine, untrained in presenting religious truths and unskilled in foreign languages. "It will no longer do," the committee said, "to pre-suppose ability in this direction because of any other attainment in education or character." What was needed, they thought, was "the most effective and scientific method known to determine in advance all that can be known of the perfections and imperfections of those who present themselves for candidates." The committee pointed to the methods of "modern industrial enterprises" which employed "highly educated and trained experts" to examine scientifically all candidates. Standardized tests could "determine with startling accuracy questions of mental, moral, physical and tempermental ability and quality that are even unknown to the candidate personally."[91] When Bishop Hare studied the China Mission for the D&FMS in 1892, he urged "the careful selection of a picked few who have ability and training sufficient to enable them to occupy important points of central influence."[92] Some called for special schools for the education of future missionaries, and in 1912 the Disciples opened a College of Missions in Indianapolis to train persons for "a more efficient, specialized ministry."[93]

In addition to the need for expertise at the top, Church leaders also believed it was important to educate the masses who supported denominational work. A Baptist centennial committee in 1900 reported that it was "useless for the Convention to hope to enlist in missions over a million five hundred thousand people in its work without spending the amount necessary to inform the people in its aims and enlist them in its work. No business man or business corporation hesitates to spend the money necessary to make their business a success. The children of light should be as wise in their generation."[94] "Church-wide study of Christian missions" needed to be developed, and missionary education for all age groups and both sexes was launched.[95] Secretary Ranshaw of the ACMS said that the "mission appeal, to have any weight at all, must be buttressed by the facts."[96] Properly devised information could yield the desired attitudes. The executives of the ACMS reported a "rising tide of influence in its favor" as a result of five years of effort spent "commending their work to the altar of the brotherhood; advertising it, creating a confidence in the management and in its future."[97] Secretary Taylor of the Methodist Board reported to the Commission on Finance that a "strong educational campaign is one of the chief safeguards which can be thrown about the new benevolence plan."[98]

As a result of the desire to educate Church members, there was a sudden increase in the interest in publicity. The agencies of the Church had developed house organs during the nineteenth century. These were usually filled with quotations from mission reports and acknowledgements for mission gifts. Often edited by the corresponding secretary, they were seldom lively reading. Due to the increased significance of education around the turn of the century, however, this type of publication began to change. Calling for the appointment of a full-time editor, an Episcopal committee reported "that 'The Spirit of Missions' was unattractive in appearance, uninteresting as to matter and that only a strong sense of duty could induce ordinary readers to peruse it."[99]   The Methodist Board had these criteria in mind for its revised magazine: "It must be popular.   Not for the student—not technical. Profusely illustrated.   Bright, comprehensive, with the world outlook. Human interest must be its constant feature."[100]

The executives also hoped to establish Information Bureaus to develop "syndicated" articles for both the religious and the secular press.[101]   In an editorial entitled "Publicity Breeds Efficiency," *The Churchman* said, "It is little short of amazing that the Church is so slow to realize the value of publicity.   The failure to take advantage of it dwarfs the efficiency of much of her administration."[102]   Churches were urged to advertise their wares much as a business would.[103]   Books and articles on methods of religious advertising proliferated.[104]   The keeping of statistical records also became more important.   "It is greatly to be desired," said *The Churchamn*, "that a more systematic method of treating records might be practiced throughout the Church, and above all that some uniform method should be generally agreed upon."[105]

The Progressive concept of organization, with its emphasis on centralized and executive decision-making appealed to denominational leaders.   This was true, in part, for pragmatic reasons.   The problems of diocesanism, inter-agency conflict, and uncertain authority described in the previous chapter, seemed amenable to solution by way of centralization.   None of the four Churches had a central executive in 1910.   Decision-making by national legislative conventions was sluggish and vulnerable to the whims of the delegates.   Executive authority granted to bishops proved little better because each was engaged in diocesan affairs and they rarely met as a group.   The Episcopalians had a Presiding Bishop, but he was always the oldest bishop in terms of seniority—seldom likely to exercise strong administrative direction.   The lack of central authority was thus obvious to the leaders.

In addition to this pragmatic reason for centralizing Church organizations, however, one can also sense that the Churches were carried further than they might otherwise have gone by the Progressive ideas circulating in these years.   In 1910, for instance, *The Churchman* argued that because the PEC had no executive head, it was "without that which in the common experience of humanity has proved essential to doing any business well—whether it be the business of a nation or the business known to mankind."[106]   A letter to the same journal compared the Church to the political world: "unlike the Republic, it has no administrative or executive head, such as the President or his Cabinet are to the republic."[107]   The editor of *The Churchman* declared that the General Convention had failed as a deliberative body due to the "vast extent of the country" and to the "cumbrous" nature of its membership. Religious leaders often spoke of agency executives as the central figures in the twentieth-century Church.   "If the end of the Church is work for the Kingdom," said *The Churchman,* "then the real business of our Church's Christianity is being centered in its Board of Missions. Here, rather than in the constitutional discussions of the General Convention, is the Church's heart, and here is to be felt the pulse of its health-giving life."[108]   A Southern Baptist field secretary echoed these sentiments when he reported that "our board is growing in the favor of the denomination more and more. One of our Texas men, who does not use our literature, said to me 'The Sunday-school Board will soon be the biggest thing in the Convention.'"[109]   Perhaps the clearest statement about the need to shift power from legislative to executive hands came from the Virginia Baptist newspaper: "It must be frankly admitted. . .that the real work of the Convention is no longer done by the Convention itself. . . . We are coming rapidly to the place, *if we have not already reached it,* when we must rely wholly upon the Boards and standing committees to do our thinking for us. This is to some extent both desirable and inevitable."[110]

The belief in centralization was expressed in a variety of ways. A Baptist Home Mission Board report as early as 1887 argued that "state Boards, however efficient," could not accomplish the work carried on by the national board.[111]   Again *The Churchman* pointed to the national government as a model: "The state has blazed the way and demonstrated the necessity for higher organization, and it has proved the absolute security of such organization. The Church cannot afford to lag behind. She cannot serve a Nation with diocesan machinery."[112]   More than once did Episcopalian leaders express a desire for the Board of Missions to serve as a "board of strategy."[113]   At the time of the San Francisco earthquake, Corresponding Secretary Wood of the D&FMS pointed out that parochial missions were no longer adequate to the task of aid. Wood believed that "with the prestige, the machinery, and the executive efficiency of a body like the Board of Missions, we could do work of this kind more thoroughly and wisely probably than any other institution."[114]   An editorial in the Methodist *Christian Advocate* entitled "Organization Essential to Power" maintained that "strong organizations require the surrender of personal rights for the sake of the strength [of the organization], and he is blind who cannot see it."[115]   Other Methodist spokesmen argued that "the tendency of to-day is organization with central control" and that "a strong and all-inclusive organization. . .is the supreme need of the hour."[116]

While the ideology of organization had captured the minds of a growing number of denominational leaders by 1910, not everyone, of course, was convinced that the new ideas were entirely salubrious. Some feared that reorganization of the Church would defile its traditional mission. Even some of the proponents of organization admitted that it had "a hard, modern ring. It seems more appropriately applied to business and party politics than to offices of state and church."[117] The editor of the *Methodist Review* warned that "the Church does not exist for itself, but is the instrument for the propagation of the kingdom of God. . . . This is so often forgotten in the zeal to build up denominational forms."[118] An article in *The Churchman* likewise warned Episcopalians of the "danger of over-organization." The writer observed that "it is one thing to have an organization which has been made necessary by increased interest and zeal springing up within the Church, but it is quite another to try and create [sic] a fictitious interest by a more complicated machinery."[119]

Other critics were concerned that too much power would come to reside in too few hands. A member of the Episcopal Board rejected unification of benevolences saying, "the absorbtion of power in a central body is not a favorite doctrine with the American people." Such a plan was contrary to "that desire for democratic rule and love for independent action which I think is prevalent throughout the land."[120] "Many brethren," reported the *Christian Standard,* "fear that the tendency of our missionary and other general organizations is to infringe on the liberties of the church."[121] One Methodist pastor had an entirely different view from the bureaucrats as to what the Church needed in the way of change: "Our Methodism must be (to put it all in a single word) *democratized.* There is too much power atop and too little responsibility on the average man, both layman and preacher."[122]

This sort of thought represents, of course, another strand of Progressive thought—one which stressed anti-organizational and democratic ideas. In the realm of politics, these ideas found expression in the "New Freedom" of Woodrow Wilson. The passage of such measures as the anti-trust acts and the amendment for the direct election of Senators were largely influenced by these ideas. In general, however, such ideas tended to be frustrated by the imperatives of organization.

In addition to these general qualms about organization, the individual denominations also had special circumstances that made it difficult to impose the bureaucratic ideology in any simple, unqualified manner. Some Episcopalians argued, for example, that more powerful agencies would be unnecessary if the power of the bishops were strengthened. The bishops could meet as a "collegium" to administer the missionary work of the Church.[123] Baptists and Disciples had more difficult obstacles to overcome since their polities continued to declare proudly the independence of the local church. A significant segment in each of these denominations had always opposed any mission effort beyond the local level. As Church agencies grew in the 1890s, protests became more strident. J. A. Scarboro, a Texas Baptist pastor, warned that the church was headed toward "Episcopacy." Denominational leaders were "not for missions *per se*," said Scarboro, "but for a system first and missions afterwards." The Boards, he added, were trying to ostracize and persecute all opponents; "their doctrine is: With and through the board He can succeed, without it He cannot. Then the success is in the board, not in God. They laugh and hoot at the very idea of mission work without a board."[124] Copies of Baptist missionary T. P. Crawford's *Churches, To the Front!* were circulated throughout the South. Crawford argued that "This 'organization craze' has gone to great extremes, and the time has come for our people 'to call a halt.' Say what you may, its tendency is to break our spiritual moorings and drive us upon the lee shore of secularization and ring-government." Calling for an end of national control by denominational agencies, Crawford denounced them as "deadly hostile" to Baptist polity.[125]

Curiously the most vocal resistance to the organizational ideology seems to have been aroused before the agencies experienced their major restructuring after 1910. In part, this may be the result of the schisms in both the Southern Baptist Convention and the Disciples of Christ between 1890 and 1906. Landmark Baptists, centered in rural areas of Texas, Louisiana and Arkansas, withdrew from the Convention to form the American Baptist Association in 1905. They acted in protest against the increasing number of state secretaries and national boards. The withdrawal of the Landmarkers has been seen by Southern Baptist historians as partly responsible for an increased sense of unity in the denomination. "A strong Landmark undercurrent," according to Robert A. Baker, "would have rendered impossible what took place in Southern Baptist organizational life between 1917 and 1972."[126] A similar development took place in the Disciples, which had long been divided on questions such as use of instrumental music and creation of mission societies. In 1889, Daniel Sommer's Sand Creek Declaration called for division of the church, and by 1906 the Federal Religious Census recognized two distinct heirs to the Campbellites—the Christian Church (Disciples) and the Churches of Christ. Again, schism seemed to leave "the way to consolidation of societies more open."[127] J. H. O. Smith, a former Corresponding Secretary, believed that the new attitude toward missions would allow the Church to organize on a "business basis."[128] Opponents of organization may in a similar if less spectacular way have left Methodist ranks as well during these years. Holiness groups were formed, in part, by disgruntled Methodists offended by "denominational executives [that] imitated the methods of business tycoons in building up the strength and income of their organization."[129]

Thus the schisms prompted a short-run increase in the criticism of organizational change, but in the long run the schisms helped to clear away some of the major stumbling blocks from the path leading toward centralized organization. Whether the pace and timing of denominational reorganization would have been appreciably different had these critics remained within the major denominations is, I think, a difficult question to settle. As yet no one has adequately studied the schisms of the late nineteenth century as a whole to tell us why so many persons withdrew at this particular time. I suspect that the schisms were merely the final confirmations of independence by local churches that had long operated autonomously. Nevertheless, their withdrawal removed at least a potential—if not actual—barrier to further centralization.

In the long run those who objected to organizational change tended to be drowned out by those demanding further bureaucratization. As we shall see in the next chapter, the problems facing the agencies and the new organizational values both played major roles in the transformation of Church structure after 1910—a process that began with the "systemization" of Church finances.

NOTES

[1] On the predominant role of business see Wiebe, *Businessmen and Reform,* pp. 1-2, 212-19 and *Search for Order,* pp. 181-85; Thomas Cochran, *Business in American Life: A History* (New York: McGraw Hill, 1972), especially Part III.

[2] Eric F. Goldman, *Rendezvous with Destiny: A History of Modern American Reform* (New York: Knopf, 1952) is the best presentation of the progressive interpretation. See also Harold U. Faulkner, *The Quest for Social Justice* (New York: Macmillan, 1931); Samuel Eliot Morison and Henry Steele Commager, *The Growth of the American Republic* (2 vols.; New York: Oxford, 1962), II, 440-545; Ralph H. Gabriel, *The Course of American Democratic Thought: American Intellectual History Since 1815* (New York: Ronald Press, 1940), pp. 331-39; and Merle Curti, *The Growth of American Thought* (New York: Harper, 1951), pp. 605-32.   To an extent George Mowry, *The Era of Theodore Roosevelt and the Birth of Modern America, 1900-1912* (New York: Harper and Row, 1958) also relies on the traditional framework.

[3] *Search for Order,* p. 161.

[4] See Gabriel Kolko, *The Triumph of Conservatism: A Reinterpretation of American History, 1900-1916* (New York: Free Press, 1963) and *Railroads and Regulation, 1877-1916* (Princeton: Princeton University Press, 1965); James Weinstein, *The Corporate Ideal in the Liberal State: 1900-1918* (Boston: Beacon Press, 1968); and Wiebe, *Businessman and Reform.*

[5] Hofstadter, *Age of Reform,* pp. 131-173.   See also George Mowry, "The California Progressive and his Rationale: A Study in Middle Class Politics," *Mississippi Valley Historical Review,* 36 (September 1949), 239-50.

[6] On the "Progressive Profile" see Mowry, *Era of Theodore Roosevelt,* pp. 85-105 and Wiebe, *Search for Order,* pp. 111-132.

[7] Wiebe, *Search for Order,* p. 112.

[8] Hays, *Conservation and the Gospel of Efficiency,* pp. 3-4.   Haber, *Efficiency and Uplift,* pp. ix-xii, calls the spirit "scientific management"; Wiebe, *Search for Order,* p. 145, terms it "bureaucratic"; and Galambos, "The Emerging Organizational Synthesis," suggests the term "organizational."

[9] *The Republican Roosevelt* (New York: Atheneum, 1971), p. xi.   See also Hays, *Response to Industrialism,* p. 1.

[10] See Blum, *Republican Roosevelt,* p. xi.

[11] Wiebe, *Search for Order,* pp. 146-147; Blum, *Republican Roosevelt,* p. xi; and Frank Freidel, *America in the Twentieth Century* (New York: Knopf, 1960), p. 34.

[12] Theodore P. Greene, *America's Heroes: The Changing Models of Success in American Magazines* (New York: Oxford University Press, 1970), pp. 319-22, 265-266; Blum, *Republican Roosevelt,* p. 19; and Hays, *Conservation and the Gospel of Efficiency,* pp. 124-27.

[13]On the changing meaning of efficiency see Haber, *Efficiency and Uplift*, pp. ix-x; Wiebe, *Search for Order*, p. 147; Hays, *Conservation and the Gospel of Efficiency*, pp. 122-27, 265-66; and Barry Dean Karl, *Executive Reorganization and Reform in the New Deal: The Genesis of Administrative Management, 1900-1939* (Cambridge: Harvard University Press, 1963), pp. 16-21.

[14]See Blum, *Republican Roosevelt*, pp. 106-07 and Wiebe, *Search for Order*, pp. 155-59.

[15]Hays, *Conservation*, pp. 265-66. Hays described the emphasis on scientific planning in the conservation movement. See similar emphases in tenement house reform [Roy Lubove, *The Progressives and the Slums: Tenement House Reform in New York City, 1890-1917* (Pittsburgh: University of Pittsburgh Press, 1962)]; in administrative reform in government [Harold T. Pinkett, "The Keep Commission, 1905-1909: A Rooseveltian Effort for Administrative Reform," *Journal of American History*, 52 (September 1965), 297-312]; in business [Haber, *Efficiency and Uplift*]; and in labor relations [Milton J. Nadworny, *Scientific Management and the Unions, 1900-1932* (Cambridge: Harvard University Press, 1955)].

[16]Freidel, *America in the Twentieth Century*, p. 34. See also Hays, *Conservation*, pp. 2-3.

[17]*The Promise of American Life* (Cambridge: Belknap Press, 1965), pp. 103-04, 131, 138-39.

[18]See Haber, *Efficiency and Uplift*; Nadworny, *Scientific Management*; Freidel, *America in the Twentieth Century*, p. 37.

[19]Blum, *Republican Roosevelt*, pp. ix, 19; Pinkett, "The Keep Commission"; and Lubove, *Progressives and the Slums*, p. 119.

[20]See Freidel, *America*, p. 55; Wiebe, *Search*, pp. 148-49; Frederick Lewis Allen, *The Big Change: America Transforms Itself, 1900-1950* (New York: Harper, 1952). Allen suggests that we had become "a nation devoted to the use of statistics," p. 57.

[21]Lubove, *Progressives and the Slums*, pp. 123-24. See also Pinkett, "The Keep Commission" and Arthur M. Johnson, "Theodore Roosevelt and the Bureau of Corporations," *Mississippi Valley Historical Review*, 45 (March 1959), 571-90.

[22]Quoted in Merle Curti, The Social Ideals of American Educators (New York: Scribners, 1935), p. 231 and in Thomas Cochran and William Miller, *The Age of Enterprise: A Social History of Industrial America* (New York: Harper and Row, 1961), p. 271. On the relation of education to efficiency see Greene, *America's Heroes*, p. 329.

[23]Wiebe, *Businessmen and Reform*, p. 9.

[24]On the use of publicity by muckrakers see Freidel, *America in the Twentieth Century*, pp. 55-56; by business see Wiebe, *Businessmen*, p. 187; by government see Johnson, "Theodore Roosevelt," pp. 571-90. See also Alan R. Raucher, *Public Relations and Business, 1900-1929* (Baltimore: Johns Hopkins University Press, 1968).

[25]Wiebe, *Search for Order*, pp. 148-49.

[26]Blum, *Republican Roosevelt,* p. 20. See also Hays, *Conservation and the Gospel of Efficiency,* p. 3.

[27]"The Keep Commission," pp. 297-98, 311-12. Karl, *Executive Reorganization,* also notes the tendency of the executive viewpoint to give efficiency a status equal to if not prior to that of economy, p. 17.

[28]Quoted in Blum, *Republican Roosevelt,* p. 110.

[29]See Cochran and Miller, *The Age of Enterprise,* pp. 189, 276; Blum, *Republican Roosevelt,* pp. 109-24; Hays, *Conservation,* p. 126; and Lubove, *The Progressives and the Slums,* pp. 139-49.

[30]"Board, MEC," June 21, 1904; "Board, PEC," May 10, 1910; "Report of the Sunday School Board," *Proceedings, SBC* (1903). Salary figures were never broken down in ACMS reports, but the Board did hire an assistant secretary in 1907 for $2200, "Board, ACMS," February 22, 1907.

[31]On professionalization see C. Wright Mills, *White Collar: The American Middle Classes* (New York: Oxford University Press, 1956), Chapter 6, and Peter M. Blau and William G. Scott, *Formal Organizations: A Comparative Approach* (San Francisco: Chandler, 1962), Chapter 3.

[32]See Richard H. Hall, "Professionalization and Bureaucratization," *American Sociological Review,* 33 (February 1968), 92-104 and Walter I. Wardwell, "Social Integration, Bureaucratization, and the Professions," *Social Forces,* 33 (May 1955), 356-59.

[33]See Joseph A. Fichter, *Religion as an Occupation: A Study in the Sociology of Professions* (South Bend: University of Notre Dame Press, 1961), p. 231 and Leonard Reissman, "A Study of Role Concepts in a Bureaucracy," *Social Forces,* 27 (March 1949), 305-10.

[34]Quoted in *The Encyclopedia of Southern Baptists,* p. 1318.

[35]"Board, PEC," February 8, 1911, p. 235. See also *Handbook, MEC* (1916), p. 182; "Board, PEC," October 12, 1897, p. 80. Interestingly, the Sunday School Board joined the Nashville Chamber of Commerce in 1899, "Board, SBC," August 16, 1899.

[36]"Board, PEC," September 28, 1909, p. 3. Baptists and Methodists kept the title of Corresponding Secretary until the 1920's before changing over to "Executive Secretary."

[37]See internal memorandum, c. 1914, in George M. Fowles file, Methodist MSS.

[38]*Journal, PEC* (1916), p. 429; *Encyclopedia of Southern Baptists,* p. 1318.

[39]Rev. William R. Huntington, "Things Old and New," *The Churchman,* 78 (September 24, 1898), 653.

[40]78 (August 6, 1898), 175-76.

[41]"The Convention's Opportunity," 108 (September 27, 1913), 406.

[42]Lloyd to Wood, October 20, 1906, Lloyd MSS.

[43]Emile L. Patterson, "How to Promote Generous, Systematic Giving," 44 (January 4, 1908), 6.

[44]"Board, MEC," September 17, 1912, p. 460. See also "Report of the Board of Church Extension," *Journal MEC* (1912), p. 733.

[45]"Episcopal Address," *Journal, MEC* (1912), p. 201.

[46]Bishop Leigh R. Brewer, "Our Mission Work and the Apportionment Plan," *The Churchman,* 85 (March 1, 1902), 267.

[47]*Journal of the Efficiency Society,* 3 (November 1913), 11.

[48]Tull, pp. 8-9.

[49]"Business Methods in Collecting and Disbursing Missionary Funds," *the Churchman,* 77 (February 19, 1898), 265.

[50]"Episcopal Leadership," *The Churchman,* 80 (July 22, 1899), 75.

[51]Rev. D. G. Downey, "Methods and Principles—A Study in Methodist Polity," *Methodist Review,* 78 (May 1896), 424.

[52]Rev. Frank W. Merrick, "The Individual in a Social Age," *Methodist Review,* 86 (July 1904), 546.

[53]"More Secretaries in the Missions House a Necessity," *The Churchman,* 80 (August 26, 1899), 227.

[54]"Why a Bishop as a General Secretary?," *The Churchman,* 77 (January 22, 1898), 111.

[55](Chicago: University of Chicago Press, 1912), p. v.

[56]Allan B. Philputt, "Organization and its Adjustment to the Present Needs of the Church," *Our First Congress,* ed. Garrison, p. 191. Philputt argued that redemption of man could not take place "without suitable organization," p. 192.

[57]"Will the Churches Survive?," *The Arena,* 29 (June 1903), 594.

[58]"Where is the Remedy?," 78 (July 30, 1898), 143.

[59]"The Church and the City," *Methodist Review,* 76 (March 1894), 223.

[60]*Age of Reform,* pp. 131-73.

[61]Such developments are traced in Aaron I. Abell, *The Urban Impact on American Protestantism, 1865-1900* (Cambridge: Harvard University Press, 1943); Charles Howard Hopkins, *The Rise of the Social Gospel in American Protestantism, 1865-1915*

(New Haven: Yale University Press, 1940); and Henry F. May, *Protestant Churches and Industrial America* (New York: Harper, 1949).

[62]For example see Charles J. Bushnell, "The Place of Religion in Modern Life," *American Journal of Theology,* 17 (October 1913), 520-40; Josiah Strong, *Social Progress* (New York: Young People's Missionary Movement, 1906), pp. 254-56; and George Allan England, "The Ebb of Ecclesiasticism," *The Arena,* 39 (February 1908), 176-84.

[63]J. H. Wright, "Ministerial Supply: The Financial Phase," *Christian Standard,* 38 (November 15, 1902), 1574.   See also "Education for the Ministry," *Methodist Review,* 67 (June 1885), 597-600; William Chauncey Langdon, "Correspondence," *The Churchman,* 40 (July 5, 1879), 12; *Journal, PEC* (1910), p. 438; and W. H. Waggoner, "The Twentieth Century Exodus," *Christian Standard,* 41 (June 2, 1906), 1078.

[64]*Journal, PEC* (1910), p. 438; and Bushnell, "The Place of Religion in Modern Life," p. 522.

[65]"Organization and its Adjustment to the Present Needs of the Church," pp. 190-193.

[66]"What Are the Functions of the Church?," 75 (July 1893), 632-33.

[67]*Review of Reviews,* 45 (March 12, 1912), 350-51.

[68]"The Function of the Church—The Function of the State," *The Survey,* 22 (September 11, 1909), 801.

[69]"Report of the Committee on the Reconstruction and Unification of our Missionary and Philanthropic Interests," typewritten copy located in the Disciples of Christ Historical Society, Nashville.

[70]Quoted in "Convention, ACMS," (1914).

[71]"Board, MEC," April 19, 1904, p. 67.

[72]"System in Parochial Affairs," *The Churchman,* 107 (May 17, 1913), 637.

[73]"Board, PEC," May 4, 1911, p. 565.

[74]"Information;" see also "The Mission Campaign," pamphlet #1109, August 1917, p. 4, both in Pamphlet Boxes.

[75]"How to Apply Efficiency Tests to a Church," *Current Literature,* 53 (December 1912), 675.

[76]"Fraternal Address," in the *Journal of the General Conference of the Methodist Episcopal Church, South* (Nashville, 1896), p. 281.

[77]"A Movement: A Message: A Method," *Independent,* 72 (May 9, 1912), 988.

[78]*Atlantic Monthly,* 109 (June 1912), 725.

[79]*Efficiency in the Sunday School* (New York: George H. Doran Co., 1912), p. 4. See also Jesse L. Hurlburt, *Organizing and Building Up the Sunday School* (New York: Eaton & Mains, 1910).

[80]"Report of the Committee on Consolidation of the Benevolent Societies," *Journal, PEC* (1901), p. 655 and "Report on the Commission on Finance," (1916), p. 1323.

[81]*Proceedings, SBC* (1890), p. 10. The increasing size of the BSSB gave "promise of enlarged efficiency," *Proceedings, SBC* (1909), p. 19. The Methodist Board sought "efficient administration" in the expenditure of funds, "Board, MEC," September 16, 1913, p. 73. See also "Efficiency," *Maryland Baptist Church Life,* 1 (July 1917), 5.

[82]*Journal, PEC* (1916), p. 1323. See also William H. Allen, "Efficiency in Religious Work," *Annals of the American Academy of Political and Social Science,* 30 (November 1907), 539-544.

[83]*Efficiency and Uplift.*

[84]For Example see George A. Andrews, *Efficient Religion* (New York: George H. Doran, 1912); Clarence A. Barbour, *Making Religion Efficient* (New York: Association Press, 1912); Henry F. Cope, *Efficiency in the Sunday School* and *The Efficient Layman* (Philadelphia: Griffith and Rowland, 1911); Carl Gregg Doney, *An Efficient Church* (New York: Fleming H. Revell, 1907); Lynn H. Hough, *The Man of Power: A Series of Studies in Christian Efficiency* (New York: Abingdon, 1916); Shailer Mathews, *Scientific Management in the Churches;* "A Church on Business Principles," *Literary Digest,* 48 (March 28, 1914), 704; "How Far Scientific Management Can Be Applied to Religion," *Current Literature,* 51 (November 1911), 533-35; "How to Apply Efficiency Tests to a Church"; Samuel W. Dike, "Shall Churches Increase their Efficiency by Scientific Methods?," *American Journal of Theology,* 16 (January 1912), 20-30.

[85]David Graham Phillips, "The Business Organization of a Church," *Harpers,* 107 (July 1903), 207.

[86]"City Missions and Social Problems," *Methodist Review,* 75 (March 1893), 238. See also Charles Otis Gill and Gifford Pinchot, *The Country Church: The Decline of its Influence and the Remedy* (New York: Macmillan, 1913). Pinchot called for "special training" for the rural minister and the "readjustment of religious doctrine in accordance with the scientific method," pp. 47, 32. *The Churchman* also noted that "specialization is now required to prepare intelligent support for mission work," in "The Extension of Missionary Work," 107 (January 18, 1913), 72.

[87]"Foreign Mission Board Report," *Proceedings, SBC* (1893), p. x; "Report of the Board of Missions," *Journal, PEC* (1916), p. 1186; "Board, MEC," November 23, 1897, p. 36, January 16, 1900, p. 119, November 27, 1900, p. 371, January 16, 1903, p. 231; and *Handbook, MEC* (1916), p. 183.

[88]"Convention, ACMS," (1914).

[89]Commission on Finance File, Methodist MSS. See also Cope, *Efficiency in the Sunday School,* pp. 32, 224-26; and Frederick B. Gruel, "Organizing the Church for

Efficient Economic Service a Present Day Necessity," *Journal of the Efficiency Society*, 3 (December 1913), 65-66.

[90]Some like Everett T. Tomlinson argued that such a standard should apply to all in the ministry, "Too Many Churches," *World's Work*, (August 1913), 478.

[91]"Board, MEC," September 16, 1913, pp. 74-75.

[92]*Spirit of Missions*, 57 (September 1892), 349-50. See also "Board, PEC," December 13, 1911, pp. 297-98; February 12, 1913, p. 85; May 10, 1916, p. 95.

[93]"Board, MEC," September 16, 1913, p. 74; "Convention, ACMS," (1912), p. 514.

[94]*Proceedings*, *SBC* (1900), p. 23.

[95]See "Board, MEC," December 7, 1917, p. 91; July 20, 1915, p. 335; "Board, PEC," November 10, 1904, pp. 23,25.

[96]"Convention, ACMS," (1904), p. 311.

[97]"Board, ACMS," May 17, 1909.

[98]Commission on Finance File, Methodist MSS., November 25, 1912.

[99]"Board, PEC," March 12, 1895, p. 156.

[100]"Board, MEC," December 17, 1912, p. 60.

[101]"Board, MEC," December 20, 1904, p. 211; June 17, 1902; December 7, 1917, p. 91; "Home Mission Board Report," *Proceedings*, *SBC* (1910), p. 254; "Board, PEC," January, 1901, p. 294.

[102]85 (January 11, 1902), 35.

[103]"Report of the Joint Commission of the Protestant Episcopal Church on Press and Publicity," *Journal*, *PEC* (1919), pp. 568-70.

[104]See W. B. Ashley, ed. *Church Advertising: Its Why and How* (Philadelphia: Lippincott, 1917); Christian B. Reisner, *Church Publicity: The Modern Way to Compel Them to Come In* (New York: Methodist Book Concern, 1913); Graham Taylor, "Advertising Religion," *The Survey*, 30 (June 21, 1913), 408-10; "The Lord's Press Agent," *Literary Digest*, 65 (April 17, 1920), 73-74; "'Selling' Religion" *Literary Digest*, 70 (August 20, 1921), 28-29; "How to Advertise Religion," *Literary Digest*, 67 (November 20, 1920), 37-38; "Religious Advertising," *Current Literature*, 29 (August 1900), 185; "Experiments in Advertising the Church," *Current Opinion*, 57 (September 1914), 188-89; "The Campaign for Church Advertising and Publicity," *Current Opinion*, 61 (September 1916), 184-85. Most of the books on efficiency in the Church also included sections on religious advertising.

[105]"The State of the Church," 85 (January 4, 1902), 5. The editor also suggested that the Roman Catholics were "considerably in advance" of the PEC in this respect. See also *Journal*, *PEC* (1907), p. 453.

[106]"General Convention Opens Hopefully," 109 (October 15, 1910), 561; "The Provincial System," 78 (September 24, 1898), 402.

[107]John H. Stotsenburg, 79 (April 8, 1899), 518. "Divided and indefinite responsibility" was "contrary to modern business methods," *Journal, PEC* (1907), p. 453.

[108]"Supremacy of the Missionary Motive," 82 (November 17, 1900), 593. Similar sentiments may be found throughout *the Churchman,* e.g. 78 (September 24, 1898), 402 and 84 (August 17, 1901), 199.

[109]W. E. Brittain to J. M. Frost, June 4, 1906, in Frost MSS., Box 21.

[110]*Religious Herald,* (May 20, 1909), 10, quoted in Barnes, *The Southern Baptist Convention.* p. 172. Italics mine.

[111]*Proceedings, SBC* (1887), p. xlii.

[112]"The General Convention and the Opportunity," 90 (July 23, 1904), 135.

[113]"Board, PEC," November 3, 1910, p. 5 and *The Churchman,* 108 (October 25, 1913), 550.

[114]Letter to Arthur S. Lloyd, March 20, 1907, Lloyd MSS.

[115]67 (April 7, 1892), 221.

[116]Rev. D. G. Downey, "Methods and Principles," pp. 424-25; Rev. P. H. Swift, "The Problem of Religious Life in the City," *Methodist Review,* 82 (May 1900), 412. See also Methodist pastor Samuel W. Dike, "Shall the Churches Increase their Efficiency by Scientific Methods?," pp. 24-25.

[117]H. A. Garfield, "The Limits of Organization," *Harford Seminary Record,* 18 (July 1908), 211.

[118]"Methodism: Centripetal or Centrifugal?," 74 (January 18, 1892), 113.

[119]"The Apostolic Way," 77 (February 5, 1898), 189.

[120]*The Churchman,* 35 (March 10, 1877), 265.

[121]"Exceeding Their Power," 42 (May 25, 1907), 873.

[122]Rev. Joseph Pullman, "Weakest Spot in Methodism," *Christian Advocate,* 67 (February 25, 1892), 192.

[123]*The Churchman,* 35 (January 27, 1877), 97; 84 (August 17, 1900), 199-200.

[124]The Bible, *The Baptists and The Board System,* pp. 61-63, 357-58, 347.

[125]In Baker, *Baptist Source Book,* pp. 178-79.

[126]*The Southern Baptist Convention and its People*, p. 284; see also Barnes, *The Southern Baptist Convention*, p. 166.

[127]Clyde Harold Evans, "A History of the United Christian Missionary Society to 1926, "unpublished M.A. thesis, Phillips University, 1944, pp. 41-42.

[128]"Organization," *Christian Standard*, 44 (May 30, 1908), 925; see also Joseph Franklin, "The Fruit of Anti-ism," *Christian Standard*, 34 (January 8, 1898), 51; "Convention, ACMS," (1906), p. 414.

[129]Timothy L. Smith, *Called Unto Holiness, The Story of the Nazarenes: The Frontier Years* (Kansas City: Nazarene Publishing House, 1962), p. 14.

CHAPTER 6

THE SELLING OF THE CHURCH

The religious leaders' adoption of bureaucratic values produced significant changes in their approach to the practical problems of Church finance. Efficiency and "systematic" fundraising became primary goals for the rising body of agency bureaucrats who made these years what one historian has called an "Age of Crusades."[1]   No longer could the impulsiveness of the traditional appeal for funds be tolerated; well-ordered and sophisticated nationwide campaigns conducted by publicity experts would take their place. A completely new means of support kown as "systematic finance" was adopted in the Churches. By the 1920s the art of religious promotion demanded national conferences to train denominational executives in the latest methods for handling Church advertising, promotional campaigns, legacies, annuities and endowments.[2]   Everywhere Madison Avenue techniques were applied both by the agencies and local churches.

The transition to "systematic finance" was not always an easy change for either the agency executives or local churches to make. Adjustment to the new techniques was never painless. Even with far greater funds with which to work, agency officials seemed unable to stay within their budgets. In part this was due to a lack of sophistication in projecting income, a problem that was compounded by the financial instability immediately following World War I. The agencies, flooded with inflated dollars, established programs and expanded staffs which they could not afford by the mid-1920s. Foreign mission boards were additionally weakened by the fluctuating exchange rates in these years. Even within the new framework of "systematic finance," competition between agencies and departments continued. From the point of view of the central agencies, moreover, local churches remained niggardly in the percentage of their contributions allotted to the national benevolences, especially during the era of church building in the 1920s.

The stuctural problems of making the transition to "systematic finance" were minor, however, compared to the effects the new methods eventually had on Americans' perceptions of the Church's role in society. When the new techniques were applied the Church was often pictured as a business institution whose principal end was to sell its religious product. New kinds of organization replaced what had once been agencies of the heart. No longer did the boards operate on the faith that God would provide, but on the assurance that financial drives would.

Local leaders resisted these trends as best they could, but they too were often swept away by the demands of organization.

How did this revolution in Protestant finance take place? In large measure it proceeded along several different and often overlapping lines in the years after about 1900. The first major innovation had been the development of the sophisticated nationwide financial drive around 1900. Shortly thereafter, leaders had begun to devise what they called regular, "systematic finance." Both of these new approaches had been enhanced by a series of non-denominational crusades that sought to bring business techniques to the Churches. Finally, after World War I the Churches had begun to coordinate their various financial campaigns through specialized and centralized promotional agencies. In effect, all of these various lines of development coalesced in the twenties and thus produced a major shift in the mode of operation of the Church.

The nationwide drive was in many ways an outgrowth of the existing annual offering. The chief differences were that the new drives occurred less often, being tied to special events, that they generally united the various boards behind one major financial crusade, and that they were better organized and promoted. On the surface these campaigns, or "forward movements" as they were often called, do not appear to have been a means for achieving more regular financial operations. Careful promotion and long-range planning, however, produced greater stability than with the older annual offerings. Sometimes church members were asked to pledge support for periods of several years in these drives in order to secure a more certain source of income. Furthermore, the enthusiasm generated by the special drive tended to produce larger contributions than ever before.

Among our four Churches, the initial drives occurred in conjunction with the opening of the new century. The theme of these particular efforts was the celebration of past accomplishments and the definition of future tasks for the new century. Methodists launched a "Twentieth Century Thank Offering," utilizing the theme of "Two Millions for Missions in 1901." Those giving five dollars or more were to receive a "Twentieth Century Thank Medal," embossed with the likeness of John Wesley. A joint committee of the Southern Baptist Convention directed the "Centennial Celebration" which sought to inform the Church's members about the work of their boards and to raise funds to "better organize and equip" them. In 1901 the Methodist Board extended its campaign another year, organizing the "Open Door Emergency Movement;" in this instance the Board carefully carved the nation into eight divisions for fundraising. Staff members were assigned to each division and three new field secretaries were hired. Each presiding elder was urged to hold one or more Missionary Conventions in his district. Those giving five dollars were offered a "color portrait in bas-relief style" of Wesley. The General Committee of the Board praised the success of the campaign and ordered that permanent field secretaries be hired in each division to continue to promote the regular offering. Episcopalians did not hold a centennial celebration, but in 1907-08 the D&FMS organized a special "Men's Thank Offering." This appeal raised $778,000 in celebration of three hundred years of English Christianity in the New World.

These early campaigns suggested that the key to success was to get local churches excited about and involved in the drive. Means needed to be found to mobilize masses of financial supporters, especially those most likely to give—the business and professional laymen. Such means were perfected in the early twentieth century in a series of non-denominational crusades that grew out of an increased lay interest in missions. This interest had produced numerous non-denominational organizations for the study and support of missions in the 1890s: King's Daughters and Sons; the Society of Christian Endeavor; the Student's Volunteer Movement; the International Student Federation; and the Brotherhood of Andrew and Phillip. Following the highly successful Ecumenical Missions Conference of 1900, sponsored by the interdenominational Foreign Missions Conference of North America, more elaborate crusades were launched: the Young People's Missionary Movement; the Missionary Education Movement; and Laymen's Missionary Movement (LMM).

Of these interdenominational crusades, the LMM, held in 1909-10, was perhaps the most influential for the course of Protestant finance. Some fifty-five Protestant boards and societies supported its plan to heighten lay awareness of missions and urged their local churches to support the movement. Each board named laymen in the cities where the campaign was to take place to serve on the planning committees. The agencies also took charge of publicizing the campaign in the denominational press, named a list of outstanding speakers to serve on the programs, and arranged their calendars to conform with the campaign.[3] The LMM was not designed to be a permanent organization, nor did it seek funds for its own operations. Its principal goal was to generate enthusiasm among laymen, especially business and professional men, that would express itself in increased giving to denominational agencies. The tactics of the campaign represented an important innovation. Meetings of businessmen were held in every major city throughout the nation. These meetings were carefully organized by the staff. The climax of the local campaign was the huge "Crusade Dinner," often attended by as many as 1000 men, in which dynamic speakers challenged laymen of all denominations to support the missions cause. A culminating Congress in Chicago attracted an estimated crowd of 65,000 laymen for three days.[4]

The success of the LMM had a profound effect on the denominations. Permanent laymen's or brotherhood organizations were established in most Protestant Churches. Pledges for the mission work of the Church were increased wherever lay movements had been held. Secretary Leonard of the Methodist Board reported: "In 18 centers where conventions have already been held our churches have pledged a total sum of $496,667, being an advance over last year of $214,113. If this increase is maintained throughout the country the result will be one of the grandest achievements of mission history."[5] The Episcopal Board of Missions also noted "a new spirit" and "a more adequate standard of giving" that were products of the movement. "The dioceses in which the largest increase in offerings has been made during the past year are the dioceses in which Churchmen have taken an important part in the preparation for, and conduct of, these laymen's meetings."[6] The methods employed by the LMM were soon the regular tools of the denominational boards. As the Corresponding Secretary of the ACMS observed: "These movements were each led by a master mind with a genius for organization."[7]

If the denominational executives needed further confirmation of the merits of new organizational and business techniques for enlarging religious incomes and stimulating interest in missions, the Men and Religion Forward Movement (M&RFM) provided that. Inspired by the vision of H. W. Arnold, Secretary of the International Young Men's Christian Association, the M&RFM organized to combat the "keen sense of the inefficiency of the churches in meeting modern needs and coping with modern perils" under the motto of "More Religion for Men and More Men for Religion."[8] A "Continental Committee" of ninety-seven members was selected in October 1910, to plan the movement. Local committees of 100 men in ninety cities were organized to prepare for the eight-day campaign. These local committees in turn organized campaigns in some 2000 smaller communities. Four teams of "experts" from the Continental Committee, including "religious leaders, social service leaders and experts in shop and factory work," were sent out to conduct the local campaigns.[9]

The primary emphasis was educational, although the movement was more concerned about social service than missions. In Dallas, for instance, Charles Stelzle urged reform in housing laws, garbage collection, and inspection of meat, milk and water. Large sums were spent to promote the campaign's events through the press, and teams were organized to canvass the communities. Lectures and institutes were held on such subjects as social service and evangelism. Extensive use of surveys and graphs was made in each city.[10] As with the LMM, a final "Conservation Congress" was held which brought together on the same platform such notable figures as William Jennings Bryan, Charles Stelzle, Booker T. Washington, Gipsy Smith and Jane Addams.

The Men and Religion Forward Movement was closely connected to developments in urban Progressivism.[11] The M&RFM's supporters included Jane Addams, Graham Taylor, Robert A. Woods, Owen R. Lovejoy and Charles Stelzle, all of whom were leading figures in the reform movements of Progressivism. The official history of the M&RFM declared it to be "the composite of those forces which have produced cooperation in business and in philanthropy, progressivism in politics, and efficiency in all administration."[12] Walter Rauschenbusch wrote that the movement had "made social Christianity orthodox."[13] Efficiency was a key word; the principles of "scientific" efficiency were at last to be applied to the Church. The movement was "the climax of that adaptation of the spirit of the times to the Christian enterprise," or as George Arthur Andrews said, "an attempt to rescue the religion of Jesus from the realm of intellectual thought, and bring it into the realm of efficient action."[14]

The movement was organized around five basic themes: social service; boys' work; evangelism; Bible study; and missions. In each area, however, the basic emphasis was on the achievement of efficiency and the development of improved forms of organization. In the area of Bible study, for instance, the "experts" argued that "the best Sunday-schools and the most efficient Bible classes are thoroughly organized." The movement stressed the merits of the "vocational evangelist" and his "concentrated campaign," observing that "the same reason for scientific specialization exists in religious work as in every other field of endeavor." In discussing social service, the leaders of the movement called for church advertising directed by "an expert manager. . .The Church should make it its business to make men think well of it."[15]

This amalgam of religious and business thought in the years before World War I seems to challenge some of the traditional assumptions about the "decline" of religion in the 1920s.[16] Religious historians, following the basic outlines of political historiography, have portrayed a Church disillusioned by the War and captured by the Babbittry of men like Roger Babson and Bruce Barton. Yet as we see here, the infusion of business values into religion began long before 1920. The Church's "secularism" was hardly a new development, even if it was manifested in more vulgar ways in the 1920s. Furthermore, business emphases in the Churches were not simply the product of a "courtship" of capitalists and fundamentalists as certain historians have maintained.[17] If anything, this early movement to bring organization and efficiency to the Church was largely in the hands of the leading Social Gospelers, men and women of liberal bent in matters political and theological.

The impact of the M&RFM, moreover, was not "temporary and limited," as another historian has argued, just because it did not succeed in converting the Churches to the Social Gospel.[18]   Its long-term implications were not to be found in the realm of ideas, but rather in the institutional changes that the movement produced.   Interdenominational nation-wide crusades such as the M&RFM, awakened denominational leaders to the potential merits of campaigns for their own Churches.   An Episcopal "Forward Movement" followed on the footsteps of the LMM in 1911.[19]   The Methodist Board also launched several campaigns in the years before World War I.   The African Jubilee Campaign of 1910 raised $330,000 in celebration of seventy-five years of work in Africa.   A Property and Equipment Movement was organized in 1912 to acquire better missionary facilities abroad.   The outbreak of World War I resulted in the establishment of an Emergency War Relief Fund to provide support for the missions of British Methodism.   In 1910 the ACMS organized its "Million Dollars by 1915" campaign and then expanded the effort in 1911 into a "Men and Millions Movement" involving all major Disciple boards.   One Disciple leader called this development "'a holding corporation' formed by our mission, benevolent and educational organizations to raise $6,300,000 in large personal gifts; to encourage the consecration and training of young life for Christian service; and to institute more business-like methods of increased regular income for congregational and general religious work."[20]

As a result of the new stress on denominational campaigns, non-denominational efforts like the LMM and M&RFM fell on hard times. Plans for a United Missions Campaign, proposed by both the interdenominational Home Missions Council and Foreign Missions Conference, was deemed inexpedient in 1913, even though its supporters planned for it to be under the direction of the mission boards.[21]   Then came the failure of the Interchurch World Movement, which was launched after World War I in an effort to combine in a simultaneous crusade all of the various denominational fund-raising drives.   By 1920 a vast organization with a staff of 2600 had been created to promote the drives and to survey the condition of the Churches.   The leaders assumed that the expenses of the organization would be paid—as with the earlier LMM   and   M&RFM—by   "friendly   citizens"   not   tapped   by   the denominational drives.   But only one million (and two million in additional pledges) of an expected forty million dollars was subscribed. An emergency appeal netted only $10,000 in cash.   The organization suddenly discovered itself 6.5 million dollars in debt and dissolved in July 1920. The denominations, whose own drives had succeeded beyond all hopes, were stuck with the bill for the Interchurch Movement. The experience was painful, and never again would non-denominational efforts along these lines be as important a part of the life of the twentieth-century Church.

The denominational campaigns following World War I were frequently inspired by the success that the government, the Red Cross and the YMCA had achieved in wartime fundraising. Some, like the Methodist Centenary, had been planned before the war, but now took on new meaning in the light of the wartime enthusiasm. An Episcopal executive said, "The mind of the nation, profoundly stirred to interest and determination, abandoned all previous habits of thought in the matter of giving."   Wartime expressions were applied to religious programs; the campaigners spoke of mission "fronts," "victories" and "defeats," "enlistment" and "training," "Christ's Missionary Army" and the formation of a "Missionary Reserve Corps" to give money. The Board of Missions was described as a "General Staff" and diocesan "Recruiting Officers" were asked to fill out the "muster rolls." Admiral David Beatty was quoted in favor of this religious drive: "If half of the zeal and passion, half of the outpouring of life and treasure, of organization and efficiency that the state has put into this War could be thrown into the cause of the Kingdom and of the eternal verities, the world would soon be won."[22]

The resulting denominational campaigns were carefully planned. The Episcopalians hired the advertising firm of Barton and Durstein, Inc. to conduct their Nationwide Campaign. Careful surveys of the needs of the churches were conducted. The Church, it was announced, would "engage in a scientific propaganda work. We would, as it were, put over this idea." Regional offices were created to carry out the campaign and an expenditure of one million dollars was originally budgeted merely for the promotion of the Campaign.[23]

The Methodist Centenary Campaign was organized by a Joint Committee of the major Methodist boards. Beginning in January 1918, the Church launched a series of organizational, educational and training programs. Then in September the financial campaign began, culminating in a "great Centenary Celebration" in June of 1919. The original plans called for raising some eighty million dollars over a five-year period, but the goal was soon raised to $140 million. A Conservation Committee was established to follow-up on pledges after the campaign.[24]   The

Foreign Board spent over $2.5 million to conduct the Centenary and another $367,000 was used to finance the Columbus Celebration at the close of the campaign. In addition, the Conservation Committee cost the Foreign Board $1.7 million in promotional expenses. Total costs of the campaign for all Methodist Boards probably came to over $9 million. Pledges by church members came to over $100 million, but as it turned out, only 60% of those pledges were honored over the next five-year period.[25]

Southern Baptists organized a five-year "75 Million Campaign" in 1919 under the slogan of "Millions for the Master." Once again the campaign was carefully planned: September was to be a month of prayer; October, "the Enlistment for Service Month;" and November, "Christian Stewardship Month." Churches were offered "Sermon Hits on Christian Stewardship." For all Churches the last week of November was designated "Victory Week," with November 30 as "Pledge Day." The *Maryland Baptist Church Life* noted: "Our nation demonstrated that democracy can be made tremendously efficient in political and military affairs. Our denomination has now demonstrated to all the world that democracy can be made tremendously efficient in religious affairs."[26] Just how democratic the Baptist campaign was remains debatable, but it was clearly an economic success, with pledges of $92 million.

The Disciples' post-war campaign was small in comparison with those of other denominations. A "War Emergency Campaign" was created as an extension of the earlier Men and Millions Movement, and pledges of $7.1 million were received. The major focus of Disciple attention, however, was on the reorganization and centralization of its major boards.

The overall success of the post-war campaigns had both good and bad effects. Coming at a time of high inflation, the pledges gave denominational leaders a false sense of wealth. Actual giving fell far short of the pledges by the end of the five-year periods. Baptists paid only $58 of the $92 million; Methodists only 60%. Denominational agencies meanwhile had expanded programs and staffs on the assumption of high incomes. By the mid-1920s the agencies faced sharp cutbacks and increasing indebtedness. Clearly better planning was still needed. On the other hand, agency incomes were definitely higher in real terms than before the war, even if expenditures had gotten out of hand. The "forward movements" had proved that organized and centralized fundraising could bring home the bacon. Moreover, as a first venture into inter-agency and long-run finance, these campaigns were a preview of the sophisticated denominational promotion that was to be undertaken after 1920 by permanent promotional agencies.

In the same years that denominational executives developed the financial drive, they also conceived new fundraising techniques that they called "systematic finance." The central emphasis of "systematic finance" was weekly giving based on each member's individual pledge. Denominational executives took the lead in the development of this new financial program. Tracts on "systematic finance" were sent to all churches, along with materials that would enable local churches to initiate the program. Executives believed that by securing pledges the local churches and national agencies would be better able to project their incomes for the coming year.

In addition, "systematic finance" used new psychological tools to increase total giving. One technique, first emphasized by the LMM, was the Every-Member Canvass. The Canvass was designed to survey personally every member of the local church in order to secure his pledge. As the Episcopal Board reported, "If everyone has been given an opportunity in personal conference to decide whether or not he or she desires to have a part in this work, there can be no doubt that there will be more than enough to meet all legitimate claims upon the Church's generosity."[27] Pastors were told to preach a series of Sunday sermons, to give explanatory leaflets to each member, to organize a men's supper at which "leading men of the congregation" would offer resolutions in favor of increased offerings, and to select canvassers to "be coached concerning their work just as salesmen and other businessmen are trained before engaging in any important business undertaking." Canvassers were encouraged not to allow members to postpone making decisions.[28]

Books on technique proliferated. A six-month planning schedule was mapped out, including directions on when to publicize, when to order supplies, and when to train canvassers. Churches were told to reject "cheap, flimsy paper" in their publicity, to conduct elaborate commissioning services "with all possible impressiveness" for the canvassers, to divide canvassers into competing teams in order to increase totals, to present pledges in a magnificent pageant climaxed by lighting candles in a darkened church for every ten dollars pledged. (The author of one book noted the sense of failure that would result if all the candles were not lit.) Churches were told that "it pays to advertise" and pastors were advised that "personal allusions and chuckles are not to be despised."[29]

The results of the Every-Member Canvass were described as "little short of startling" in terms of both parish and national giving.[30] The Episcopal Board reported: "While the annual offering has achieved much in the past, its inadequacy in the present day of missions opportunity is universally recognized. Thousands of business men over the country have pronounced the Every-Member Canvass for offerings on a weekly basis the best method of mission finance."[31]

Another important device in the program of "systematic finance" was the "duplex envelope." These envelopes were two-pocketed, numbered, dated and boxed. Each was persuasively designed; they were "large enough to contain contributions many times larger than the average contributor is willing to give." One pocket was for contributions to local expenses, the other for national benevolences. The envelopes, it was hoped, would be constant reminders of the individual member's pledge. In addition, those who had neglected to support the national benevolences would feel guilty each time they left their envelope empty.[32] Denominational leaders were lavish in their praise of this new device. Arthur Gray of the D&FMS said that the envelope was "efficient."[33] The Corresponding Secretary of the BSSB noted that "if generally adopted in our churches, [it] would do much to solve the question of systematic giving."[34] Boards offered to provide the envelopes free of charge to any local church that would use them. An Episcopal Easter Bulletin in 1914 showed increases in missionary offering of from 150 to 700% through use of the duplex envelope.[35]

A "systematic" approach was also suggested for dealing with the problem of specials. Denominational executives discontinued their hitherto fruitless efforts to eliminate special gifts and sought, instead, to channel those contributions along a selected course. In 1902, the Methodist Board adopted a "Station Plan" that was designed to allow an individual church to provide support for a certain missionary. The Board was thereby relieved of the cost that would otherwise have been part of the general budget, and at the same time, the local church retained a sense of personal involvement in the work of the Board. The Plan proved so popular that a Station Plan Secretary was hired in 1904. At the General Conference of 1908, the Methodist Board was ordered to insist that its missionaries submit all requests for special assistance to the Board. Missionaries were not to make any other special appeals. All funds were to pass through the general treasury of the Board. Mission treasurers were to report any direct gifts to the Board's Treasurer by special voucher "in order that the Church may have presented to it annually a complete statement of all receipts and disbursements."[36] In 1910 a "well-equipped Special Gift Department" was established at the Board; one of its aims was to stimulate greater giving consistent with long-term stability.[37] Churches were categorized by the amount given to missions. Those giving less than $600 were offered the "privilege" of supporting a single missionary at a cost of $800-1000. Churches giving less than $1000 were given the "privilege" of maintaining a married couple at $1200. Other churches were to have the "privilege" of sustaining schools, hospitals, orphanages, newspapers or entire mission districts. Churches were asked to pledge this support for periods of three to five years in order to ensure the stability of the new scheme.[38] In 1912 a "Parish Abroad Plan" similar to the Station Plan was added. The Disciple Board adopted a "Living Link" program similar to that of the Methodists and the D&FMS soon followed the same course. In 1912 the Episcopal Board advised all churches of the amounts necessary to support native priests, schools or hospital beds. The new system of specials seems to have proved very efficacious; board minutes fail to mention the problem after 1912.

The heart of "systematic finance" was its emphasis on education and effective promotion of the national interests of the Church. Much of the agencies' time was spent in developing methods that would increase their constituencies' interest in the central Church. Barton and Durstein advised the Episcopal Board that the primary task would be "getting our people to comprehend our program." In order to accomplish that end, they advocated use of "all avenues of publicity to make our people thoroughly familiar with what we are attempting to do. We would in a sense, engage in a scientific propaganda. We would, as it were, put over this idea." Nor did they have any doubt as to where solutions to problems should be found. "The central office would see that just as soon as possible efforts be made to solve certain problems which we have today. . .The central office would see to it that that was done. That's the plan. It's simple."[39] Boards invested large sums in "missionary education," especially among young people in the churches. Agencies often created a special publicity department to promote this work. The Baptist Home Mission Board, for instance, formed such a department in 1910.

This kind of national work seemed also to demand a higher degree of cooperation among the various agencies of the Church. In 1906 the three Disciples Boards created a Committee on Calendar to oversee their fundraising operations. Cooperative ventures such as the Men and Millions Movement and the War Emergency Drive demonstrated the value of collaboration and eventually led to the formation of the United Christian Missionary Society (UCMS) in 1919. By 1925, this new Society had a promotional division with ten full-time employees to direct through a central agency the entire work of denominational finance. Methodist Boards made joint appeals for funds after 1906 under a Joint Committee on Apportionment and later a Commission on Finance. Over time the Commission acquired greater independence from the Boards until by the 1920s, with its name changed to the World Service Commission, it was responsible for all Methodist promotion. When the Episcopal Church created its National Council in 1919, two new departments—publicity and finance—symbolized the new role that merchandising was beginning to play in the modern Church. Baptists created a Conservation Commission following their 75 Million Campaign; in 1925 the organization became the Commission on Future Program (later the Cooperative Program). This agency was responsible for soliciting unrestricted funds for all the boards and commissions of the Convention.

Another means of assuring greater stability for the operations of the national agencies was to emphasize the development of permanent endowments. Elaborate plans for annuities and legacies were drawn up and publicized by boards desiring permanent sources of income. By the 1920s most Churches had adopted standards for all agencies to follow in the writing of such agreements. A national conference advised Church treaurers on the latest techniques in 1925.[40] Agencies were apparently successful in securing endowments; in 1909 some 4.6% of their income came from these sources; in 1923, 5.7%; and by 1929, 10.7%.[41]

Indeed, the entire program of "systematic finance" appears to have been an outstanding success—in monetary terms—during the years I have examined. Studies made during the 1920s suggested the effectiveness of the new fundraising techniques. "From the standpoint of the denominational executives," said C. Luther Fry (in a study of fluctuations in giving to benevolences by rural churches), "the moral [is] that church leaders through concerted action can decidedly influence the policies of rural churches."[42] An examination of giving by eleven Protestant denominations from 1913 to 1927 concluded that in constant dollars "benevolences are seen to make a far more erratic, though, in some respects a better, showing than congregational expenses." The study went on to reveal that although giving in constant dollars fell from 1915 to 1919, it caught up in 1920 and by 1927 it "still more than compensated for the decreased value of the dollar."[43]

In each of the four Churches examined there was substantial growth in constant dollar benevolent giving in the years from 1890 to 1930 (See Graphs 1 - 5, pp. 105-109).[44] In each Church there was a fairly steady growth in giving from 1896 to 1914, primarily reflecting increased membership. The rapid inflation during the war years (1914-1919) saw the agencies suffer slightly, but the post-war deflation combined with the drives to produce substantial growth during the 1920s. Even more impressive was the effect of the new methods on constant dollar per capita giving (Graphs 6 and 7, pp. 110-111) in those Churches where accurate and uninterrupted membership statistics are

GRAPH 1: ACMS Receipts, 1926 Dollars

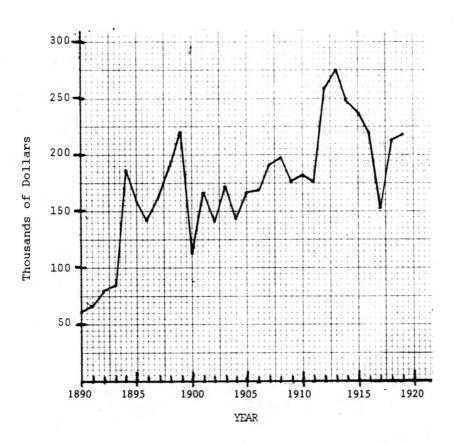

Sources: Disciples of Christ Yearbook, 1890-1920
         Wholesale Price Index, Historical Statistics
         of the United States: Colonial Times to 1970
         (Washington: Bureau of the Census, 1975),
         p. 200.

GRAPH 2: Total Benevolent Giving, Disciples
        of Christ, 1926 Dollars

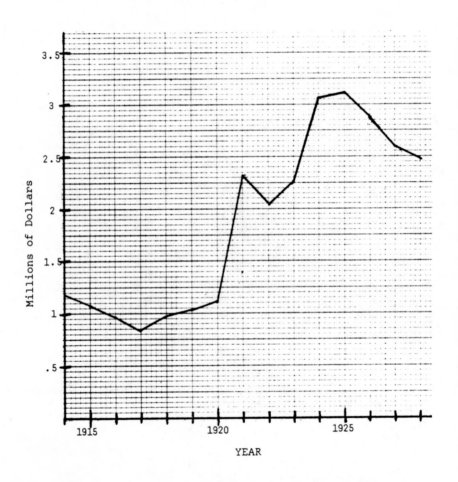

Sources: Disciples of Christ Yearbook, 1914-1929
         Wholesale Price Index, Historical Statistics

GRAPH 3: Total Benevolent Expenditures, Methodist
Episcopal Church, 1926 Dollars

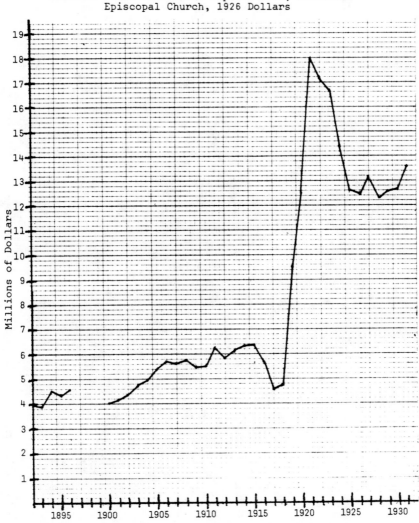

YEAR

Sources: Methodist Yearbooks, 1926 and 1931
Wholesale Price Index, Historical Statistics

GRAPH 4: Total Benevolent Giving, Southern
          Baptist Convention, 1926 Dollars

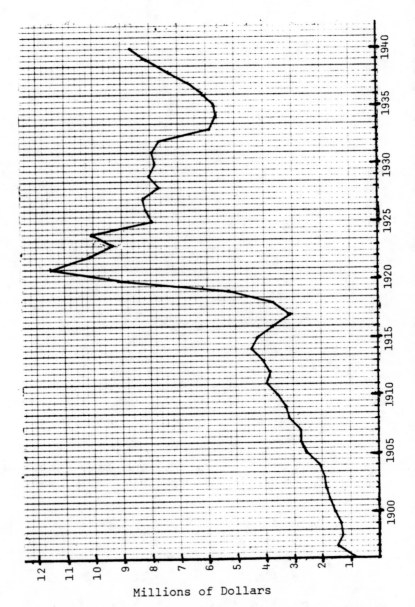

Millions of Dollars

Sources: Encyclopedia of Southern Baptists, pp. 1256-57
         Wholesale Price Index, Historical Statistics

GRAPH 5: Total Expenditures, D&FMS,
1926 Dollars

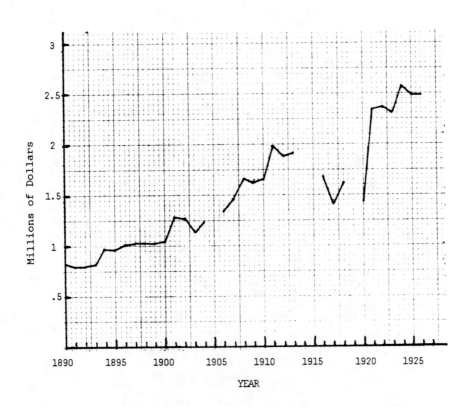

Sources: Annual Report, PEC, 1892-1919
          Annual Report, National Council, 1920-1927
          Wholesale Price Index, Historical Statistics

GRAPH 6: Per Capita Benevolent Giving, Southern
Baptist Convention, 1926 Dollars

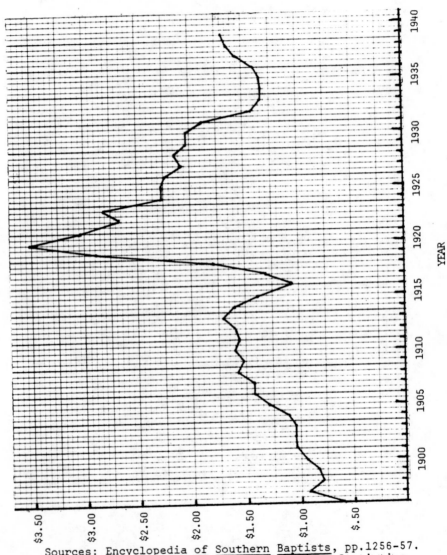

Sources: Encyclopedia of Southern Baptists, pp.1256-57.
Wholesale Price Index, Historical Statistics

GRAPH 7: Per Capita Benevolent Giving, Methodist
          Episcopal Church, 1926 Dollars

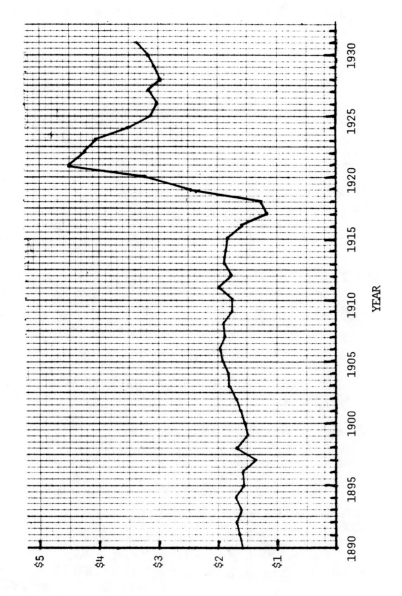

Sources: Methodist Yearbooks, 1926 and 1931
          Wholesale Price Index, Historical Statistics

available.[45]   Per capita giving to national causes by Methodists and Baptists grew greatly in the years after 1918. In the period from 1913 to 1927, denominational benevolences performed far better than either the general price index or local congregations, as Table 1 shows.

TABLE I

Year	Price Index	Benevolences	Congregational Expenditures
1913	1.00	100	100
1914	1.008	100	102
1915	1.007	102	99
1916	1.09	104	100
1917	1.29	117	104
1918	1.52	134	109
1919	1.76	181	114
1920	1.98	267	136
1921	1.69	256	148
1922	1.58	241	153
1923	1.60	238	160
1924	1.60	231	171
1925	1.65	213	180
1926	1.66	209	183
1927	1.62	194	188

Source: Fahs, *Trends in Protestant Giving*, p. 31.

Evidence of Protestant financial successes was everywhere. In the first forty-five years of the twentieth century, for instance, Disciples of Christ giving for national causes multiplied twenty times while membership grew only 53%.[46]

    While I have focused on the significance of more successful techniques in the growth of Protestant benevolent giving, this increase also reflects certain basic changes in the general economic context. During the late nineteenth century, for example, Gross National Product per capita increased. In the twentieth century the rate of growth in product per capita also increased. Both of these statistics suggest a greater supply of money was available for the Churches to tap. Moreover, the growth in the number of middle-class, urban professionals also gave the Church a new class of individuals to be "approached."[47]

These supply-side changes, however, seem less important than the increased demand produced by "systematic finance."

Although the depression years of the 1930s lie beyond the boundaries of this study,, there is some reason to believe that even during these hard times, Protestant denominations performed significantly better, at least in a financial sense, than most historians have believed. An Institute of Social and Religious Research study in 1935 reported that "the average income of the national benevolent boards of the major denominations has not been reduced as much as have the personal incomes of the American people, or their personal expenditures and savings." In truth, denominations may have profited on a relative basis during the years of depression. The study further noted that reductions in mission support had yet to fall below the amount that would have been reached "by steady proportional rise in financial support since the beginning of the present century."[48] If these conclusions are correct, and my own statistics in part bear this out, then the notion of a "religious depression" from 1925-35 seems to need serious qualification. Protestant leaders naturally complained about falling incomes during the 1930s, but judging from my research, "systematic finance" left them better off than has commonly been supposed.

For all its monetary success, "systematic finance" was of course not without its drawbacks. As we have already noted, the decreases in income following the post-war financial campaigns forced sharp curtailments in the expanded staffs and new plans that had developed. The indebtedness of the agencies became a heavy burden. At a meeting of the Methodist Board in 1924, board members offered to pawn their watches in order to symbolize their personal concern for the financial plight of the agency.[49] Too much control over offerings still remained in local hands to suit denominational leaders. Local churches were engaged in formidable church building and local improvement campaigns "that denied funds to the 'larger work of the church.'"[50] The Episcopal Board complained that parishes and dioceses "camouflaged" their expenses and were "stealing" children's offerings for missions to avoid paying their fair share of benevolent finance.[51] Secretary S. Earl Taylor of the Methodist Board charged that pastors let benevolent interests slip, always increasing "their salaries at the expense of the benevolences."[52]

Interagency rivalry was certainly not eliminated by centralized budgeting. The Methodist Missionary Society, while supporting the principle of central fundraising, constantly complained that it did not receive its proper share of the total raised. Too many other small agencies were getting a piece of the pie—without paying an adequate share of the costs—to suit the mission executives. Indeed the Missionary

Society's percentage of total funds distributed after the creation of the Commission on Finance gradually fell. In addition, the central agency now handled all specials and in effect made up for one agency's shortfall in designated monies by giving it a greater total of the undesignated funds. Since the Missionary Society received the greatest amount in specials, it again felt cheated. The Board complained that the new method was a denial of "democracy" and that donors would soon channel their funds in other directions where more "freedom is offered." Hundreds of thousands of dollars, said the Board, were going down the drain.[53] There were further complaints about the necessity of handling all monies through the Chicago office of the World Service Commission. Treasurer Fowles of the Society grumbled about the loss of "initiative in promoting the interests of the Board." A. E. Chenoweth of Fowles' office cited instances of delay, added expense, inadequate information, and red tape due to the intervention of the Chicago office. "In many instances," said Chenoweth, "the routine work is handled by clerks who do not appreciate the fact that the New York office needs to know exactly what the donor may have said, or written, even to the punctuation of his letter."[54]

More important, in my judgement, than interagency rivalry was the long-run effect that "systematic finance" had on the way the Church defined its goals in the twentieth century. In many respects, the new programs seemed to transform the Church, making it as much a business as a religious institution. Church leaders were opting for the successful marketing of their product, but they did so at the cost of sacrificing the Church's prophetic role as critic of society.

For the centralized promotional agencies, fundraising was an art. Denominational fundraisers experimented with gimmicks of all kinds to increase giving at the local level. Churches were urged to give "as much for others as ourselves." Denominational leaders shied away from the Budget and Apportionment system that had proved objectionable to local churches as a form of "taxation." Instead, churches were now categorized by the percentage given to benevolent causes. Charts showing local church "successes" and "failures" in terms of support for the central church were regularly published.[55] Individual churches and dioceses were ranked by their benevolent gifts. The 1927 SBC *Annual* classified churches into five categories, ranging from Class A (those giving more than 50% to missions) down to Class E (those giving nothing). 75% of the churches fell into classes D and E and another 10% submitted no report. The Baptist leaders hoped, no doubt, that the appearance of local failure would prove a powerful psychological stimulus for local church action on behalf of the central organization.[56]   Larger churches were actually asked to give a greater percentage of their incomes to central expenses.[57]

Contributions to central expenses often became the principal means of evaluating a local church's attainments.   In 1911, the D&FMS informed the parishes that the apportionment was not merely "an end to be aimed at," but indeed "a measure by means of which all concerned might know that they had not fallen short in their proportionate share of the common obligation."[58]   H. C. Weber's book on the *Every-Member Canvass* noted that the success or failure of the canvass ought to tell the congregation a great deal about its "temperature."[59]   Local pastors realized that success or failure within the denomination often depended on their fundraising abilities.   The *Journal of Religion* noted in 1921 that a pastor who "is able to raise the figures of his budget (especially for the support of his denominational machinery), is invariably pronounced successful.   The quicker and greater his returns, the better chance he stands of favorable recognition."   Ministers were in competition with one another and needed to advertise.   "Novel methods, new 'stunts,' striking innovation, ingenious competitions and pleasing variations are not to be disdained if the curiosity of the crowd is to be aroused."[60]   Roger Babson suggested that the successful minister in industrial centers "must be one of the salesman type rather than of the academic type."[61]

There was, I think, a decidedly non-Christian aspect to the thought of those denominational fundraisers who carefully evaluated alternative courses of action to stimulate giving.   The Episcopal General Secretary debated whether it would be wiser to "ask the Church to give a million dollars," knowing that a lesser sum would suffice, or to request a smaller amount that would be "more likely to succeed if the burden is now made to fall as lightly as possible on the Dioceses."   The Board decided not to ask for too great a sum, but it did so only because of fear that it would alienate local churches.[62]   In 1916 the Methodist Commission on Finance discussed means to shift power away from the district superintendents who were seen as "responsible for the church's losses" by their constant tendency to set aside the official apportionments of the central church.   Various means to make the district superintendents subservient to the national agencies without alienating them were considered.[63]

During the 1920s "scientific" research was conducted to determine the type of church which gave the most to national causes. This research confirmed what denominational leaders had already discovered: wealthy churches did not sacrifice as much for missions as poorer churches.   A "sliding scale of apportionment," such as many Churches already had, was suggested to persuade wealthier churches to give more on a percentage basis. In addition, smaller churches (fewer than fifty members) had greater contributions per capita, but gave less to missions since most of their funds were needed to keep the local church alive. Contributions per member to missions and benevolences rose considerably in churches larger than 150 members. Churches with resident ministers gave larger sums as well. These facts suggested more care in avoiding "overchurching" and the merger of local churches if denominational budgets were to benefit. Moreover, denominational executives were urged to prevent the construction of "too large and expensive churches." In effect, denominational executives had created for their local churches a demographic profile that would produce maximum national support—instead of maximum effectiveness in terms of the direct relationship between the individual and the church.[64]

Denominational fundraisers also perfected "stewardship" techniques that would ensure that local churches would achieve the maximum support from their members. The Baptist Cooperative Program, for instance, designated 1929 as "Stewardship Year." Each pastor was issued a handbook on promotional methods. "Attractive wall posters" were sent to local churches in support of the national theme. Two new tracts on the Cooperative Program and on Stewardship were available for insertion in church bulletins. The journal, *The Baptist Program*, planned to feature ideas on "cash ingathering" in its April issue. All churches were to conduct the annual Every-Member Canvass during December 2-9. Local pastors strongly supported the program, knowing that larger budgets also meant larger salaries for themselves. Congregational independence was threatened by the power of such central planning, but what other options did local churches have?[65]

The language of denominational leaders came to be permeated with business terms, with the vocabulary of the counting house. Charles Stelzle declared that "the supreme duty of the modern church is to get new business. The church must realize that it is in exactly the same position as any other solicitor of custom, and it must advertise its goods."[66] The Rev. D. E. Weigle of Philadelphia declared that "we must be about our Father's *business*. The church," he said, was like a "great corporation."[67] Local churches began to describe church-going as a "business asset." "It is obvious," said one advertisment, "if you are known as a steady, sober-minded churchman, those with whom you deal have greater confidence in you. . . . This is a decided business advantage, a personal asset, and worthwhile in every way."[68] A New York City pastor purchased a billboard that urged: "Come to Church. Public Worship Increases Your Efficiency."[69]

Few, of course, were so callous as to proclaim fundraising an ultimate end. But "all unconsciously," as one astute critic noted, "money has won a false place in the Christian kingdom." The Church was no longer a "revolutionary force:" it prayed for missions but measured possibilities in terms of the offertory; it called for faithful ministers, but labeled them as so many "hundred or thousand-dollar-a-year men;" it demanded vision, but ran its organization on the "same principles as the ordinary countinghouse." The Church showed "in practice, what most would last of all admit, that God can do just as much as man can do, and no more, and that man can do just as much as money will admit—no more and no less!"[70]

In an attempt to camouflage the secularism embodied in the techniques of "systematic finance," the new methods were often couched in the language of Scripture. Advertising was the "Modern Way to Compel Them to Come In."[71] After all, Christ told his disciples, "Let your light so shine before men, that they may see your good works and glorify your Father which is in Heaven."[72] At the 1916 Convention of the Associated Advertising Clubs of the World the new Commission on Church Advertising and Publicity heard what one journal called "a new petition to the liturgy" that declared it "a sin to preach to empty pews when proper advertising fills the churches." One pastor called God the first great advertiser whose burning bush made "$50,000-a-year electric signs look insignificant" by comparison.[73] The head of the Presbyterian Department of Promotion told the 1925 FCC Conference on Financial and Fiduciary Matters that raising money for endowments as an end in itself was doomed, but if "endowments spelled S-O-U-L-S" then funds were easily obtained.[74] The Methodist Board informed its members that their estimates were not to be viewed as "an apportionment, but as the call of God."[75] The Methodist Board's 1912 report to the Commission on Finance is a perfect melding of the old and new: "If by prayerful, concerted effort the facts may be fully presented to our membership, and if a well-systematized financial plan can be presented to the local church, we have every confidence that the church will respond in abundant measure."[76]

The boards sought reassurance by constantly reminding themseves that the answer to their problems was not in machinery alone—even as they obsessively discussed techniques and organizations. The Methodist Board's Campaign on Relief and Reenforcement in 1912 ended its twelve-page report on organization and procedure by urging all campaigners that "at all times it must be remembered that 'This problem is not one of machinery but of life.'"[77] Secretary S. Earl Taylor of the Methodist Board told the Commission on Finance that they must "deal with business principles, methods of work, organization and finance, and still subordinate the machinery to the spirit and motive of it all."[78] One clever fundraiser went so far as to urge "systematic finance" as a means to "prevent both the absorbtion of the Church in itself and the bestowal of the chief thought of the Church on the temporalities." He pointed out that if funds were quickly raised, there would be little distraction "from the work of winning men to God."[79] These themes in the discourse of the Church reflect, I think, the leaders' awareness that a substantial and potentially dangerous shift in emphasis was actually taking place. They reassured themselves, but promptly returned to the organizational (as opposed to religious) tasks at hand.

Most often, the question asked of the new techniques was not from Scripture but rather from business: "Does it pay?"[80] Inevitably the answer from denominational leaders was yes. "'It pays to advertise' is just as true of the Church as of business," reported the Literary Digest. All too often the language of business became the message of the Church. One sold the Church like any commodity, such as bread. Everyone needed it; it was "the bread of life."[81] Joseph A. Richard, a Madison Avenue specialist, told ministers gathered for the Church Advertising meeting that he would recommend a "survey" for any church that wanted to determine "what goods you have to advertise, just how they are packaged, just how you propose to deliver them."[82] Canvassers were to adopt the "techniques of salesmanship, of approach and personal contact, on which secular business is based. . . . An enthusiastic seller makes the best salesman."[83] Occasionally the business jargon was indiscrete, if not profane. A Methodist internal memorandum in 1922 rejoiced that "Dr. North has succeeded in landing his $50,000 annuity and the money and Liberty Bonds are in the bank."[84] Disciple officials, upon realizing that a number of churches had not given their regular contributions "undertook a great campaign to bring these churches into line."[85]

The application of business methods to Church finance was promoted on the grounds that it would help to restore the image of the twentieth-century Church. As one observer noted, "The Church should make it its business to make men think well of it."[86] Many believed that if Churches conducted their financial affairs "as in a factory," then the confidence of members in the institution would be restored. Members wanted the "assurance" of good accounting systems, of double entry bookkeeping, of professional advertising.[87] Men of the world would be impressed by a Church of wealth and power. Frank H. Mann, treasurer of the FCC and President of the Union Guarantee and Mortgage Company, informed the 1929· Conference on Financial and Fiduciary Matters that religious endowments represented a "staggering volume of wealth." Mann admitted he had guessed that the figure was two hundred million dollars but had learned the real total was "nearer two billions," a sum that clearly pleased the gathered fundraisers.[88]

Techniques seemed more acceptable to Churchmen if they had been employed successfully by business.   Frank H. Mann, FCC Treasurer, told the 1925 Conference of Financial and Fiduciary Matters that annuitants should be issued "handsomely engraved" contracts. Mann admitted there was no inherent value in the "elegance of the workmanship," but suggested that "it reflects business-like methods which inspire confidence and have a decided value to those officers of the organization who are responsible for the promotional program."[89] Pastors were urged not to insist on payments of pledges in cases of evident distress since it "would be neither Christian nor good business."[90] But one wonders what conclusion might have been reached had such demands indeed been good business.

Many perceived the Church as competing in a market for Sunday time, and advertising was thus the best means to win the Church's proper share in the market. Churches must learn to advertise, it was said, in order to counter the glaring posters of the theatre, the electric marquee of the motion picture, and the message of the Sunday press which lured men on excursions in their new automobiles.[91] One critic of the process noted that Churches were "at their wits' ends to devise and invent means to draw and hold people." Churches resorted to the crudest fads and inventions of the amusement world "to interest and draw the public, to increase their size and strength, and to command respect and influence in the nation's life."[92]

Religious leaders realized how "radically" different the new fundraising techniques were. Episcopal spokesmen frankly admitted that they were now "spending money for the purpose of securing a larger income."[93]   The new methods were costly, but in the rhetoric of business, Church leaders saw the expense as an "investment" that would yield benefits beyond even the money raised.[94]   In 1908 the General Missions Committee of the Methodist Board urged the Church to invest money in promotion. "Businessmen do not hesitate to invest vast sums of money in great enterprises and wait for dividends." Members were assured that "the investment will pay."[95] Educational Secretary Sturgis of the D&FMS pointed out that the businessman "was prepared as a starter, to spend the bulk of his capital in arousing and stimulating the need" for his product.[96] As a result of the campaigns "great numbers of men and women" were enlisted in active support of the various causes. More Churchmen than ever learned about "self-sacrifice."[97]

The selling of the Church became a part of the celebration of business values and of the accomplishments of man epitomized in the 1920s in the popular works of Bruce Barton and Roger Babson. God played only a supporting role in the new faith. Asking if the Sunday schools paid, Henry Fredrick Cope admitted that "such a statement leaves out for the present the consideration of divine cooperation, because we may be assured that if we do our work rightly and submit it to the great tests of life, the tests which the Master Himself set, there will be no question as to the cooperation that is from above."[98] None was more callous, however, than William S. Beard, Secretary of the Layman's Advisory Committee of the National Council of Congregational Churches. Beard appeared at the 1929 Conference on Financial and Fiduciary Matters as an expert on raising funds for endowments. Beard stressed the importance of laymen's dinners. Such dinners should be billed as meetings of the "stockholders" of the most "significant corporation in the world." The "stockholders" would hear of past dividends and future forecasts of growth; emphasis would be placed on the Church as a "billion dollar proposition." Beard urged that such meetings be held in hotels and clubs, not in churches; and that the guests sing popular songs like "Swanee River" and "Old Black Joe," not religious hymns. Concluding his message, Beard noted that "nothing has been left to chance. At no point have we trusted that the Lord will provide. He won't."[99]

Thus by 1930 the central agencies of the Churches had put themselves on much firmer financial ground than fifty years before. They had produced more stable incomes through "systematic finance." Permanent endowments provided security in times of financial stringency. Church leaders now "invested" millions of dollars in centralized promotional agencies.

American Churches paid a price, however, for this prosperity in the form of a diminished sense of the Church's traditional religious goals. Local church success tended to be measured by giving to benevolences, not by preaching good news to the poor or by healing the wounds of the broken-hearted. Professional promoters wanted to know whether their plans would "pay," not whether they were in accordance with the plan of God. The Church was often an institution to be packaged and sold like any other commodity. The money changers were certainly back in the Temple.

Thanks to their financial success, agencies and boards were becoming the principal sources of power in twentieth-century American Protestantism. The older pastoral structure still remained an important nexus of power at the local level, but even it was increasingly influenced by the national agencies. The two structures coexisted as best they could, with local institutions becoming more slaves than masters of the boards they had orginally established. As we shall see, the financial power of the agencies paved the way for yet another, and often synergistic, change in the Church in these years: a change toward centralized forms of adminstration.

NOTES

[1]Gaius Glen Atkins, "The Crusading Church at Home and Abroad," *Church History*, 1 (September 1932), 131.   See also "Convention, ACMS," (1912), p. 514.

[2]See Alfred Williams Anthony, ed., *Safeguarding Funds: Financial and Fiduciary Matters* (New York: J. E. Stohlman, 1925) and *Changing Conditions in Public Giving* (New York: Federal Council of Churches, 1929).   Conferences on Fiduciary and Financial Matters were held in 1925, 1927 and 1929.   Representatives of Church boards, religious colleges and social work agencies were in attendance. Transactions of the conferences sold about 1000 copies.

[3]"Board, MEC," February 16, 1909.

[4]On the Laymen's Missionary Movement see "A Significant Religious Movement," *The Century*, 80 (June 1910), 313-15; W. S. Rainsford, "Getting Together for Foreign Missions," *Review of Reviews*, 41 (June 1910), 731-33; and *The Survey*, 24 (June 18, 1910), 479-80.

[5]"Board, MEC," December 21, 1909, p. 159.

[6]*Journal, PEC* (1910), p. 460.

[7]"Convention, ACMS," (1912), p. 514.

[8]"A Permanent Awakening?," *The Outlook*, 101 (May 4, 1912), 9.

[9]"Men and Religion Forward Movement," *The Survey*, 26 (May 6, 1911), 205-08.

[10]"Campaigning with the Men and Religion Teams," *The Survey*, 27 (December 23, 1911), 1393-96; Fred B. Smith, "The 'Forward Movement,'" *The Survey*, 28 (April 6, 1912), 33; Graham Taylor, "Advertising Religion," pp. 408-10; Ellis, "A Movement: A Message: A Method," pp. 984-88.

[11]George Mowry suggests that the California Progressive "often thought of the political movement he had started as part of the 'Religious Forward Movement.'" See "The California Progressive and his Rationale," p. 246.

[12]Allyn K. Foster, "The Dream Comes True," *Making Religion Efficient*, ed. Barbour, p. 8.

[13]Quoted in George H. Nash, III, "Charles Stelzle: Social Gospel Pioneer," *Journal of Presbyterian History*, 50 (Fall 1972), 221.

[14]Foster, "The Dream Comes True," p. 8 and *Efficient Religion*, p. 17.   See also Ellis, "A Movement: A Message: A Method," p. 988.

[15]Barbour, *Making Religion Efficient*, pp. 71, 92-93, 200.

[16]See Paul A. Carter, *The Decline and Revival of the Social Gospel: Social and Political Liberalism in American Protestant Churches, 1920-1940* (Hamden, Connecticut: Archon Books, 1971), especially Parts 1 and 2; Robert Moats Miller, *American*

Protestantism and Social Issues, 1919-1939 (Chapel Hill: University of North Carolina Press, 1958), especially Chapter 2; Donald B. Meyer, *The Protestant Search for Political Realism, 1919-1941* (Berkeley: University of California Press, 1960), especially Chapter 3; and Robert T. Handy, "The American Religious Depression, 1925-1935," *Church History*, 29 (March 1960), 3-16.

[17]Miller, *American Protestantism and Social Issues*, p. 18.

[18]Nash, "Charles Stelzle: Social Gospel Pioneer," p. 221.

[19]"Board, PEC," November 4, 1919, pp. 92-93; *Annual Report, PEC* (1911), pp. 4-5.

[20]"Convention, ACMS" (1916).

[21]"Board, PEC," May 14, 1913, pp. 196-97.

[22]"Board, PEC," October 2, 1918, p. 20; December 11, 1918, p. 35; February 12, 1919, pp. 15-22. The effect of World War I may also be seen in Manross, *A History of the American Episcopal Church*, p. 352.

[23]"Board, PEC," May 14, 1919, pp. 187-89, 287-93.

[24]"Board, MEC," December 7, 1917, pp. 91-93.

[25]*Journal, MBFM* (1923), pp. 64-67. See also *Handbook, MEC* (1928), pp. 535-36.

[26]4 (January 1920), 3; 3 (July 1919), 4, 16; 3 (October 1919), 6; 3 (November 1919), 7.

[27]*Annual Report, PEC* (1911), p. 14.

[28]Episcopal Leaflets #1109 (March 1911) and #1115 (March 1911) in Pamphlet Boxes, Episcopal Archives.   See also *Yearbook, Disciples of Christ* (1917), p. 10.

[29]H. C. Weber, *The Every-Member Canvass: People or Pocketbooks?* (New York: Fleming H. Revell, 1932).   Paradoxically, Weber's central thesis was that the purpose of the Canvass was to relate people to religion, not to raise money. The thrust of the book, however, belied his warnings. He urged churches to single out the wealthy for special approaches and to adopt the "techniques of salesmanship."

[30]*Annual Report, PEC* (1913), p. 6; Episcopal leaflet #1109, p. 13, Pamphlet Boxes.

[31]Episcopal Leaflet #1109, p. 11, Pamphlet Boxes. See also "Board, MEC," June 18, 1912, p. 356 and *Annual, SBC* (1927), p. 46.

[32]Episcopal Leaflet #1107, p. 14, Pamphlet Boxes.

[33]"Information," p. 60, Pamphlet Boxes.

[34]R. J. Willingham to J. M. Frost, July 12, 1901, Frost MSS.   Box 14.

[35]Episcopal Leaflet #901, p. 4, Pamphlet Boxes.

[36]"Board, MEC," October 19, 1909, p. 121; May 17, 1910, p. 281.

[37]"Board, MEC," April 19, 1910, p. 255.

[38]"Board, MEC," September 20, 1910, pp. 339-40.

[39]"Board, PEC," May 14, 1919, p. 188.

[40]For example see *Handbook, MEC* (1920), p. 382; "Board, SBC," February 6, 1919; *Yearbook, Disciples of Christ* (1915), p. 10; Anthony, *Safegarding Funds.*

[41]C. Luther Fry, "Changes in Religious Organizations," *Recent Social Trends in the United States* (2 vols.; New York: McGraw-Hill, 1933), II, 1049. Walter Charles Giersbach's *Protestant Finance in Metropolitan Chicago as Revealed by a Study of Four Denominations* (Chicago: University of Chicago Libraries, 1936), pp. 206-07, also points out the larger endowments of denominational agencies. Giersbach feared that such involvement in the social and economic order would undermine religious values. Religious leaders would have to play up to the wealthy, and their failure to secure large contributions could bring their administrative ability into question. I found little evidence to substantiate those fears, however. The rise in endowments came more from better planning and techniques than from larger contributions from wealthy donors.

[42]*Diagnosing the Rural Church*, p. 209.

[43]Charles H. Fahs, *Trends in Protestant Giving: A Study in Church Finance in the United States* (New York: Institute of Social and Religious Research, 1929), pp. 28, 31.

[44]One should note that denominational statistics are very sketchy prior to 1900. Even after that time the basis for computing income varies from year to year. Totals are further complicated by the consolidation of benevolences, especially after 1900. I have used only those figures which seemed fairly consistent from year to year in the various denominational handbooks, almanacs and board reports.

[45]Membership in the Disciples of Christ, for instance, varies widely in these years due to the official loss of the Churches of Christ in 1906.

[46]Garrison and DeGroot, *The Disciples of Christ*, p. 413.

[47]On general ecnomic trends in this period see Simon Kuznets, "Notes on the Pattern of U. S. Economic Growth," *The Nation's Economic Objectives*, ed. Edgar O. Edwards (Chicago: University of Chicago Press, 1964), pp. 15-35 and Harold G. Vatter, *The Drive to Industrial Maturity: The United States Economy, 1860-1914* (Westport, Connecticut: Greenwood Press, 1975), especially pp. 61-84.

[48]H. Paul Douglass and Edmund deS. Brunner, *The Protestant Church as a Social Institution* (New York: Harper, 1935), pp. 208, 226.

[49]"Minutes of the United Christian Missionary Society," December 22, 1921 and June 12, 1923, hereafter "Board, UCMS." See also *Handbook, MEC* (1924), p. 88 and *Journal, MBFM* (1924), pp. 66-70.

[50]"Board, UCMS," June 12, 1923.

[51]Educational Secretary Sturgis, "Board, PEC," February 12, 1919, pp. 16-17.

[52]Commission on Finance File, Methodist MSS., June 19, 1913.

[53]*Handbook, MEC* (1924), p. 94; Memo of S. Earl Taylor to Frank Mason North, January 11, 1919, Taylor file, Methodist MSS.

[54]Memo to Fowles, November 2, 1922, Fowles file, Methodist MSS. In the same see memo of North to Fowles, February 13, 1923; in Taylor file see memo of North to Taylor, May 26, 1919.

[55]*Annual Report,* National Council, PEC, 1920-1926.

[56]See also *Yearbook, Disciples of Christ* (1921); *Annual Report, PEC* for 1925-26 and "Board, MEC," June 21, 1910 for similar rankings in other churches.

[57]"Board, PEC," December, 1900, p. 91; May 1915.

[58]*Annual Report, PEC* (1911), p. 5; see also "Board, PEC," December 13, 1911, p. 13.

[59]p. 51.

[60]William E. Hammond, "The Economic Struggle Within the Ministerial Profession," 1 (September 1921), 515-16.

[61]*New Tasks for Old Churches* (New York: Fleming H. Revell, 1932), p. 164.

[62]"Board, PEC," December 1900, p. 90.

[63]Commission on Finance File, Methodist MSS., especially the report of Executive Secretary Hollingshead in 1916.

[64]See Fry, *Diagnosing the Rural Church*, pp. 92-94, 129, 144-55, 232-34. Franklin H. Giddings wrote the Foreword to this book.

[65]"Minutes of the Executive Committee, Southern Baptist Convention," January 11-12, 1928. Hereafter "Executive Committee, SBC."

[66]Quoted in Reisner, *Church Publicity*, p. 19.

[67]*Ibid.*, p. 74.

[68]"Church Going as a Business Asset," *Literary Digest,* 50 (June 26, 1915), 1540.

[69]Jesse Rainsford Sprague, "Religion in Business," *Harpers,* 155 (September 1927), 436.

[70]P. Gavan Duffy, "Is Modern Organized Christianity a Failure?," *The Arena,* 41 (February 1919), 174-75.

[71]Reisner, *Church Publicity.*

[72]"Selling' Religion," p. 28.

[73]"Combined Church Advertising," *Literary Digest,* 53 (November 25, 1919), 1411. See also Ashley, ed., *Church Advertising,* pp. 23-24 and "The Campaign for Church Advertising and Publicity," pp. 184-85.

[74]O. W. Buschgen, "Endowments," *Safeguarding Funds,* pp. 38-39. See also Barbour, *Making Religion Efficient,* p. 23.

[75]"Board, MEC," February 21, 1911, pp. 29-30. "The call of God" was nonetheless "carefully arranged" and "printed in suitable form."

[76]"Board, MEC," September 17, 1912, p. 460.

[77]"Board, MEC," July 16, 1912, pp. 402-13.

[78]Commission on Finance File, June 19, 1913, Methodist MSS.

[79]*Journal, MEC* (1916), p. 1330.

[80]For example see "Does Publicity Pay?," Chapter 2 in Reisner, *Church Publicity;* Russell H. Conwell, "How to Make a Church Pay," *The Independent,* 54 (March 27, 1902), 730-33; "Do Our Sunday Schools Pay?," Cope, *Efficiency in the Sunday-School,* p. 5; "Does it pay the 'Church of Today' to adopt unusual methods of publicity?," Ashley, ed., *Church Advertising,* p. 23.

[81]"Selling' Religion," p. 28.

[82]Quoted by Sprague, "Religion in Business," p. 436.

[83]Weber, *The Every-Member Canvass,* pp. 40, 45.

[84]Sutherland to Fowles, August 12, 1922, Fowles File, Methodist MSS.

[85]"Board, ACMS," October 5, 1906.

[86]Barbour, *Making Religion Efficient,* p. 200.

[87]For example see Conwell, "How to Make a Church Pay," pp. 730-33 and William H. Leach, *Toward a More Efficient Church* (New York: Fleming H. Revell, 1948), pp. 99-105.

[88]Anthony, ed. *Changing Conditions in Public Giving.*

[89]*Ibid.,* p. 22.

[90]Leach, *Toward a More Efficient Church,* p. 105.

[91]"The Campaign for Church Advertising and Publicity," p. 185.

[92]Ordway, "Will the Churches Survive," pp. 593-600. Ironically despite his criticism of the Church's commercialism, Ordway concluded that the Church's main problem was

"unsystematic and unbusinesslike methods of administration." He called for "business keenness and mastery of detail" and "systematic methods and diligent attention."

[93] "Board, PEC," June 13, 1905, p. 626.

[94] For example see "Executive Committee, SBC," February 19, 1920, p. 10; *Journal, PEC* (1919), p. 570.

[95] *Handbook, MEC* (1908), p. 179.

[96] "Board, PEC," February 12, 1919.

[97] John Crosby Brown in *Safeguarding Funds*, pp. 117-18. Brown was head of the advertising firm of Tanblyn and Brown. See also "Executive Committee, SBC," February 19, 1920, p. 10.

[98] *Efficiency in the Sunday-School*, pp. 5-6.

[99] *Changing Conditions in Public Giving*, pp. 81-84.

CHAPTER 7

THE ADMINISTRATIVE SOLUTION

The resolution of the agencies' financial problems was accompanied by changes in the organization of the agencies themselves. In many ways these developments were but two dimensions of the same phenomenon. New systems of finance and administration acted symbiotically on each other. Larger budgets and centralized finance demanded trained staffs capable of expending the funds. By the same token, high-salaried experts, long-range planning, and an increasing variety of programs made stable financial support a necessity.

The effort to resolve the administrative problems of the denominations went on at two levels. At both levels the ideology of organization which religious leaders adopted shaped the solutions to the Church's problems. On one level, individual agencies engaged in a process of internal bureaucratization, manifested in departmentalization, specialization, and intensified oversight and coordination. The values of "expertise" and "system" provided the primary rationale for these changes. On a second level, the Churches moved to streamline the existing maze of agencies and to coordinate them all under the direction of a central executive. In this development the Progressive confidence in executive authority and central management served to justify the action of the denominations.

Each of the four agencies underwent a gradual department-alization in the years after 1900. The boards began to hire individuals to perform specific task-oriented functions, at first chiefly related to the new systems of finance. In the beginning departments developed on an *ad hoc* basis, with little thought given to formal organizational structure. As the number of departments proliferated, however, more explicit formulations of departmental structure emerged, eventually resulting in the establishment of a hierarchy of divisions, departments and sections.

The experience of the Missionary Society of the Methodist Episcopal Church was fairly typical of this process of development. As we have noted before, the Methodist Society was the largest and wealthiest mission board in America. Its receipts averaged $1,223,000 annually in the decade from 1893 to 1903. In 1900 it already was supporting four hundred missionaries overseas, as well as a number at home. If any agency had reason to need a large central staff, it was this one. Yet the size of the staff had hardly grown over the years, numbering only twelve in 1892 and fourteen in 1900. The chief object of the administrators seems to have been to keep the percentage of central expense at as low a level as possible. In addition, between 1904 and 1908 the Society divested itself of its domestic operations, transferring them to a new agency. The corresponding reduction in staff which might have been expected did not occur, however. Instead, the Society expanded phenomenally after 1908. The evidence suggests that the bureaucratization of the Church was in this instance (as in others) less a response to administrative problems created by size and complexity than it was an effort to adopt the institutions and values of the larger society.

The departmentalization of the Missionary Society's work began in 1893 with the appointment of J. W. Young as director of the new Apportionment Plan. Up until this time the Society's operations had been managed by three corresponding secretaries without any specific delineation of duties. As in other denominations, the executives of the agency were generalists. In 1896 the work abroad was divided geographically among the secretaries for the first time, although there is some evidence that this may have been done on an informal basis previously. In 1900 a Missionary Editor and two assistants were hired to establish a Literature Department and a Bureau of Missionary Information and to edit two missionary magazines and the annual report of the Board. (Eventually this department became known as Publication and Publicity.) In the same year the Board hired a field secretary to be responsible for the development of Young People's Work. Offices charged with Accounting and Shipping were also mentioned for the first time in the agency's report. In 1901 an Open Door Emergency Commission was created. This department (later known as Home Cultivation) had charge of the Society's field work. The Station Plan (later the Department of Income) was established in 1903, and in 1904 Treasurer's and Office Stenographer's divisions were set up. Although most of these "departments" began with only a one-person staff, they quickly enlarged their operations. The organizational charts on page 129 show the rapid expansion of these departments between 1900 and 1908. In these eight years the central staff grew from fourteen to forty-six. For the first time employees were formally divided by departments and the staff members in large departments like Young People's Work and World Wide Missions Magazine no doubt were directly responsible to departmental heads rather than to the corresponding secretary.

Once begun, the process of departmentalization accelerated in the years after 1908. In 1912 departments for the One Day's Income Plan and for Candidates (later Personnel) were established. An office manager was hired to coordinate the work of the Society's stenographic and clerical forces. A formal Treasurer's Department (uniting Bookkeeping and Cashiers) was formed in 1913, with subdepartments for Allotment, Parish Abroad, and Special Gifts. A College Department to care for

Chart 1: Staff of the Board of Missions, MEC, c. January 1, 1900 (14 employees)

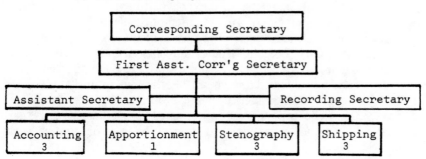

Chart 2: Staff of the Board of Missions, MEC, c. January 1, 1908 (46 employees)

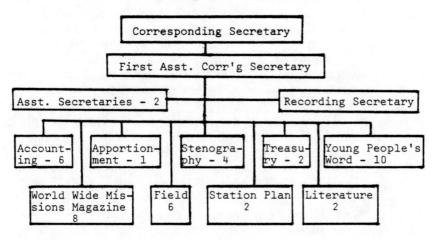

NOTE: There were no organizational charts before the 1920s. The division of staff shown above is based on examination of agency budgets. Lines of authority are unclear except that most employees answered directly to the Corresponding Secretary. Departments are for the most part ad hoc creations at this point.

Methodist students on campus was organized in 1915, and in 1919 the Church set up new Legal and Medical Departments, as well as ones for Foreign Field, Research and Survey, and Transportation and Shipping.

By this point, more than a dozen departments were reporting to the corresponding secretaries. In an attempt to simplify the existing conglomeration of agencies, in 1919 the work of the Society was divided into three divisions: Foreign, Home and Treasury. The Home and Foreign divisions were headed by the two corresponding secretaries, while the Treasurer directed the third. Each division included six or seven departments, each headed by a supervisor in that area (see chart on page 131). The central staff now totaled approximately sixty; six years later 102 persons were employed to execute the administrative work of the Society.

The story of departmental accretion was the same for the other agencies studied. The D&FMS, like its Methodist counterpart, had no formal departments before 1900, but there was an explicit division of duties. The General Secretary had assigned details of the office to one of his associates and supervision of correspondence and business affairs to the other in 1898. In addition, there was an assistant editor for the *Spirit of Missions*, the agency's magazine. After 1900 the work expanded rapidly. By 1920 some 300 missionaries served where there had been but 80 twenty years before—an increase of 375%. The Board's administrative staff grew even faster, however. Fourteen employees had labored at the Church Mission House in 1897; by 1918 the agency was served by 87 (an increase of 621%). A system of eleven departments (including specialized work for such areas as education, publications, students, and foreign-born Americans) was formally organized in 1916.

The ACMS had no departments or specialized staff in 1900, although it spent $64,000 in support of 54 missionaries. In 1917, at the time of its formal departmentalization, there were twelve executives to direct the work of ten departments. The staff's primary responsibility was to provide support for 208 missionaries, but staff experts now managed specialized offices for evangelism, social service, statistics, immigrants, the rural church, pastoral maintenance, and education.

The Baptist Sunday School Board in 1897 was administered by the corresponding secretary, a bookkeeper and four clerical assistants. The central staff remained small in the early years of the twentieth century, but over the years a number of field men were hired. The principal function of the Nashville office was to publish and distribute educational literature.[1] Following the death of Corresponding Secretary J. M. Frost in 1916, however, formal departments were established, and they soon began to expand. New departments included Church Architecture, Statistics and Information, Baptist Young People's Union,

Chart 3: Staff of the Board of Missions, MEC, c. January
1, 1919 (63 employees)

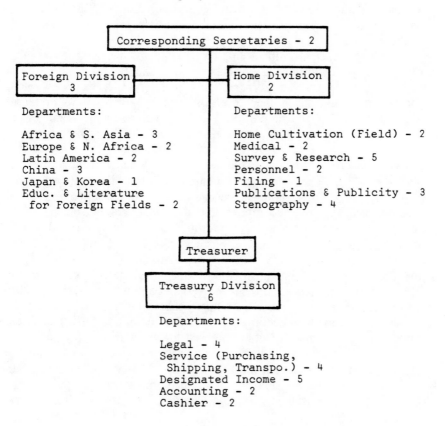

Corresponding Secretaries - 2

Foreign Division
3

Home Division
2

Departments:

Africa & S. Asia - 3
Europe & N. Africa - 2
Latin America - 2
China - 3
Japan & Korea - 1
Educ. & Literature
  for Foreign Fields - 2

Departments:

Home Cultivation (Field) - 2
Medical - 2
Survey & Research - 5
Personnel - 2
Filing - 1
Publications & Publicity - 3
Stenography - 4

Treasurer

Treasury Division
6

Departments:

Legal - 4
Service (Purchasing,
  Shipping, Transpo.) - 4
Designated Income - 5
Accounting - 2
Cashier - 2

Sunday School Administration, Vacation Bible School and Book Editing. Specialists in Sunday School work for elementary, intermediate, young people's, adult, and organized classes were available to the local churches. The staff of three secretaries, which handled receipts of $516,000 in 1917, had by 1927 grown to seventeen secretaries with an income of $1,806,000.

The principal rationale for the creation of departments was that of achieving efficiency in a business sense. The Baptist Committee of Seven which investigated Corresponding Secretary I. J. Van Ness' plans for reorganization stated that "the affairs of the Board have in recent years assumed such proportions as to require some changes in organization and methods. There is some laxity and a lack of complete efficiency which needs to be overcome. Complaints are made on the field of mistakes which give the Board a bad name from a business standpoint."[2]   The Methodist Board reported that prior to its departmentalization, "prominent business men were consulted and, based on the data received, committees of the Board drafted plans for a reorganization which has greatly contributed to the ease and facility with which the enormous volume of business has been handled."[3]   When President Lloyd of the D&FMS urged a reorganizaton, a committee of the Board reported "that no methods which have stood the test in the affairs of men of progress should be overlooked, but that agencies should be multiplied and all parts of the Church should be reached to secure the requisite force for new ventures. . . . " The committee further exhorted the agency to put into operation "unused forces" and to apply "new and improved machinery and a larger capitalization (as men speak) with the plain intent that the Church must go forward."[4] The head of the ACMS explained that the decision to create departments resulted from the complexity of the problems and the variety of activities confronting the society.[5]

By the 1920s religious agencies fully understood the value of bureaucratic organization. The Methodist Board of Education reported that "the organization of departments with definite assignment of duties relieved the Executive of many details." The report went on to observe that "division of labor is an effective means of multiplying achievement in big enterprises. The larger an organization, the more completely it must be departmentalized. . . . Activities that do not belong together have been separated, and responsibility has been fixed in departmental heads."[6]

With the expansion of staffs came all the accoutrements of a modern business enterprise. Labor-saving machinery of all sorts was employed; typewriters and duplicating equipment were purchased; telephones installed; electric lighting introduced.[7]   To facilitate the smooth operation of a more complex office, board administrators installed the latest filing and accounting systems.[8] The executives fashioned personnel departments (first known as Candidates Departments) to select individuals to meet the new organizational requisite of expertise.[9] The demands of these experts in turn led to the creation of facilities to provide information. Libraries were constituted and bureaus of "statistics," "research and survey," or "information" were formed.[10] Agency officials organized specialized departments to handle logistics, supply and record-keeping in central locations.[11]

One of the most significant evidences of the increasing business influence on the agencies was the reliance by both managers and staff on management consultants. No longer did the boards call on their own members or committees when evaluating the operations of the agency as had been common in the nineteenth century.[12] The Finance Committee of the Methodist Society conferred wth "experts in business organization" and "efficiency experts" in its reorganization of the Treasury Department in 1913.[13] The BSSB also hired a "professional consultant" to examine its business methods in 1924.[14] In 1915 the Episcopal Board secured the services of Price-Waterhouse & Co. to investigate the "Business Methods of the Church Mission House." A lengthy report analyzing the existing organization and administration of the Board and suggesting certain more efficient policies was published.[15] When the same Board organized its Nationwide Campaign following World War I, it engaged Barton & Durstein, Inc., referred to as "advertising agents and infrequently publicity counsellors."[16] The decision of the Disciples of Christ to create a United Christian Missionary Society in 1920 led to the hiring of John Williams, "an organization expert," who had served as managerial consultant to the Interchurch World Movement. Williams was to advise the new Society as to the most efficient form of organization.[17]

As staffs expanded in size and work became more diversified and specialized, increasing attention had to be devoted to the problem of internal coordination. Departmental rivalries were common. The Methodist Secretary for Latin America, for example, complained that the Personnel Department was communicating directly with the field in recruiting new missionaries, thereby "bypassing the Secretary interested." He was clearly jealous of the influence Personnel had over new missionaries, but he couched his argument in organizational terms. The result, he observed, was a "confused state as to what sort of a unified office management we have."[18]

One of the primary means utilized to improve internal coordination was communication. Office staffs began to meet for regular "conference and exchange of ideas" and for "closer coordination and strengthening" of the organization.[19]   Various staff meetings were instituted with the goal of "heightening the efficiency of administration, in our getting the point of view of the other department and the other man, and in deepening our personal fellowship."[20]   Already, it seems, employees were feeling the impersonality of the bureaucratic structures. Official forms for internal correspondence were adopted, along with rules governing their use.[21]   The agencies hired office managers to coordinate the labors of the expanding numbers of stenographers, clerks, office boys and receptionists.[22]   Employee newsletters were established "to serve as a medium of communication between the Administration and all departments of the Board."[23]   Staff cafeterias allowed workers to meet on an informal basis to discuss their work.

In addition to improving communication, executives tried to strengthen internal oversight.   Sets of rules proliferated as the agencies began to adopt legal definitions of responsibility and authority.   Agency heads urged departments to create "definite statements of procedure which they use in transacting business of the Board," and devised standardized reports for submission on a monthly basis.[24]   The Methodist "Office Bulletin" hoped to serve "as the place of record and reference for all policies and procedures which should govern the staff of the Board."[25]   Individual departments were ordered to submit all communications with local churches to the promotional divisions, to requisition all supplies through purchasing divisions, and to funnel all literature through the editorial divisions.[26]   Executives called field men back to the home office in order to direct their work more closely and to restrict their independence.[27]   Those who remained in the field were required to submit standardized monthly reports and to attend an annual meeting of all the field staff at the central headquarters.[28]

This rapid evolution toward a bureaucratic system of authority was not without its critics, even within the organizations themselves. There were complaints of red tape and the problems of departmental power struggles.   The tendency, however, was to gloss over problems by reference to the liturgy of business efficiency.   When the Episcopal administration decided that no bills would be paid without the approval of the Purchasing and Shipping Agent, departments complained of a loss of independence. Secretary Burleson replied that "we are sure that we can help, not only in the way of economy but of efficiency, and wish everyone connected with the Mission House to understand that this arrangement is merely for better service and not to impede progress nor to create new authority. . .[the goal was] not to pass judgment but to find the cheapest price."[29]   Of course, the result was indeed new authority which had to exercise judgement about expenditures, but efficiency proved a powerful rhetorical tool for justifying such changes.

The bureaucratization of the four agencies made them more efficient, but the problems of interagency rivalry and overlapping authority remained. There was still no chief executive to coordinate activities throughout the Church or to provide long-term planning. Each agency was busy setting up its own statistical, promotional, personnel and procurement arms, giving little thought to the possibility that duplication might well be eliminated if these services were provided by a central headquarters.

In response to these problems, each of the four Churches acted to unify and centralize its bureaucracies in the decade from 1910 to 1920. The process, however, was neither as smooth nor complete as the internal bureaucratization of individual agencies. Interagency rivalries hindered efforts at consolidation. Individuals with personal empires at stake were reluctant to agree to change. In addition, the polities of each Church restricted in certain ways the degree of centralization that could be achieved.

Calls for reorganization and consolidation of benevolences had been heard in the late nineteenth century, but without response. The ACMS Convention considered proposals for coordination of all existing boards under a united missionary society as early as 1887. These early proposals urged that the agencies remain "independent" departments, subject to their own managers, but with a central treasury.[30] A Congress on Unification was held in Indianapolis in 1900, but the Foreign Christian Missionary Society opposed any sort of merger.[31] Before the Episcopal Convention of 1877, Episcopal leaders, including a number of bishops, engaged in a lively debate over General Secretary Twing's proposed unification of the general charities of the Church.[32] Other recommendations in favor of a reorganization of Episcopal benevolences preceded the General Convention in 1901.[33] An appeal to streamline Methodist structure was tendered by the "General Conference Commission on Consolidation, Unification and Reorganization of Church Benevolences" in 1888. The commission proposed grouping Methodist agencies along functional lines. Two major boards would have been created, one for foreign missions and the other for home missions. A single general committee would have overseen the entire operation.[34] In 1900 another special committee attacked the problem but finally reported that it was unable to agree upon a plan of unification.[35] The Southern Baptist Convention of 1890 appointed a "special committee of seven" to "examine into the methods and workings of the two Boards of the Church."[36] A committee of cooperation between the three Baptist boards operated in 1898 to direct the Convention's centennial celebration, but the Conventions of 1900 and 1901 rejected proposals to make the committee permanent and to hire a secretary of cooperation to coordinate board activities.[37]

There is no clear explanation for the failure of these early attempts to unify and centralize the benevolent work of the Churches. One might surmise that Baptist and Disciple conventions were hesitant to endorse any plan which might leave the impression of undermining the principle of local autonomy. Methodist and Episcopal bishops were also unlikely to support a stronger central authority which might endanger their prerogatives. There is, however, little specific evidence to corroborate these suppositions. One reason for Church inaction is of course the inertia that is always a powerful force in religious organizations. There seemed as yet to be no compelling reason to overhaul a system that had developed and worked well throughout the nineteenth century. Bureaucratic ideas did not become irresistable overnight. But even more important was the fact that agency executives were usually too busy with the supervision of their own activities to consider long-range strategies. The main thrust of bureaucratic development at this stage was in the creation of relatively autonomous agencies. A unified organization might not appeal to executives who stood to lose the power and prestige of governing their own independent operations.

By the first two decades of this century, however, denominational leaders more and more were convinced of the necessity of achieving a higher degree of centralization. By this time agency executives had achieved many of the bureaucratic goals they sought in their own domains, and they took the lead in supporting the formal consolidation and centralization of the various Church benevolences. One of the primary tasks was the streamlining of existing organizations. Disciples, Methodists and Episcopalians constantly shuffled existing agencies to produce what they felt was a more rational pattern of organization in the early decades of the century. In the Methodist Church, for instance, major agency reorganizations were promulgated at nearly every General Conference from 1904 to 1924. In 1904, as we saw before, the Mission Society was divided along functional lines into home and foreign missions. The new Board of Home Missions also assumed the activities hitherto directed by the Church Extension Society and the City Evangelization Union. Various committees concerned with the welfare of pastors and their dependents were united as the Board of Pensions and Relief in 1908. The General Conference of 1908 amalgamated publishing interests previously divided between agencies in New York and Cincinnati. The 1920 Conference formed the Board of Hospitals and Homes and Deaconness Work out of the maze of charitable institutions within the Church. The existing Board of Education was expanded in 1924 to incorporate within its jurisdiction the work of the Epworth League, the Board of Negro Evangelization and Education, and the Sunday School Board.

Normally agency officials began to confer with one another on an *ad hoc* basis long before any formal central organizations existed. An "unofficial inter-board Secretarial Council" was established by executives of the Methodist Boards some time between 1904 and 1912.[38] In 1913 the Episcopal Board of Missions named a committee to meet with representatives from the Board of Religious Education to coordinate their separate plans for student work.[39] Two years later the three major Episcopal agencies authorized an interboard council "to consider all questions concerning the relations of the three boards."[40] Disciple leaders formed a "joint budget committee" to secure funds on a cooperative basis some time after 1900. The four major societies also united in support of the Centennial Convention of 1909 that celebrated the first 100 years of the Church's existence.[41] Baptist executives apparently "talked frequently about the three Boards working jointly in some matters," although efforts along these lines were limited by their fears of alienating the autonomous local churches.[42]

Eventually the Churches created official bodies to centralize the affairs of the various boards. In 1906 the Disciple conventions agreed on the formation of a permanent Committee on Calendar to coordinate the fundraising of the societies. In 1911, upon the recommendation of this committee, the Church established a single delegate convention that finally placed the agencies on a "denominational" rather than a "society" basis of organization.[43] The Methodist Church formally established a Commission on Finance and an Intersecretarial Council in 1912 to improve communication between its boards. At first these central bodies had little power other than to make recommendations. The Methodist Commission on Finance saw its principal function as ending "isolation," and establishing a "closer touch" and a "larger degree of cooperation."[44] The official duties of the Commission on Finance were to "advise and cooperate with the several Benevolent Boards in promoting the unity and efficiency of their financial plans."[45] Interagency committees of this sort were hindered in the task of centralization because of their composition. Each agency's representative on the committees had a vested interest in the work of his own benevolence, an interest which usually made him unwilling to compromise on questions involving power or money.

Thoroughgoing centralization could not be achieved until the Churches created independent central executives that (to varying degrees) could oversee the financial and administrative affairs of the various agencies. It was at this point in their organizational development that the individual denominations displayed the greatest differences (at least in the short run) in approach. In the Methodist Church support for centralization came mainly from the newly-formed Commission on Finance. In 1915 its Committee on Investigation was critical of the existing organization of the Church, citing three major problems: "The multiplication of agencies;" the failure of local churches to recognize the "paramount importance" of connectional benevolences; and the danger of General Conference legislation inconsistent with the best interests of the boards.[46] The problems were so acute that the Commission's General Secretary, Fred Fisher, resigned in 1915 in protest against what he called "divergences of interest among the Boards represented by the Commission on Finance."[47]

    As a result of these complaints, the General Conference of 1916 created the Inter-Board Conference, composed of representatives of fourteen boards and societies. In addition, the Commission on Finance was authorized to set the percentage of general income allotted to each board. The staff of the Commission grew to include departments of stewardship; apportionment and survey; general office and audit; publicity; and field work. Its budget expanded from $7,000 in 1914 to $45,000 in 1920. The Commission moved to create uniform voucher forms, uniform annuity rates, and standardized business methods and accounting procedures for all the agencies.[48] For the first time, each agency was required to adopt a "complete budget." The growing power and expense of the Commission, which was funded by surcharges on each agency, perturbed certain agency leaders. On the other hand, the Commission's executives chaffed under what they saw as their financial dependence on the very agencies they were supposed to control. In 1919 the Commission urged the General Conference to create a General Board of Benevolence for "coordination, correlating and unifying the plans and activities of the several Constituent Boards." The General Board's functions would be to receive reports, determine general policy, fix total budgets and apportion askings of the local churches. A minority report advocated a General Board of Finance that would continue to coordinate financial operations but would otherwise abstain from policy-making decisions by the boards.[49]

    The decision of the General Conference of 1920 was to create the Council of Boards of Benevolence. The Council was composed of 132 members, 70 of whom were selected by the constituent boards. Its purpose was "to secure (a) one harmonious and unified world program of missions, education and benevolent activities, (b) one unified financial policy and appeal, (c) the elimination of duplication of all activities, and (d) a larger measure of economy and efficiency." The Council met annually to receive board reports, coordinate board activities, set budgets, and determine apportionments. An executive committee exercised power *ad interim*, and there was now a committee on Conservation and Advance that served as the promotional arm of the Council.[50] Late in the quadrennium the Council also established a centralized department to recruit personnel. In 1924 the Council's membership was reduced to facilitate better direction, and it was renamed the World Service Commission (WSC). Headquartered in Chicago, the WSC directed Methodist activities until the 1950s. The WSC and its predecessors generally left decision-making in the hands of the boards, except for the important power of the purse. Centralized operations were not an inexpensive proposition; the Council spent some $3,740,000 in its first four years of operation.

The Methodist pattern of achieving central control of finance but not of administration was also followed by the Southern Baptist Convention. Baptist executives were fearful that the establishment of anything resembling an ecclesiastical hierarchy might split the loosely-organized Convention. In 1915 an Efficiency Commission rejected consolidation of the three boards. Such a plan "would be a serious mistake. . .a movement in the direction of centralization which is inherently objectionble to Baptists and likely to encourage agitations and criticisms which would be injurious to missionary offerings."[51] J. M. Frost desired "simpler" machinery. He urged that "each concern had better be left to attend to its own affairs but work in full cooperation with all the others."[52] Frost rejected the idea of replacing the existing system with an "untried experiment" that seemed "utterly unbusinesslike and even reckless." According to Frost, "Many able and successful business men" also had deemed the plans for consolidation "hazardous." Paradoxically, Frost criticized those who wanted consolidation for reasons of economy and efficiency, declaring that "there should be modesty and reserve when discussing business and efficiency as applied to religious and educational institutions. Much of their business simply cannot be forced into the moulds of the business world or be determined by its standards and regulations. Let us not deceive ourselves by talk about business methods and efficiency;" a unified operation, Frost said, would be "a physical and psychological impossibility" for any one man to control.[53]

A compromise on the question was effected in 1917; the boards were allowed to remain separate but an Executive Committee of the Convention was established "to act for the body between its sessions."[54] This committee had very limited power at first. It arranged meetings of the Convention, acted on matters of general business for the Convention, and could serve in an advisory capacity if any of the boards of the Convention requested such assistance. The Committee directed the Convention's 75 Million Campaign following World War I and established a schedule of annuities for the boards in 1922. The Committee also supported efforts to consolidate benevolent giving, which in 1925 resulted in the Cooperative Program. It regularly urged the Convention "to review and study the question of the unification and correlation of the work of the Convention," but at first these pleas went unheeded.[55] When the Convention's boards incurred substantial debts in the 1920s, however, calls came demanding that "the work of the agencies of the Convention shall be more closely correlated in order to achieve 'efficiency of administration.'"[56] Finally, in 1927, the Convention expanded the power of the Executive Committee to include the setting of budgets for the agencies and authorized the Committee to hire a full-time Executive Secretary to oversee its day-to-day work.[57]

When the Disciples decided to create a central organization, their solution was to unite the three existing boards into a single national society. In some ways this is surprising in that Disciples like the Baptists had a strong belief in local church autonomy. The Christian Church, however, also had long been committed "in thought and desire for union."[58] Proponents of centralization played on this theme of union in their arguments in favor of a single society. In addition, the leaders of the Disicple societies were convinced of the advisability of uniting their efforts. The reason is unclear—perhaps Disciple agencies had not matured as much as those of other denominations. In any event as early as 1912, Corresponding Secretary McLean (earlier an opponent of unified organization) proposed consolidation to the other societies.[59] Shortly thereafter the three major boards worked together successfully in support of the Men and Millions fund-raising effort and in 1917 agreed on a Joint Apportionment Committee for finances. That same year a Committee on Cooperation and Unification representing the three societies met for the first time. During the course of the next two years this committee worked out the details of a united organization, resolving legal difficulties, considering various administrative strategies and designs, and consulting with other denominations. An "organization expert" was hired to guide the process of unification. In 1919 Disciple leaders completed the consolidation and the new United Christian Missionary Society (UCMS) moved into a central headquarters in Indianapolis (in 1923 the UCMS transferred its operations to St. Louis).

The UCMS originally rejected the advice of its "organization expert" in one respect. Instead of establishing a hierarchical structure as in business, the Society organized its work into committees for the various divisions. Staff members served on several committees although each had primary responsibility for one area of work. The system was apparently one of equals and decision-making was by committee. In many respects, the idea of "joint responsibility " might have been a suitable model for other agencies to adopt since it stressed the Christian goals of brotherhood and love. By 1922, however, the President of the UCMS concluded that the system was "clumsy" and "ineffective" since it did not achieve "results." A reorganization was ordered to create departments with a "responsible head" for each.[60]

After 1922 the President of the UCMS was directly responsible for the work of the various divisions and departments. The President required regular monthly reports from the department heads on a "standardized form."[61] An interoffice newspaper was created and an officer council formed. Staffs were shuffled and budgets readjusted as the President directed. The new organization grew rapidly in size and cost. The first year of its existence, the United Society spent 21% of its budget ($439,000) on administration and promotion. Even this total did not include other administrative costs hidden in various departmental budgets. Five years later administrative costs had risen to $447,000 or 23% of the total expenditures of the Society. By way of comparison, the ACMS had spent only 11% of its budget ($17,000) on administration in 1916. The general office staff of the Society grew to an average of fifty employees in the mid-twenties, and when budget reductions were forced by insufficient revenues, cuts came only in areas other than those of promotion and general administration.[62]

The Episcopal centralization was similar to that of the Disciples. When a proposal to revise the canon on church extension was discussed at a meeting of the D&FMS in 1913, President Lloyd declared that if the Church was to "have the ability to work efficiently to this end, it must work as a unit." Lloyd urged that all the general administration of the Church be turned over to the Presiding Bishop and a council of advisors. This group would present plans and budgets to the General Convention and act as "permanent executive of the General Convention between its sessions."[63] At the General Convention of 1916, the Committee on Missionary Organization and Administration advocated the unification of the three major boards of the Church under an elected Presiding Bishop. Such a plan could not be instituted, however, until after the death of the current Presiding Bishop. The boards did cooperate, nonetheless, in the Nationwide Campaign following World War I. At the General Convention of 1919, the organizations were united as the Presiding Bishop and Council (soon retitled simply the National Council).

As was the case with the other denominations, this change resulted in a considerable growth in cost and size on the part of the national administration. Central expendiures grew from $164,000 to $246,000 in the first year of united operations, an increase of 50%. Publicity, Finance and Field Departments were established in addition to the older work in missions, religious education, and social service. In fact, the entire Church hierarchy was revamped to resemble the national organization. The Bishop and Executive Council and the Rector and Council were established at the diocesan and parish levels as units analogous and subordinate to those of the national body.[64]

By the 1920s, then, religious agencies had departmentalized their operations and hired experts to handle specialized forms of work. Staffs grew enormously in these years, confirming what sociologists have suggested about large-scale organizations: that the proportion of administrative personnel increases in the early stages of organizational growth.[65] In the MEC, for instance, administrative personnel were 3.6% of the Board's work force in 1897, but 5.9% in 1920; 7.1% of the D&FMS' American employees were administrators in 1890, but 28.7% were in 1918. If time and money spent on administrative problems, administrative hierarchy, and proportion of administrative personnel are accurate measures of bureaucracy,[66] then Churches were certainly so by the 1920s. In addition, the Churches had intensified their means of control through field inspections, the adoption of rules, requirements for statistical reports and improvements in internal communication, another indication of bureaucratic organization.[67]

The bureaucratization of America's mainline denominations proved economically and administratively advantageous to the Churches. Most religious leaders believed a more orderly and efficient operation had resulted. The first President of the UCMS, Frederick W. Burnham, explained that "in a little, private enterprise it is possible for the owner or manager to obtain first-hand knowledge of everything concerning it, and to direct all its operations. . . . But as an enterprise grows in size and in the variety of its operations, organization like the UCMS becomes necessary." Burnham believed that a larger organization like the UCMS would be "far more efficient and trustworthy than is the smaller, individual enterprise. Witness the railway systems and the department stores."[68] The Executive Committee of the UCMS also reported that "unification itself has brought orderliness and efficiency into these multiplied tasks formerly handled by separate Boards. It has achieved unity and harmony in the administration of the several fields of service, and eliminated elements of friction, or overlapping and of waste. It has brought comprehensiveness and mutual sympathy for each other's fields and tasks to all the secretarial group."[69] In the first year of the National Council's existence, its Field Department reported "a marked increase in the spirit of understanding and sympathetic cooperation. . . . It can be truly said that there is a deeper national consciousness and more cohesion in the Church than there was a year ago."[70]   The Methodist Council of the Board of Benevolences reported that centralization had secured "economy of time and space, together with efficiency in the work."   The Council noted savings achieved through centralized procurement and reduced overhead.[71]

The executives of the newly centralized administrations began to develop long-range plans for their Churches.   The Baptist Executive Committee asked the boards "to make a thorough survey of the purposes" for which they planned to use their portion of the 75 Million Campaign. Boards were to present "a sufficiently itemized statement of the needs to be met in order that the denomination may be able to understand and evaluate all these benevolences."[72]   In 1922, the Executive Committee further urged that agencies plan ahead on a five-year basis.   As early as 1909, the Methodist Laymen's Missionary Movement urged that the Board of Foreign Missions prepare five-year estimates of its requirements for personnel and income as well as its plan for future expansion.[73] With the organization of the Finance Committee in 1912, all of the Methodist boards began to submit five-year budgets.[74] In 1910 the Episcopal Board of Missions adopted the role of a "board of strategy" to survey existing "conditions and progress of the work," to investigate "the resources" of the Church, and to create uniform policy throughout the Church.[75] The power of the Board of Missions was of course limited.   With the creation of the National Council, however, leaders believed that "there is perhaps for the first time in the Church's history a universal disposition and purpose to plan for the future in definite terms of needs, budget, organization and methods."[76] President Lloyd of the Board of Missions added that "the church has finally found out that a headless body cannot have intelligence, and it has really and indeed created an organization with intelligence and with authority to act."[77]

The bureaucratic solution to the administrative problems of the Churches also produced startling changes in the role expectations of agency leaders. In part this shift reflected a general decline in the value placed on individualism in American society. The "other-directed" man in the Churches (and elsewhere) was replacing the "inner-directed" one; individuals were beginning to respond to a Social rather than a Protestant Ethic.[78] Religious service began to be less a calling than a career. Business experience and specialized training came to be more highly prized than religious piety in the hiring of employees. Leaders hardly paid more than lip service to the old notion of the "call of God."

Descriptions of religious leaders changed remarkably in the years under study.   In the late nineteenth century, leaders were most often praised for certain personal traits that had made them successful.   Again and again the key words were an "attention to detail."   The Episcopal Board lauded Associate Secretary Joshua Kimber for twenty-five years of service by noting his "carefulness; close inspection of details; the discipline of memory; and an interest which takes in the whole but does not overlook the smaller things: accuracy, made such by integrity; and the ability to make ready use of his material, itself the outcome of an unselfish interest in his work."[79]   Upon the death of Bishop W. L. Harris, who had served the Methodist Board for twelve years as Assistant Corresponding Secretary, a eulogy declared him "a genius in ecclesiastical administration."   Those qualities which made him so included "his immense power of work, his thorough mastery of its details, his talent for the prompt yet careful decision of important questions, his wonderful knowledge of precedents, his wide acquaintance with men, his ability to dispatch business. . . ."[80]   Other Methodist Corresponding Secretaries were praised for *"indomitable energy,"* for the ability to "arrange, present and prosecute business affairs with a mastery of detail and unusual skill in matters both delicate and intricate," for being "assiduous in the work of the office, attending to every detail of business and performing with conscientious fidelity the duties entrusted to him," for administering "all the affairs of the Society with which he was entrusted with singular fidelity," and for a *"conscientious devotion to duty."*[81]

Agency executives were also esteemed for what today we would call charisma.   The ability to move the masses from the pulpit was judged a worthy skill.   The first Corresponding Secretary of the ACMS was praised upon his death as "a great preacher, teacher and evangelist."[82]   A Methodist Corresponding Secretary was lauded for "the charm of his *personal magnetism*" and "that earnest and persuasive *power of speech* which moved and controlled audiences and greatly increased the funds of the Society."   Another was called "one of the most eloquent and successful preachers of the gospel in the Church."[83]   C. C. McCabe, perhaps the most famous of Methodist secretaries in the years after the Civil War, was eulogized as "one of those irresistable personalities, which in the presence of the public congregation carried everything before it."[84]

The manner in which leaders dealt with their employees in the nineteenth century is less clear, but one glimpse indicates that social relations were hardly the impersonal sort associated with bureaucratic authority.   According to Corresponding Secreary, I. J. Van Ness of the BSSB, his predecessor, J. M. Frost, "bore toward all these employees a relation similar to that of a father.   Everyone had free access to him, and they went to him with their troubles as well as with their successes and joys. He was solicitous about them when they were sick."[85]

Fatherliness was hardly the quality sought when selecting leaders in the early years of the twentieth century. Instead the modern Church executive was most often characterized by his businesslike qualities. As S. M. Cooper told a group of Christian businessmen, "We want not only religion in business, but business in religion."[86] Candidates for positions with the Sunday School Board were frequently commended for their "considerable business experience" before entering the ministry.[87] Corresponding Secretary Van Ness was seldom described without notice of his work for J. P. Morgan before entering the ministry. As early as 1898 *The Churchman* declared that "from whatever side the position of the General Secretary may be viewed, it is in the main an office which requires administrative gifts and not necessarily the grace of Holy Orders. . . . He is, as it were a chief organizer. Let the Board call some man who has proved himself 'eminently successful in organization and in the handling of financial problems,' to give up his work in the world and devote himself to the organization and development of our missions system."[88] The Episcopal Missionary Council urged its Board to select men whose "aptness and business capacity" would enable them to present the work and produce "a definite income."[89] Businesslike qualities were noted in retiring executives. The ACMS praised Corresponding Secretary I. N. McCash for having "adopted scientific plans of survey and the inductive method used in the mechanical, industrial, educational and charity departments of life and applied those to Home Missions."[90] Speaking ability was no longer as highly prized in religious leaders. Hight C. Moore was hired by the BSSB even though he was "not by any means at his best on the platform." Instead, "in publicity, in resources, in machinery, in suggestions, in all that we call inspirational, editorial leadership, his equal is not to be had."[91] An article in *The Churchman* on "The Extension of Missionary Work" noted that "specialization is now required to prepare intelligent support for mission work."[92] Field agents of the D&FMS were to be "chosen for technical knowledge, missionary zeal, aptness to impart information, and activity and perseverance in presenting causes."[93]

The agencies sought to foster career orientations in their employees. A career orientation demanded changes in agency hiring policies. Boards apparently sought to appoint men to staff positions who would be permanent employees.[94] Employees were expected to give full-time service to the agencies. The need for expertise led boards to favor men of skill. As part of its reorganization in 1916, the Episcopal Board decided "that no one be named as secretary for any specific department of work except a man of maturity and experience who has rendered service entitling him to so important an office."[95] In 1917 the Methodist Board instituted a policy that promoted men who had served on the mission field to positions in the home office as regional specialists in the handling of missionary communications—a move that had the dual advantage of securing expertise and cementing employee loyalty.

Career orientations and expertise demanded better benefits for employees. Boards began to adopt standardized scales of salaries and allowances for the first time around 1910.[96] Agencies also established mandatory retirement ages and plans for support of retirees.[97] The BSSB noted that "we must attract and hold superior and trained talent. We compete in management with large businesses and must have the equipment, the men and the resources to adequately meet the needs of our constituency."[98] Boards needed the talents and expertise of laymen and therefore "must be prepared to pay the larger salary for similar work to a layman in its employ than to a priest."[99]

Employees were recruited for their expertise or trained in special schools. The BSSB subsidized Chairs of Sunday School Pedagogy at the seminaries, and the Disciples launched a College of Missions.[100] "A more efficient, specialized ministry is expected of our future theological graduates," reported Corresponding Secretary McCash. Specialists to work with the foreign-born, rural churches and Bible schools would be needed. "It has long been recognized as a fact," said McCash, "that special preparation for mission work in America was not an essential. Such is a false idea. Only workers of ability and adaptability can render effective service."[101] Training replaced "the call of God." An Episcopal Committee termed the old sense of calling "undesirable and sometimes mischievous" in that it required an "inexperienced" person to choose "life service before training." In addition, the call made "it difficult for the Board to control *the output of missionaries* in any one year and direct it toward the point of greatest need." The committee urged that the Church adopt a sense of "general" calling instead.[102] In a similar narrowing of the meaning of calling, a Methodist leader urged that missionaries henceforth be "sent out on trial for three years."[103] In the new system missionaries were less "called" than solicited. The D&FMS declared that "in order to secure men and women of the right quality the call needs *to be presented* more personally and systematically."[104] Evidently God's call was producing inferior fishers of men and had to give way to a systematic means of selection. Recruitmen was in the same sense secularized. Methodist leaders were told not to "wait for men and women to volunteer for the mission field; . . . Secretaries, Bishops,

Managers and members of the General Committee should be urged to be on the lookout for suitable material."[105]

In essence, the central institutions of the modern Church were in the process of abandoning the calling for the career, the charismatic type of authority for the bureaucratic. This is not to say that old styles of leadership did not still play major roles in the pastoral structure that had dominated the nineteenth century. Local churches still sought men of faith and inspiration, although even local churches, especially in cities, needed pastors with administrative skills. The agencies continued to need certain charismatic individuals who were able to deal with pastors and churches outside of the agency structure.

The general drift, however, was toward bureaucratic leadership. The individual's calling was no longer, in R. H. Tawney's terms, "a strenuous and exacting enterprise to be chosen by himself and to be pursued with a sense of religious responsibility,"[106] or in Max Weber's words, "a task set by God."[107] Weber himself suggested that in the modern world, the calling was "bound to the technical and economic conditions of machine production which to-day determine the lives of individuals" and was, as a result, generally devoid of all its traditional meaning.[108] Instead, Weber noted, the bureaucratic leader "is subject to an impersonal order" and "only a person who has demonstrated an adequate technical training is qualified to be a member of the administrative staff of such an organized group."[109] This was the type of leader the Church began to seek. In this sense the Church was deciding to follow the world in terms of its organization and values. As *The Churchman* admonished: "It would be equally impossible to accentuate too strongly the necessity of selecting men who possess the power of organization, and not merely the power of attractive and striking personality. It is not a question of personal eloquence or personal magnetism or personal influence, but it is a question of a body of specialists who can patiently gather statistics, persistently push organization, and unwearyingly instruct and inspire others."[110]

By 1930 America's religious agencies had been bureaucratized along the lines that Weber had suggested were typical of modern organization. Agency leaders had formulated rational rules governing personnel and administrative procedure. Work had been divided into specialized departments, and experts had been hired. Employees increasingly perceived their work as a career rather than a calling. The Churches were also more centralized in 1930 than fifty years before. The agencies gave the Churches a full-time executive authority that they had not had fifty years earlier. Greater amounts were spent on administration than ever before. Power had passed from the hands of the pastoral structure to the denominational bureaucrats in the agencies.

There were, however, perceptive critics who sensed the new meanings that the agency structure had produced. Administrative centralization and systematic finance produced problems of authority that the organizers had not always foreseen.

NOTES

[1] Baker, *Sunday School Board*, pp. 96-97.

[2] "Board, SBC," March 8, 1917, p. 140.

[3] "Report of the Board of Missions," *Journal, MEC* (1916), p. 1185.

[4] "Board, PEC," November 4, 1910, p. 48.

[5] *Yearbook, Disciples of Christ* (1917).

[6] *Journal, MEC* (1924), pp. 1353-54.

[7] "Board, PEC," January 9, 1900. Lloyd urged use of the telelphone to "save time and avoid confusion" and for the "convenience and efficiency of all engaged in the office." See also "Board, MEC," July 16, 1912, p.. 411; "Board, ACMS," April 21, 1893.

[8] The Methodist filing system was completely revamped in 1912 as a visit to the Methodist Archives in Lake Junaluska, N. C. will show. Files of the ACMS have apparently been lost, but the Board advised changes in record management in 1909, "Board, ACMS," December 17, 1909. On bookkeeping methods see "Board, MEC," January 16, 1900, p. 119; August 18, 1903, p. 300; April 19, 1904, p. 67.

[9] "Board, PEC," October 1916, p. 613; "Board, MEC," September 17, 1912, p. 453; "Board, UCMS," May 24, 1921; "Board, PEC," May 8, 1912.

[10] "Board, PEC," December 11, 1912; "Board, SBC," September 9, 1920; "Board, MEC," June 17, 1902, June 21, 1904, September 16, 1912, p. 412, and July 16, 1912, p. 411.

[11] "Report of the Sunday School Board," *Annual, SBC* (1917); "Board, PEC," December 8, 1915, October 6, 1913, p. 55, December 10, 1913, p. 75; "Board, MEC," September 16, 1912, pp. 410-11.

[12] For example, "Board, MEC," July 21, 1896, p. 202.

[13] "Board, MEC," October 13, 1921, p. 467. See also *Journal, MEC* (1916), p. 1186; *Handbook, MEC* (1916), p. 183.

[14] Baker, *Sunday School Board*, pp. 109ff.

[15] Price-Waterhouse Report, December 1, 1915, Episcopal Archives.

[16] Nationwide Campaign Report in "Board, PEC," May 14, 1919, pp. 181-90.

[17] "Board, UCMS," June 22, 1920, February 24, 1920.

[18] Internal memorandum, Harry Farmer to Frank Mason North, August 24, 1921, North File, Methodist MSS.

[19]"Board, PEC," October 3, 1917; "Board, UCMS," January 19, 1922; "Report of the Corresponding Secretary to the Annual Meeting of the Sunday School Board, 1919," p. 5.

[20]Internal memorandum, A. B. Moss to A. E. Chenoweth, re: General Staff Council, October 20, 1919 in Chenoweth File, Methodist MSS.; "Board, SBC," June 18, 1919, for discussion of Headquarters Council.

[21]See Methodist files beginning in 1918, Methodist MSS.

[22]"Board, UCMS," June 22, 1920 and February 22, 1921; "Board, MEC," July 16, 1912, p. 411.

[23]"The Office Bulletin," No. 1, October 31, 1919, p. 1; In October, 1921, the UCMS created an interoffice newspaper to boost "morale," "Board, UCMS," October 25, 1921.

[24]"The Office Bulletin," No. 1, October 31, 1919, p. 1; "Board, UCMS," February 22, 1921.

[25]No. 1, October 31, 1919, p. 1.

[26]See for example, "Board, UCMS," November 13, 1923, p. 178; "Board, PEC," October 6, 1913, p. 55.

[27]H. C. Moore to Frost, August 9, 1907, Frost MSS. Box 22; B. W. Spilman to Frost, April 10, 1916, Frost MSS. Box 32; Van Ness to B. W. Spilman, June 6, 1917, Van Ness, MSS., Box 6; Lynn E. May, Jr., "A Brief History of Southern Baptist Sunday School Work," unpublished paper in Dargan-Carver Library, BSSB, June 1, 1964; "Board, PEC," September 16, 1913, pp. 328-29.

[28]"Board, SBC," March 8, 1917, p. 141; Van Ness to B. W. Spilman, June 19, 1917, Van Ness MSS., Box 6.

[29]"Board, PEC," October 6, 1913, p. 55.

[30]"Convention, ACMS," (1887), pp. 416-17; (1893), p. 330f; (1899).

[31]Garrison and DeGroot, *The Disciples of Christ*, p. 427.

[32]*The Churchman*, 35 (January 13, 1877), 33; (January 27, 1877), 86-87; (February 10, 1877), 144, 152; (February 24, 1877), 208 and (March 10, 1877), 265.

[33]*The Churchman*, 84 (August 17, 1901), 195, 199-200; (August 24, 1901), 229-32.

[34]*Journal, MEC* (1888), pp. 749-53.

[35]"Report of the World Service Commission," *Handbook, MEC* (1928), pp. 534-38. This report provides an excellent history of Methodist centralization.

[36]*Proceedings, SBC* (1890), p. 10.

[37] Barnes, *The Southern Baptist Convention*, pp. 169-70; *Proceedings, SBC* (1901), p. 34.

[38] *Handbook, MEC* (1928), p. 534.

[39] "Board, PEC," December 10, 1913. Four Baptist boards cooperated in a similar manner on student work in the 1920s, Baker, *Sunday School Board*, pp. 106ff.

[40] "Board, PEC," May 12, 1915, p. 77.

[41] Garrison and De Groot, *The Disciples of Christ*, p. 428.

[42] Frost to F. H. Kerfoot, December 22, 1899, Frost MSS., Box 11.

[43] Garrison and De Groot, pp. 428, 524-26.

[44] *Handbook, MEC* (1916), p. 182.

[45] *Journal, MEC* (1912), p. 747.

[46] Commission on Finance File, Methodist MSS.

[47] *Ibid.*

[48] "Report of the Commission on Finance," *Handbook, MEC* (1920), pp. 400-07; "Report of the Board of Home Missions and Church Extension," *Handbook, MEC* (1920), pp. 382-85.

[49] Commission on Finance File, December 13, 1919, Methodist MSS.

[50] *Handbook, MEC* (1920), p. 568; *Journal, MBFM* (1924), p. 67.

[51] Letter of E. C. Dargan, Chairman of the Efficiency Commission, to Frost, January 28, 1915, Frost MSS. Box 29.

[52] Frost to J. Clyde Turner, Chairman of the Committee on Consolidation of Board Magazines, January 25, 1916, Frost MSS., Box 31.

[53] "From a Business Viewpoint," Frost MSS., Box 33.

[54] *Annual, SBC* (1917), p. 34.

[55] "Executive Committee, SBC," June 5, 1919, p. 9; September 7, 1921, p. 3; June 28, 1922, p. 6; March 21, 1923, p. 3.

[56] *Annual, SBC* (1926); Barnes, *Southern Baptist*, pp. 224-30.

[57] "Executive Committee, SBC," March 5, 1929, pp. 6-7.

[58] "Board, UCMS," January 8, 1918.

[59]See Lair, *Christian Churches and their Work*, p. 147. Corresponding Secretary Wright of the ACMS also expressed early support for unification, "Board, ACMS," December 17, 1909.

[60]"Board, UCMS," July 25, 1922.

[61]*Ibid.*, February 22, 1921, p. 81.

[62]"Board, UCMS," 1919-1926.

[63]"Board, PEC," May 14, 1913, pp. 560-66.

[64]*Annual Report of the National Council*, (1920), p. 247; (1921), p. 212. Hereafter *Annual Report, NC.*

[65]See Blau and Scott, *Formal Organizations*, pp. 20-25 and Theodore Caplow, "Organizational Size," *Administrative Science Quarterly*, 1 (March 1957), 502.

[66]Blau and Scott, pp. 25-26.

[67]On the use of such impersonal means of control in organizations see Blau and Scott, pp. 171-83, 232. The two authors suggest that strict enforcement of administrative procedure is also an indication of bureaucratization, pp. 25-26.

[68]"Unification," Pamphlet Boxes.

[69]*Yearbook, Disciples of Christ*, (1921), p. 8.

[70]*Annual Report, NC* (1921), p. 212.

[71]*Handbook, MEC* (1924), pp.. 483-91; (1928), pp. 538, 567. See also memo in Chenoweth File, July 1, 1922, Methodist MSS.

[72]"Executive Committee, SBC," June 5, 1919, p. 9; June 28, 1922, p. 6.

[73]"Board, MEC," October 19, 1909, p. 121.

[74]"Board, MEC," September 17, 1912, p. 455.

[75]"Board, PEC," November 3, 1910, p. 5.

[76]*Annual Report, NC* (1920), p. 247.

[77]"Board, PEC," December 10, 1919, p. 16. See also "Manual of Suggestions for Use in Connection with the General Survey of the Episcopal Church" (New York: 1920), p. 14, Pamphlet Boxes.

[78]See Theodore P. Greene, *America's Heroes*; David Riesman, et al., *The Lonely Crowd: A Study of the Changing American Character* (New Haven: Yale University Press, 1950); Whyte, *Organization Man;* and Mills, *White Collar.*

[79]"Board, PEC," May 10, 1892.

[80]"Board, MEC," September 20, 1887, p. 212.

[81]*Ibid.*, March 10, 1880; May 19, 1894, p. 248; May 19, 1896, p. 141.

[82]"Convention, ACMS" (1908), p. 390.

[83]"Board, MEC," March 10, 1880; May 19, 1894, p. 248; May 19, 1896, p. 141.

[84]*Ibid.*, December 20, 1906, p. 332.

[85]c. 1916 in Van Ness MSS., Box 5.

[86]"Church Businessmen in Conference," *Christian Standard*, 35 (July 22, 1899), 912.

[87]Z. T. Cody to Frost, February 1, 1900, Box 11; numerous letters to Frost re: G. S. Dobbins, June-July, 1916, Box 32, Frost MSS. See also the description of Harry L. Strickland in P. E. Burroughs, *Story of the Sunday School Board* (Nashville: BSSB, 1931), p. 43.

[88]"Why a Bishop as a General Secretary?," p. 111; see also January 29, 1898, p. 147.

[89]*Annual Report, PEC* (1900), p. 17.

[90]"Convention, ACMS," (1913).

[91]Bailey to Frost, August 6, 1907, Frost MSS., Box 22.

[92]107 (January 18, 1913), 72.

[93]*Annual Report, PEC* (1901), pp. 24-25.

[94]W. A. Jarrel to Frost, September 9, 1907, Frost MSS., Box 22. See also "Convention, ACMS" (1895), p. 151, which discouraged "frequent changes" in secretarial positions.

[95]"Board, PEC," December 13, 1916, p. 202.

[96]"Board, MEC," July 21, 1914, p. 333; "Board, SBC," June 8, 1932, pp. 211-17.

[97]"Board, MEC," October 19, 1915; *Annual Report, SBC* (1926); "Board, UCMS," July 25, 1922.

[98]*Annual Report, SBC* (1928), pp. 4-5.

[99]"Report of Educational Secretary Sturgis," in "Board, PEC," February 12, 1919, pp. 19-20.

[100]"Board, SBC," April 12, 1906; "Convention, ACMS" (1912), p. 514.   Beginning in 1895 all women appointed by the D&FMS were required to have six months' training in one of the Church Training Schools, "Board, PEC," November 12, 1895, p. 53.

[101]"Convention, ACMS" (1912), p. 514.

[102]"Board, PEC," February 12, 1913, p. 85.   Italics mine.

[103]"Board, MEC," September 16, 1913, p. 386.

[104]"Board, PEC," December 13, 1911, p. 297.   Italics mine.

[105]"Board, MEC," September 16, 1913, p. 386.

[106]"Foreword," to Max Weber, *The Protestant Ethic and The Spirit of Capitalism* (New York: Scribners, 1958), p. 4.

[107]Weber, *Protestant Ethic*, p. 79.

[108]*Ibid.*, p. 181-83.

[109]*The Theory of Social and Economic Organization*, pp. 324-56.

[110]"More Secretaries in the Mission House a Necessity," p. 227.

CHAPTER 8

THE PROBLEM OF AUTHORITY

As the denominational agencies moved to resolve the administrative and financial problems they faced by expanding the size, power and complexity of their operations, they upset the precarious balance of interests that was important to stability. Problems of authority multiplied, and denominational executives stood at the center of a cluster of parties which had vested interests in the operation of the agencies. We have already observed, for example, the agencies' financial dependence on the local church and its pastor, but the power configuration in the denominations included the religious press, the national conventions, the boards of managers, and board employees as well. It was only natural, then, that these other interests became alarmed by an increasingly bureaucratic Church.

It was also over problems of authority that denominational differences were most apparent. As we have seen, all four Churches developed quite similar solutions to the problems of administration and finance. Legitimacy, however, demanded that executives pay greater attention to their denomination's own values and symbols.

In many ways the problems of authority were the direct result of the new ideology of organization that pervaded the thoughts of agency leaders. Since order and efficiency were now to be obtained by administrative expertise and centralization, the executives found it more and more difficult to tolerate breeches of their mandates by other interests in the Church. From the boards' perspective there were growing indications of unsubmissiveness and recalcitrance within the Church. Leaders began to complain bitterly of "parochialism."[1] There is little evidence that suggests that local churches were any more provincial than before; their localism had just become progressively less acceptable to the bureaucrats. We have already noted the frequent complaints about the failure of local churches to provide financial support for the agencies. Denominational executives denounced pastors who "always increase their salaries at the expense of the benevolences" or who endeavored "to make the parish church more beautiful" while producing only meagre "missionary offerings."[2] The executives frequently apprehended a "tendency toward local interests," despite their constantly improving financial situation. Local officials were accused of making unauthorized changes in the denominational apportionments to congregations.[3] Board officials discovered that "diocesan needs are met before National needs are met," and tried to discourage any benevolent developments at that level. In some states, the ACMS believed it was little better that a "mendicant" whose appeals were seen as "little short of affrontery."[4]

The agencies were also displeased by what they described as resistance to administrative centralization. The 1900 Annual Report of the D&FMS attacked "an individualism which, in its own conceits, rejects agencies, however appointed, and refuses intimate relationship to administrations, however authorized, disintegrating the Church's force, and scattering seed in unnecessary, or little fertile or ready fields."[5] At the Disciples' lay congress in 1900, one delegate noted "our lack of general oversight and our false ideas of the absolute independency of the individual church and preacher. . . . We are so fearful of ecclesiastical tyranny that we are dangerously near to individual anarchy."[6] The forty-two state and district societies, each "a law unto itself," "entirely independent of each other and of the National Board, their work unreported and unknown," perturbed the leadership of the ACMS.[7] An Episcopal pastor observed: "Each bishop is immersed in the affairs of his diocese. But there are a large number of important questions of an interdiocesan character that are outside any diocesan jurisdiction."[8] Secretary Arthur R. Gray of the Episcopal Board in a study of Specials reported that "it very frequently happens that what the Church [meaning the Board] thinks should be done is quite different from what this or that parish or individual prefers to do."[9]

Denominational officials also objected more and more to what they regarded as irresponsible decision-making by the denominational conventions that ultimately governed the Churches. Unlike the local church which could do little by itself to threaten the legitimacy of the agencies, the national convention had the power to restructure the agencies and elect their boards of managers. The stability, and even the very existence, of each agency rested in that governing body. If persistent, the conventions could make binding decisions about their Church's agencies. The conventions' prerogatives were not new; the major change had taken part in the national agencies themselves. Their growing power seems to have exacerbated what were long-standing patterns of tension. Conventions were a source of concern because as mass legislative bodies they might easily be influenced by persuasive individuals or popular causes; they were, in effect, akin to anarchy in the minds of denominational leaders. Arthur Lloyd of the D&FMS feared that the General Convention would allow the popular Bishop of Chicago to "dictate anything he pleases," including the nomination of all of the Board's officers.[10] W. B. Crumpton of the BSSB's Executive Committee called the SBC an "unthinking multitude" dominated by "untried speakers, who can get up a whoop at almost any radical remark."[11]

Corresponding Secretary Van Ness added that "they seem to follow along any line which proposes to make changes, whether these commend themselves or not."[12]   The Methodist Commission on Finance noted that the General Conference was constantly in "danger of passing new legislation without coordination with what has gone before."[13]

Denominational executives lived in fear of what the conventions might do. The Minutes of the Sunday School Board reveal an ever-present concern that the SBC would use the Board's financial surplus for some hare-brained scheme. Corresponding Secretary Frost complained that the Convention did not understand the Board's policies: "I sometimes wonder if they read our reports."[14]   Secretary Wood of the D&FMS noted to General Secretary Lloyd that there were some in the General Convention "who would take pleasure in digging the grave [of the Board] wide and deep and patting down the sod with a long handled shovel!"[15]   Such fears were not without cause, as in the case of the ACMS Convention of 1903. Benjamin Smith, Corresponding Secretary of the ACMS, was a member of that Convention's Special Committee on Evangelism. The committee had apparently agreed with Smith's desire to create a Bureau of Evangelism in the ACMS, but when Smith absented himself at one meeting, the Committee and later the Convention approved an independent National Board of Evangelism. Smith was incensed, but little could be done to change matters until the subsequent convention.[16]

Agency bureaucrats also seemed to have had little patience with the missionaries under their control. Throughout the nineteenth century there had been power struggles between administrators and missionaries over the degree of control to be exerted by the central board. Missionaries had generally accepted the agencies' right to select and station candidates, to expect regular reports from the field, and to handle most of the finances (although Specials were a bone of contention). Missionaries, however, had long claimed dominion over what they saw as local policy making, a prerogative that was buttressed by the slowness of nineteenth-century communication. As the Boards grew in size and as communications with the field improved, however, Church administrators had become increasingly intolerant of what they deemed employee truculence. Missionaries, said General Secretary Lloyd, saw the Board as a "'cow to be milked until she kicks' (as one of the Bishops put it) by anyone shrewd enough to work it." While the D&FMS was willing to allow local decision-making in the field by the bishops, it maintained that "the episcopal prerogative" must not "overshadow or override the authority of the Board. Sometimes I am disposed to think that it does, and that we suffer accordingly, particularly in the domestic work."[17]   A variation of the same image was employed by the ACMS' Corresponding

Secretary who declared his "hardest work" was "to get churches that have once tasted the sweet milk of Missionary help to consent to any reduction of that help."[18]   Corresponding Secretaries Taylor and North of the Methodist Board concluded that Methodist mission forces gave "an impression of lack of unity and definiteness of purpose" because "we have largely left to the bishop the formulation of policies, if any policies were formed at all."[19]   Visits to the field revealed that local missionaries often were involved in operations of which the agencies were completely ignorant.[20]

From the agencies' point of view, the local missionary simply could not fathom the complexity of the entire missionary operation. Missionaries tended to perceive their own problems as preeminent; they lacked general and objective vision and a sober understanding of the boards' limited financial resources.   Agency officials maintained that it was the "right and duty of the Board to administer the missionary appropriations."[21]   "Most mistakes" in mission work, it was believed, "were made at the local level."[22]

Denominational leaders also complained, although less frequently, about the power that the denominational press had over Church opinion.   The Baptist Home Mission Board urged the Southern Baptist Convention not to eliminate the Boards' house organs in favor of the state journals.   "Much as we esteem our denominational press," they said, "we trust the Boards of the Convention will never be placed so largely under its control."[23]   The Disciples Boards felt they were constantly being harrassed by a denominational press that was, as we have noted, particularly powerful in that Church.   In 1906, for instance, the ACMS complained of "direct attacks" and "intemperate discussion" in the "religious papers."[24]

Agency bureaucrats were disgruntled with their lack of authority, and they fully understood how difficult it would be to overcome this problem.   President Lloyd of the D&FMS probed this dilemma when he asked how the Church's national interests could be "conserved without encroaching on diocesan rights."   Lloyd knew that some means had to be found to achieve "harmonious relations and cooperation" throughout the Church in order to unite it in the "development of its national and world-wide interests."[25]   The chief task for the bureaucrats was to find means to exercise their new power without alienating the key interest groups in the Church.   Their approach to the problem was perforce subtle.

There were, of course, a few occasions when boards resorted to strong-arm tactics to achieve their ends.   In 1909, for instance, the Episcopal Board obtained a legal opinion holding that in fiduciary and financial matters, the "Bishops have no power to act except with the advise and consent of the Board of Missions."[26] In another case, the ACMS threatened to cut off all support for one of its missions unless it submitted its candidate for pastor to the Board for approval.[27]

Such overt actions were rare, however, since they pained the Christian consciences of the bureaucrats and, more importantly, threatened the Boards' image as servants of the Church. Instead, denominational leaders learned that oversight and direction of denominational affairs were best achieved by low-key institutional constraints employed under the guise of improved communications and efficiency. The most fruitful denominational cooperation came not from overt displays of power, but from artful manipulation of symbolic values. Agency independence would be established by circumventing existing interest structures and avoiding power struggles.   In other words, denominational leaders discovered first hand that normative organizations could not directly coerce their members.

Effective agency operation thus called for institutional means of promoting Church responsiveness without producing alienation or conflict. One such means was improved communication with the various interest groups through regular correspondence and solicitation. We have already observed, for instance, the increased use of advertising and promotion by the agencies in their financial operations. In the minds of denominational executives, such "personal conversation with pastors" had a very clear aim: "It makes them feel that they are watched, and that we are interested in their work; it also makes them feel that they are of some importance in the eyes of the brotherhood and that their work does not go for naught."[28]   The goal of effective communication was to establish agency authority and yet to reassure other interests of their worth.   As one BSSB Board member said, "We must make every minister feel that the Board from top to bottom is his personal friend."[29] Episcopal leaders noted that contacts with local churches would "personalize missions" and give the churches a "sense of responsibility" for the Board's work."[30] An "enlarged free circulation" of the boards' publications would overcome "the lack of interest in missions [that] is due to a lack of information."[31]

Communications were improved and stabilized by adopting institutional arrangements that would on a regular basis produce greater intercourse with the various interest groups in the Church.   The promotional departments of the boards were one example of this new strategy. In addition, most agencies established field forces in the early years of the century to serve in a liaison capacity with state and local religious authorities.[32] As many as ten men were hired on a full or part-time basis to be responsible for "the promotion of the Sunday school cause" or for the dissemination of missionary "information."[33]   Their talents as "intermediate agents" of the boards would ensure larger offerings as well. The D&FMS noted sagely that in business such agents "have within the past few years increased enormously the volume of business of employers."[34]

Bureaucrats also sought to co-opt local leaders through the power of the purse. This approach proved especially popular with Baptist and Disciples boards which could not use ecclesiastical hierarchies to effect their ends. When Christian churches in the East felt they were being cheated by the ACMS' emphasis on establishing churches in the West, the Corresponding Secretary was "deluged with letters about the danger of the secession of the Atlantic Coast." The Society could have cut back on work in the West; instead, it quickly responded by voting to support two missionaries to Newark, New Jersey![35]   A study of dependent churches and institutions in urban areas found that "authority comes with the financial aid given by the society. This is both psychologically and practically true in all denominations and in all cities."[36] The BSSB used its publications income to underwrite the salaries of fulltime Sunday school and Baptist Young People's Union secretaries hired by state conventions.[37]   Beginning in 1895, the ACMS wrote "contracts" with State Boards that provided for "mutual support, advice and consent, and regular reports."[38]   Episcopal Bishop Thomas F. Gailor of Tennessee admitted that the $1200 that his diocese received in missions aid was "one of the bonds that hold the people in loyalty to the General Work of the Church."[39]   There was no explicit *quid pro quo* in these arrangements, but the proverb about biting the hand that feeds certainly applied.

Agencies also facilitated their control by obtaining better information from the field. Mission executives began to make more frequent visits to the field and to appoint special fact-finding emissaries to tour the missions.[40]   Missionaries were required to submit more frequent and detailed reports.[41] Denominational officials pressed local churches and diocesan officials for more accurate information about church membership and financial contributions. As the *Maryland Baptist Church Life* noted, "the keeping of good records is one of the laws of efficiency."[42] Baptist Sunday schools adopted a special six-point record system and began to submit reports in triplicate.

The information obtained was used in subtle ways to influence action. We have already seen how the boards ranked churches according to their contributions. In another case, the Reverend J. W. Young urged Methodist bishops to ask when making appointments, "What is his record respecting the benevolences? and then all things being equal, let the answer determine the appointment; then a remarkable waking up will occur."[43] In the 1890's, the D&FMS sent all bishops an annual list of those parishes which failed to support the cause of missions.[44]   The Methodist Corresponding Secretaries noted: "We need to keep in personal touch with every church at least once a year.   Pastors who do well ought to be commended; pastors who are not doing so well ought to receive friendly counsel and such help as could be afforded."[45]   There was, of course, no compulsion in all of this, but the system placed pastors under considerable pressure to do what was expected of them.

The rules drawn up in these years by the boards were another form of subtle sanction.   Promulgated as means to rationalize the boards' operations, the rules had an air of impersonality which made them seem less threatening.   Thus there were new regulations to provide for the fair treatment of all employees by standardizing salaries and furlough systems.   Employees could be sure of their obligations to the board in such matters as financial reporting.[46]   A spokesman for the Methodist Board reported that missionaries would "welcome" the Board's determination of all budgets.   Such a plan would "save them much perplexity and very much responsibility" as well as "clarifying and simplifying the work."[47]

The religious agencies also had all the advantages that issued from their staffs' ability to develop long-range plans.   The Churches' central organizations had programs and institutions that left the local churches increasingly dependent on the agencies for direction.   As a study of *The Protestant Church as a Social Institution* concluded in 1935: "Like it or not, denominations have come to mean more than they used to.   They exercise wider functions and their functioning is more necessary to the well-being of the local churches than ever before.   Denominations increasingly supply the competent planning for their subordinate units and furnish the technical experts.   The interdependence of part and whole is ever increasing."[48]   An investigation of local churches and institutions in urban areas also found that those organizations tended "to develop a sense of dependence" on the central denominations."[49]

In addition to these structural means of assuring oversight and cooperation, denominational bureaucrats skillfully labored to create the right image for their agencies.   Religious agencies were portrayed as knowledgeable and efficient; members were to perceive them as successful.   Moreover, agency decision-making was presented as an exercise in democracy.   Since executives could not strong-arm other interest groups, they thus learned to manipulate various symbolic values to achieve their ends.

Public statements of denominational bureaucrats were carefully crafted to give the impression of agency self-assurance.   The planning that went into "systematic finance" was but one example of this new understanding of image-making on the part of agency officials.   Messages to local churches were "simplified and unified;" nothing was sent out "without careful coordination between departments."[50]   The D&FMS adopted a rule forbidding any of its appointees to "publish any criticism on the work under the charge of the Board or of the conduct of the Missionaries appointed through and serving under it without previously submitting the proposed publication" to his bishop or to the Board.[51] Communications were phrased so as to put the best light on existing conditions in the Church.   In 1912, for instance, Methodist fundraisers were told to omit "the idea of debt or possible deficiency" in their appeals.   On another occasion they were enjoined to make "no allusion" to previous methods, "but always to proceed upon the assumption that only one method and that the one adopted by the Board, has any existence."[52]   Episcopal apportionments were not to be called "assessments on parishes," but rather "reasonable expectations."[53]

The thrust of agency reports to the Churches was on agency successes, particularly those that could be quantified.   One spokesman wrote that "we should measure its growth or its decline just as we measure the growth or the decline of any other organization, by a study of its statistics and by such facts and conditions as indicate strength or weakness."[54]   Charts showed the growth in the number of missionaries supported or Sunday schools begun.   Economy of administration was computed down to hundreths of percentage points.   As Oldham and North of the Methodist Board reported: "Secretaries are keenly aware that their administration will be judged by the Church at large for the present at least, partly by the percentage of missionary income spent upon the home administration.   They are not willing to increase this amount largely until the income grows."[55]   Too much administrative economy, however, might be dangerous, it was pointed out.   "Business efficiency" was not synonymous with "missionary efficiency"; "Efficient administration" was preferable to "cheap administration."   Too great an emphasis on "saving money," the Churches were told, could mean low administrative costs, but also failure of the work as a whole.   The true test of the Church's work was not "economy of administration," but rather effectiveness in appealing to the Church as a whole.[56]   Size and complexity were signs of agency efficiency, the churches were told.   The new systems of finance paid dividends to both central and local treasuries.   The Church's salvation was assumed to be in its agency structure.

The agency officials tried to maintain just the right appearance to gain support from all sides.   Too much success might speak of pride, so denominational bureaucrats also adopted the show of humility.   The Episcopal Board realized that "this body is not like a political legislature clothed with powers of taxation, and therefore must depend on voluntary contributions."[57]   It was therefore incumbent on Episcopal leaders to give the appearance of democracy when adopting diocesan quotas for the apportionment system.   Hence they maintained that all quotas, though originally designated by the Board, were established "in every case, [by] the consent of the diocese itself" since all were represented in the Missionary Council.[58]   While noting that "our people are everywhere conforming their machines and plans to this policy," the BSSB obsequiously maintained that "Baptist democracy is observed everywhere, and we have no desire to change this long-established method of doing our work."   According to its leaders, the BSSB "never attempts to dictate, or work from the top down, but always takes its cue from the great Baptist body of the Southern Baptist Convention."[59]   The Seventy-five Million Campaign would show to all the world, as World War I had in political and military affairs, "that democracy can be made tremendously efficient in religious affairs."[60]   UCMS leaders realized that they must at times demonstrate deference. As the retiring chairman of the Promotional Division warned his colleagues in 1923:   "If the churches come to the point where they think of the Society as a big organization outside of or apart from the church, then both the Society and the churches lose ground."[61]   On another occasion, the UCMS declared that it had no "desire to interfere directly with the autonomy of any international, state, district, provincial or other society that now exists." The Society was "the servant of the churches and the individuals who support it."   Having said the magic words, the policymakers then added that "the greatest efficiency, economy, and permanency of our great communion can be secured best through a well-organized and unified effort such as the UCMS."[62]   The choice was simple, said President Burnham: "organized representative democracy versus religious chaos and inefficiency."[63]

Denominational leaders also sought to demonstrate that they acted in accordance with the will of God.   The *Christian Standard* informed the Disciples that "the only Scriptural, and therefore the only businesslike, method of church support is generous systematic giving."[64]   When the Disciples debated replacing the society type of organization with the denominational type, Corresponding Secretary, J. H. O. Smith, argued that the latter was "a spiritual, Scriptural and business basis, rather than a money basis."[65]

Once the executives had established that the boards were both successful in their assigned tasks and subservient to the wishes of both God and Church, they had sufficient leverage to deal with challenges to their authority.   The boards seemed all too often to assume that all virtue and Christian values lay in their hands and, accordingly to assign the worst of motives to their opponents.   Those who opposed the boards clearly were enemies of efficiency, order and success. Criticism was described as an attempt to undermine the boards. One of the Episcopal managers, for instance, said that "nothing will more certainly weaken the hands and paralyze the energies of the Board and its committee than a spirit of fault-finding or captious criticism upon its plans and methods."[66] Local officials were guilty of "jealousy," desiring to "carry everything their own way and to be prominent above all others in the denomination."[67] When the Episcopal Bishop of Tennessee complained that the Board had reduced stipends to his diocese, the General Secretary pointed out that other "unselfish" dioceses, "ably" led by far-seeing bishops, had dropped such aid altogether. He congratulated the latter for actions "sure to redound to the lasting credit of those who framed and passed it."[68]

The cornerstone of agency authority, however, was in its skillful use of the concept of Christian harmony in its appeals for conformity. In the name of "internal peace and harmony of the denomination," Baptist leaders sought to limit criticism. As the Commission on Efficiency's report said, "While we fully recognize the necessity and great value of the free discussion of all intra-denominational questions, we would earnestly insist that all such discussions should be brotherly and illuminating." The net effect was to put opponents to board policies in the uncomfortable position of disturbing denominational peace.[69] Christians must seek to be of "one spirit and one mind striving together for the faith of the gospel."[70] The Disciples executives stressed Christian harmony and brotherly love, reminding their members that the denomination had been founded on the principle of Christian unity, as well as local autonomy. What was needed, said one leader, was "harmonizing and adjusting in the minds of our people."[71] The selection of the name "united" for the new society proved singularly salubrious to the early success of the organization. Bert Wilson, head of the Promotional Division of the UCMS, reminded members that "one of the great needs of the United Society is to become really united in experience and practice as well as in name."[72]

The careful planning that went into securing reponsiveness at the local level was applied in slightly different ways to the governing conventions and boards of managers. Denominational bureaucrats did not have to answer directly to local churches or missionaries, but their independence was subject to control from above. If they were to maintain their autonomy, Church leaders discovered that they must avoid at all costs any testing of their powers by conventions or boards. They must be extremely cautious in all their dealings with interest groups that had legal authority over them.

Fortunately for the executives, the structure of the Conventions seldom allowed these bodies to make substantive demonstrations of their authority; their functions tended to be more inspirational than legislative. The sheer size of the meetings militated against meaningful deliberation.[73] Committees studying agency reports were often hand-picked by the executives and generally produced glowing reports of agency successes. Even if a convention adopted an undesirable piece of legislation, agency executives could always "interpret" it so as to minimize its impact. Secretary Wright of the ACMS, for instance, proceeded with his agency's reorganization plans even after the Convention had rejected them. As he told his Board of Managers: "It is my opinion that the convention knew nothing about the division of labor and that several changes are absolutely necessary."[74] In another case, the Episcopal Board blocked the creation of a Department of Immigration (as proposed by the General Convention of 1916) simply by claiming there were no funds for such a project.[75] Since conventions met only as often as once a year and always with a somewhat different membership, there was normally no one determined and able to ascertain whether the agencies followed their orders strictly. Rarely indeed did a Convention rebuke an agency for ignoring its wishes, even though grounds for such a charge certainly existed in all of the denominations at one time or another.[76]

The passivity of the governing bodies was also a product of increasing agency complexity. As the work of the agencies expanded, the details that once were handled by boards of managers were now dealt with in weekly staff meetings and presented to managers as *fait accompli.* The managers, who were busy men themselves, seem to have objected little to this change. Because of their experience in business and church administration, they tended to identify more with the executives whom they governed than with the national conventions which had appointed them. Criticism of the agency seemed to be criticism of themselves as managers. Executives could therefore play off managers against the convention by noting the "expertise" of the former vis-a-vis the latter. As George Sutherland of the Methodist Board reported, one of the managers told him that "we have so much confidence in the Administration that we simply come and rubber stamp what they recommend."[77] Lloyd of the D&FMS chuckled with his counterpart in the Anglican Church when the latter confessed that his executive committee "did not seem anxious to know" about internal affairs, although Lloyd admitted that they should "know everything in a general way."[78]

Some executives shared Lloyd's concern that their new-found independence might undermine the sense of shared responsibility for actions of the boards, but this attitude seems not to have been strong enough to convince the executives to stop striving for greater autonomy. Secrecy became an important consideration in agency decision-making. The Episcopal staff objected to public meetings of the Board because they led to "inaccurate and misleading reports in the daily press."[79] Copies of the Methodist Campaign on Relief and Reenforcement in 1912 were "to be regarded as ABSOLUTELY PRIVATE for the information of team workers only."[80]   Internal memoranda asked whether proposed letters should "go indiscriminately to the members of the Board?"[81] Annual reports were shortened in order "to get away from the mass of detail" that made such reports "increasingly bulky."[82]

Agency executives also were meticulous in their preconvention planning in order to assure swift approval of their operations. Denominational leaders sought to avoid conflict wherever possible. A mistake—for example, inviting a "liberal" theologian to speak at the convention—could generate hundreds of angry letters of protest.[83] Board secretaries considered it their "duty to counteract" any controversies that might upset the convention. Plans might be changed in order to avoid conflicts on the floor of the convention.[84]   Corresponding Secretary Wood of the D&FMS wrote about a matter of missionary policy: "I am convinced that we ought not to take the thing up in the General Convention without a good deal of preliminary education along this specific line, and pretty good backing in the Convention." Wood added that the Board "could not afford. . .to be turned down by the General Convention on any reasonable proposition that it makes."[85]   Acting Corresponding Secretary W. J. Wright urged the ACMS' Managers to select a new Corresponding Secretary prior to the convention. "If this is not done," he said, "there is great danger that the Convention, without actual knowledge of the working of this Society, or the qualifications of the man, shall select some man who is not well fitted to the place and install him to take up the duties of the Secretary." Wright feared that the existing staff might resign or be fired, and that as a consequence the work "would be crippled for many years."[86]   A retired corresponding secretary advised Frank Mason North of the Methodist Board to make the "largest possible appropriations to the field" in the light of an impending investigation by the General Conference of the handling of agency funds. It was "bad strategy," he said, "to 'play safe' in meeting all home demands."[87]

The response of agency executives to the problem of authority seems to confirm most of Philip Selznick's conclusions about the relationship between bureaucratic leaders and the rank and file which hires them.[88] Once created, said Selznick, organizations tend to take on a life of their own. Rank and file members are needed only to provide support, and hence propaganda becomes a major part of the bureaucrat's job. The ranks soon become dependent on the professional work of the bureaucratic leaders. The leaders have special advantages: they are acquainted with organizational "mysteries."   Leaders work to protect these advantages. Actions are taken and policies adopted with an eye to power relations inside the organization, not in accordance with professed goals. Bureaucratic leaders, according to Selznick, construct an ideology to defend their role. They identify their administration with the group as a whole; opponents are seen as enemies of the group and its values. The leaders emphasize centralization as an exigency for disciplined action. Finally, they stress collective submission to the collective will, as represented by the leader. Hence democracy is the "ideological bulwark of autocracy" within the group.   In general, these conclusions seem characteristic of the events we have just described.

Selznick's conclusions are invalid in certain ways in the Churches we have studied. Selznick believed that bureaucratic leaders tended to be conservative. Yet in the period before 1930, the Church executives were very innovative, at least in terms of structures. Conservatism within the Church was at the local level, in the older pastoral structure. Denominational bureaucrats are often more liberal theologically and politically than their ranks. In addition, Selznick suggested that power struggles tend to become struggles between leaders at the top for support from the ranks. In the Church, however, power struggles in these years were more often between the two organizational structures within the Churches, i. e., ,between agency heads and charismatic local leaders. I might also add that Selznick overlooked another important characteristic of interaction between bureaucrats and ranks; bureaucrats, it seems, tended to resolve problems of authority by institutional means, even though such solutions often meant further exacerbation of them. Rank and file complaints were not answered by less organization, but rather by more, albeit what leaders thought was more efficient organization.

That the agencies were successful in establishing their authority is borne out by the anguished perplexity of those outside the agency structure. These outside interests were keenly aware that the Churches were rapidly changing, but they seemed at a loss to halt the process. Power was slipping from their hands, but the process was so gradual and subtle that it defied opposition, especially from parochial groups which little realized their common interests. The agencies had too many organizational and ideological advantages on their side.

Nonetheless, the outside interests did over the years produce a remarkable indictment of the agencies. If their motives were often those of jealousy and provincialism, they nonetheless saw the myriad of dangers that lurked in the modern, large-scale Church. To these critics, reports and regulations were not evidences of order, but of red tape and over-organization. Centralized power did not produce better decision-making, but rather monopolistic dictates from insensitive bureaucrats. Business values did not mean greater efficiency but conformity to the world or secularization instead. In effect, these critics perceived the problem of authority, but they saw in the agencies' solutions a threat to the Church as they understood it.

One of the most common complaints about the bureaucratization of the Church was that it produced "overorganization." Board staffs seemed unnecessarily large and complex. Increasing amounts of time were spent filling out reports, attending committee meetings, planning financial campaigns. Bureaucratic organization had not meant fewer communications from on high, even with more centralized operations.[89] Pastors and local officials longed for the "simplicity of church organization of a generation ago."[90] One Methodist pastor of the 1920's estimated that at least one-third of his time was spent on the financial program and concluded, "I see myself inevitably becoming little more than the well-paid executive of a large business organization, and that my dreams of spiritual influence are not coming true and, apparently, have small chance of ever coming true under existing circumstances."[91] The pastorate now demanded a "good business manager." The agency ideal of the "other-directed" leader filtered down to local churches; the minister was esteemed not for piety and humility, some complained, but rather for being "neat in appearance, a good mixer, an expert organizer, an adept advertiser, qualified to run every department under his care, tactful, sociable, and jolly, especially with the young people, and an entertaining talker."[92] Local interests were left with the feeling that they were becoming cogs in an ecclesiastical machine.

In addition, the "increasingly difficult executive task" which local leaders faced tended to divert attention from what they considered their more important priestly and pastoral functions.[93] Professor Theodore G. Soares of the University of Chicago's Divinity School warned that instruction in church administration threatened to undermine the "prophetic office" of the ministry "in a general fussiness about an ecclesiastical machine." Soares reported that "a good deal of the so-called work is a mere effort to make the wheels go round."[94] Preachers, Harry Emerson Fosdick said, were being "swept off their feet by the demands of their own organizations, falling under the spell of bigness, and rushing from one committee to another to put over some new scheme to enlarge the work or save the world." Fosdick observed that pastors were "doing everything except their chief business, for that lies inside individuals."[95]

These concerns reflected, I think, a widespread feeling that the central organizations were not responsive to local interests. There was little of the feeling of partnership that had pervaded the work of the nineteenth-century agencies. Fundraising plans were no longer "approved by the clergy who will have to do most of the work, and by the laity who will have to give most of the money."[96] Denominational leaders seemed to pay little attention to local affairs. The Secretary of the State Board of Missions of the Alabama Baptist Convention told Frost "to get off of the railroads and go to some backwoods Associations" because his "eyes were not open."[97] A study of Protestant organization in the cities revealed that while work in urban areas had passed into denominational hands, "responsibility accompanying such control has never been adequately assumed by the national boards." Control was now "in the hands of those who are far removed from the practical problems of the individual city."[98] In a similar vein, W. M. Jones, a Baptist state leader, complained to the BSSB about its so-called "specialists." He pointed out that the local pastor faced "the problems of his sunday school every Sunday in the year" while the expert "deduced certain principles or theories" on the basis of his experience with many schools. Pastors found it difficult "to reconcile the theory with the practice."[99]

In certain quarters there was very strong antipathy toward the central agencies. Some believed that the agencies had become monopolistic, exercising despotic powers over both local churches and mission stations. These sentiments were particularly common among Disciples who associated administrative centralization with such other trends as theological liberalism, open church membership, and church federation. One disgruntled Disciple called the UCMS "the St. Louis monopoly" and observed that it was "the verdict of history that all such centralized institutions, without exception, become corrupt and oppressive, a menace to the commonweal."[100] The organization had a "lust for power" and a "mischievous policy of subjugation" that one day would, as another critic said, "destroy the autonomy of the local churches, control the local preachers, and have as autocratic power as any ecclesiasticism in the world today."[101] Some Baptist ministers expressed similar, if less strident, fears. A state leader commented that while he considered the Boards a "benevolent despotism," the individual minister believed that in his relation to the boards, "he is merely grist for its mills." Local leaders, he reported, often saw the boards as "an autocratic, ecclesiastical overlordship."[102] While Methodist and Episcopal churches were accustomed to control from above, local bishops sometimes complained that the annual apportionment was "a steadily increasing burden on the parishes and the dioceses."[103]

Of special concern to local leaders—Baptists and Disciples in particular—was what they thought to be agency interference in local affairs. At first glance such statements may seem inconsistent with the complaints that the agencies were not responsive to local needs, but actually both criticisms merely reflected a general belief that the central boards were insensitive to and unaware of local situations. One Baptist leader called for the Boards to cease their attempts "to manipulate our ministry from denominational headquaters."[104] The *Christian Standard* accused ACMS officials of "brow-beating" pastors. One preacher allegedly received a letter informing him that "you will never rise above where you are while your attitude toward our missionary work is what it is."[105] A member of the UCMS' Executive Committee claimed that its administrators operated on this principle: "Either submit to and support the U.C.M.S. or become *taboo* in the brotherhood."[106] Critics were also aware of agency cooptation: "By scattering petty appropriations among many preachers and churches in many states, the favor of many preachers and churches and state missionary societies is purchased." The organization "controls the church and corrupts the Christian ministry," it was said, "with its allies in state offices and educational institutions, with secret pipelines, with a controlled press, with a legion of itinerant politicians, with retainers and paid propagandists in every corner of the land."[107]

There were fears that large-scale organization tended to stifle local church initiative. The Methodist Bishops reminded church executives that "as the advent of machinery robs the artisan's hand of its skill, and individual art of its inspiration, so does the mechanical functioning of Church life tend to arrest individual developments."[108] George A. Coe's study of Christian education noted that Church institutions had "an inherent gravitation away from creativity toward self-imitation." Churches tended, he said, "to acquire a momentum that is repetitious and mechanical rather than personal and creatively variant."[109]

Episcopal Bishop Fiske complained that the Church's executives endeavored "to magnify their office, and brains are busily occupied in formulating plans, projects, and programmes for churches and associations, until those who are supposed to put these programmes into practical operation are driven near to madness."[110]

Local officials also worried about the increasing influence that denominational executives had over the selection of pastors. A Disciples' elder charged that the agency secretary was tempted "to use his office in putting up and taking down men of the ministry." The executive, he said, tended to "favor the preacher who does the most for him" in terms of supporting the cause financially.[111] South Carolina Baptist leader, W.

M. Jones pointed out that the BSSB field workers had "become instrumental in pastoral changes" due to their close contact with local churches. Jones feared that such influence would alienate many pastors and in addition create a "caste system" in the ministry. He urged the Board to hold aloof from church politics, much as the judiciary did from state politics.[112]

Denominational bureaucrats were accused of exercising unwarranted controls over mission stations. This was especially true among Methodist and Episcopal critics, although it is unclear why these two denominations should have been more concerned than the others. Perhaps these two churches, which had had larger mission operations in the nineteenth century, had stronger traditions of local mission prerogatives; it may also have been the case that Baptist and Disciple polities permitted greater freedom for operations outside of the formal institutional framework of the church, thus lessening the degree of control and conflict. Whatever the reason, Methodist and Episcopalian agency bureaucrats were accused of being "above criticism" from the field, charging "fat bills" to mission stations in order to make their own accounts look good, and "acting *ultra vires* in refusing to consummate" the appointment of candidates personally selected by the local bishop.[113]

This problem came to a climax in the Episcopal Church in 1916. In the spring of that year the Board received a letter from six of its bishops denouncing the "tendency to centralize the control of distant Missions in the Board and its Executive Committee." The bishops wanted to preserve "the venerable and well-tried organization" that had worked for years; autocratic rule, it was pointed out, had led to the American Revolution and was the "essence of Papacy." The bishops turned the ideology of organization against the agencies: in matters of local administration, they said, the "Boards are amateur, the missionaries expert." Errors would result, local initiative would be stifled, and faction would be promoted as a result of central control. Missions were said to be "in a state of disruption" and missionaries suffered from "dampened ardor."[114] Sensing the crisis that was brewing, the board called a Special Meeting to air complaints. At the October gathering the Bishops reiterated their complaints, saying they were tired of hearing that "this is a Board of strategy and not a Board of supply."[115]

For their part, agency executives pointed out that they were charged with the task of managing the Church's money so as to prevent bankruptcy due to local "waste and confusion." President Lloyd asserted that "we simply want the information so as to keep our books straight." Lloyd vowed to "get rid of that word 'approval'" in his dealings with mission stations, and a resolution was adopted saying that the differences were the "result of mutual misunderstanding." The final exchange between the two sides suggested, however, that the conflict was left far short of resolution:

> Bishop Graves—Is what the Board wants from me, or any other bishop in my position, full information, consultation and the right of advise, or does it claim the right to veto?
>
> President Lloyd—Absolutely the first, sir.
>
> Bishop Graves—Then I can only say you are unfortunate in your phraseology.
>
> Bishop Francis—I think there has been a tendency on the part of the Board of Missions to claim a right in such matters to say 'You ought not to do it this way, you ought to do it that way.'
>
> Secretary Wood—That is no veto.[116]

In this instance, and others, the Churches papered over the differences, without making basic changes in the agencies.

Critics also charged that the new structures emphasized secular values. Often the complaint centered on what seemed the agencies' conformity to a business ethos that was inimicable to the essence of Christianity. The use of religious advertising was seen as "competition which smacks of the commercial."[117] A Methodist pastor pointed out that "it is not relying on the Holy Spirit for success" to employ such techniques.[118] Methodist bishops were concerned about the manner in which the Church was developing as an institution. The Church, they pointed out, was "not a human institution." The object of the Church was not "to create great ecclesiastical governments, dispensing patronage through expensive administrative machinery," but rather "to bring men to a saving knowledge of Him." The Bishops reminded Church bureaucrats that "it is only by the unfailing operation of the Holy Spirit that these institutional means can be made effective for the divine purpose. Let history warn us against magnifying ecclesiasticism. Jesus created no ecclesiastical state."[119] A Baptist critic wrote that instead of subordinating "the business world to the reign of Christ," the Boards were "freezing our Baptist work into the moulds of business." The BSSB was "fast becoming a modern corporation" that was "mechanized, standardized, sterilized, and ritualized." It was nothing more than a "Christless organization to raise large sums of money."[120]

Denominational executives, it was charged, had shifted their primary goal from building missions and saving souls to maintaining the ongoing machinery of the organization itself. Why else all the attention to questions of organizational legitimation? A critic of the UCMS showed that while income and numbers of missionaries had risen, the numbers of converts had fallen due to what he termed the "change in emphasis from evangelism to social service, educational and institutional work."[121]   Church executives tended to choose courses of action that left control in their hands but often did not further the traditional work of the Church. Episcopal executives were accused of preferring to "print circulars" rather than involve themselves in the "personal contact" of organizing the dioceses.[122]   Their Baptist counterparts were too busy holding teacher training institutes to spend time in what was seen as the more essential task of organizing Sunday schools.[123]   A UCMS committee had to remind the various departments that their annual reports should "emphasize and magnify the work rather than the organization which is carrying on the work."[124]   When the Episcopal Board reduced its missionary force due to insufficient income, one pastor wrote that the Board merely "did what any good business corporation might have done under somewhat similar circumstances." The Board, he said, "showed more business ability than faith" when it made this decision.[125]   Bishop Fiske of the Episcopal Diocese of New York complained that religion had become nothing more than "sanctified commercialism":   God had become a "Magnified Rotarian;" social Christianity a "substitute for devotion;" efficiency the "greatest of Christian virtues."[126]   The Methodist bishops warned that "our distinctive doctrines are not being emphasized as they once were," despite the elaboration of organization in their Church.[127]

Sociological studies conducted in these years made the same point about the kind of alienation that resulted when instrumental values became ends in themselves. Douglass and Brunner, although favorable to modern forms of organization, reported that ecclesiastical leaders were thought to be "more concerned with externals of the church as an institution than with the great realities behind it."[128]   Wilbur C. Hallenbeck's study of urban church institutions concluded that "the emphasis of the denominational organizations has come to be upon their own maintenance. Their great vested interests in power, prestige, jobs, and money have come to be carefully and zealously perpetuated."[129]

One suspects, moreover, that institutional constraints made interdenominational efforts increasingly difficult, even though most agency leaders believed in the ideals of church federation, church comity and ecumenism. Denominational leaders did not mean to undermine ecumenical efforts, but administrative and financial considerations compelled them to put their own organizations first. The primary loyalty of agency officials was to their own denomination. Educational Secretary Arthur R. Gray of the Methodist Board, for instance, feared that the Missionary Education Movement would become an "independent missionary society" and urged that all money be solicited only "in the name of the Boards."[130]   The United Missionary Campaign was seen by

Frank Mason North of the Methodist Board and the Managers of the D&FMS as an "attempt practically to eliminate the Boards in their united action."[131]   North also noted that few religious agencies cooperated in any meaningful way with the Interchurch World Movement.[132] The Lynd's findings in their study of *Middletown* seem to confirm the view that Church lines may have tightened in the 1920s as fundraising campaigns increasingly stressed denominational loyalty.[133] A Federal Council of Churches investigation of *Six Thousand Country Churches* discovered that denominational officials tended to underplay interdenominational projects in the attempt to retain official power in their hands.[134]

Critics also deplored the tendency of religious organizations to quantify the religious norms of success.   Agency administrators were caught up in statistical demonstrations of their accomplishments.   Price-Waterhouse's report on the business methods of the D&FMS observed that the Board tended to present its work in considerably more detail than the typical commercial establishment. The report pointed out to the Board that "the ends attained are not capable of being measured in money values," but such a finding did not seem to deter the executives.[135] A bookkeeper for the BSSB reported that Corresponding Secretary Frost frequently told him to let the traveling expenses run up "so as to make a favorable report as to the amount of work done in the field."[136]   The Methodist bishops complained that the pulpit was being commercialized in a "worldly scramble for numbers and gaping crowds." The test of the individual pastorate had become "the salary it can command."[137] Bishop Greer told the D&FMS that "I am getting pretty tired myself of all this talk about raising money. It would seem that the whole business of the Church today, represented by this Board, was simply to press and emphasize, until all the machinery creaks, money, money, as though that were the root of the whole trouble." Greer urged the executives to forget about money and concentrate instead on "reviving the faith of the Church in the Church itself, and in the Gospel which has been committed to the Church."[138]   As Douglass and Brunner's study noted, Church leaders had become "very sensitive to membership gains and losses, while the common man unhesitatingly judges the Church in large measure by its institutional size."[139] What was lost in this "modern demand for concrete results" was the sense that ministerial success depended on "an expert knowledge of the Bible, a broad outlook on life, an uncommon insight into the deep things of God, and a sane interpretation of life's varied problems. . . ." As a result, William E. Hammond said, church rolls were filled, but with "watered stock"; Bibles were revered but seldom read; members gave money but would not teach Sunday school.[140]

One of the most interesting aspects of these complaints about the agency structure is how seldom the critics challenged organization and bureaucratic values per se. Criticisms tended to concentrate on the effects of organizations rather than on their right to exist in the first place. Even P. H. Welshimer, a vocal critic of the UCMS, said, "The fact of organization is not objectionable. It is the way the organization is run. Everything depends on the personnel and the policy."[141] What the critics did not recognize was that the organizations themselves were shaping the personnel and the policies, molding them to fit bureaucratic (as opposed to religious) needs. This was a problem that could not be dealt with by merely shaking up the agency personnel or changing some agency programs. The critics could not, I think, cope with this situation because they themselves were ambivalent about the organizations. C. B. Titus, a Disciples missionary to China, for instance, complained about the "Czar-like propensities" of the "official machine," but then he called for "tenure of office based on training"—just what the agency bureaucrats wanted.[142]

Thus these religious agencies achieved their power and legitimacy, I believe, because most Americans had accepted the ideology of organization, to some degree or another. As a Fundamentalist told Walter Lippman, "Nothing holds the liberals and fundamentalists together except the billions of dollars invested in church property."[143] Despite the flaws of the new style Church, bureaucratization was by 1930 a widely accepted phenomenon in American religious life, even among those who were most critical of its effects.

NOTES

[1] "Clergy Relief Fund, *The Churchman*, 83 (February 9, 1901), 162. A speaker in "Convention, ACMS" (1901), p. 11 described the "perils of provincialism"; an editorial on "The Necessity for More Complete Organization as a National Church" in *The Churchman*, 84 (August 17, 1901), 195, noted the "evils of diocesanism" and the "kindred evils of parochialism and individualism"; and the Methodist *Baltimore and Richmond Christian Advocate*, 36 (March 18, 1901), 2, cited a "lack of connectionalism."

[2] Methodist Corresponding Secretary S. Earl Taylor, June 19, 1913, Commission on Finance File, Methodist MSS., and *Annual Report, PEC* (1899), p. 20.

[3] Report of Secretary Hollingshead, May 5, 1915, Commission on Finance File, Methodist MSS., and Treasurer King in "Board, PEC," December 11, 1918, p. 27.

[4] See John Wood of D&FMS to Morris W. Ehnes, Treasurer of the Methodist Board, December 30, 1924, Ehnes File, Methodist MSS.; *Handbook, MEC* (1928), p. 143; "Report of Committee on Unifying Our Home Work," in "Convention, ACMS," (1896), pp. 42-43; and "Board, UCMS," June 12, 1923.

[5] *Annual Report, PEC* (1900), p. 272.

[6] *Our First Congress*, ed. Garrison, p. 213.

[7] "Convention, ACMS" (1896), p. 42; (1898), p. 37.

[8] Rev. Percy Stickney Grant, "How Shall We Reorganize the Church?," *The Churchman*, 84 (August 24, 1901), 230.

[9] "Information," p. 30, Pamphlet Boxes.

[10] Letter to Corresponding Secretary John Wood, May 1, 1907, Lloyd MSS.

[11] Letter to J. M. Frost, July 17, 1916, Frost MSS., Box 33. See also the remarks on "radicals" in the letter of Rev. Livingston Johnson to Van Ness, July 2, 1916 in Van Ness MSS., Box 5.

[12] Van Ness to W. B. Crumpton, May 29, 1916, Van Ness MSS., Box 5.

[13] "Report of Committee on Investigation," 1915, Commission on Finance File, Methodist MSS.

[14] Frost to E. K. Cox, June 5, 1916, Frost MSS., Box 32. See also "Board, SBC," on Poteet resolution of 1917, June 12, 1917, p. 156; "Board, SBC," March 13, 1928, p. 125; and the Frost MSS. and Van Ness MSS. throughout, but especially 1915-1917. Burroughs' *Story of the Sunday School Board*, p. 89, notes the tendency of the SBC "under pressure [to] make gradual encroachment and place ever-increasing demands upon its Sunday School Board."

[15] June 25, 1907, Lloyd MSS.

[16]"Board, ACMS," December 18, 1903, pp. 500-01. Disciple Boards also felt "coerced" by the Conventions to support superintendents for a National Bible Association and the Society of Christian Endeavor, two favorite projects of the delegates, "Board, ACMS," April 16, 1909, December 17, 1909.

[17]Lloyd to Wood, October 20, 1906, Lloyd MSS. See also "Board, PEC," September 25, 1912, pp. 67-68, and in the same collection, Wood to Lloyd, September 28, 1906.

[18]"Board, ACMS," July 23, 1901, p. 373.

[19]Notes of an interview with Dr. Julius Richter by Secretaries Taylor and North, September 23, 1912, North file, Methodist MSS.

[20]"Board, MEC," October 16, 1907, p. 65. Missionaries sometimes called attention to the agencies' ignorance of operations in field and of the need for regular inspections; see "Board, PEC," December 14, 1909, pp. 457-58; August 14, 1903, p. 448.

[21]"Board, MEC," July 20, 1880, p. 189.

[22]George William Brown, "The Machinery of Mission Government," *Christian Standard*, 46 (April 9, 1910), 602.

[23]*Proceedings, SBC* (1895), p. lxiii.

[24]"Board, ACMS," June 8, 1906, p. 88. See the many examples of agency dissatisfaction in Henry C. Webb, "A History of the Independent Missionary Movement of the Disciples of Christ," unpublished Th.D. dissertation, Southern Baptist Theological Seminary, 1954.

[25]"Board, PEC," November 3, 1910, p. 5. See similar statements of the dilemma in Tull, *Church Organization and Methods*, pp. 5-6 and in F. W. Burnham, "Address to the Board of Managers," January 18, 1922.

[26]"Board, PEC," September 28, 1909, p. 33.

[27]"Board, ACMS," March 20, 1896, p. 156. See also *Handbook, MEC* (1884), p. 36, for the adoption of a Board of Education Constitution as another example of the same threat.

[28]"Board, ACMS," August 11, 1904, p. 6. An SBC Committee on Financial Matters recommended that "the Boards should seek *to know* these pastors. They should hold frequent communications with them by correspondence and otherwise," *Proceedings, SBC* (1892), p. 24.

[29]W. M. Jones to Frost, September 25, 1914, Frost MSS., Box 29.

[30]"Board, PEC," May 4, 1911, p. 566.

[31]"Board, PEC," November 14, 1899, p. 111. See also "Board, PEC," November 4, 1904, p. 25; May 13, 1915, p. 584; and "Convention, ACMS," (1904), p. 312.

[32]See *Annual Report, PEC* (1900), p. 17; *Proceedings, SBC* (1900), p. 146, (1903), pp. 176-77, (1904); and Lynn E. May, Jr. "Brief History of the Sunday School Board," p. 27.

[33]*Proceedings, SBC* (1900), p.146.

[34]*Annual Report, PEC* (1901), pp. 24-25.

[35]"Board, ACMS," June 29, 1900, pp. 315-16; March 2, 1906, p. 59; "Board, PEC," June 12, 1900, p. 502.

[36]Hallenbeck, *Urban Organization of Protestantism,* pp. 108, 117.

[37]"Board, SBC," July 1893, December 14, 1905.

[38]"Board, ACMS," September 17, 1897, p. 224; "Convention ACMS" (1895).

[39]Letter to the D&FMS, March 29, 1905, Lloyd MSS.

[40]*Annual Report, NC* (1921), p. 176; letters from mission tour by Lloyd, 1906-07, in Lloyd MSS.; "Survey of Home and Foreign Fields" in "Board, UCMS," February 13, 1923 and November 13, 1923; "Board, PEC," April 14, 1903, p. 448, December 14, 1909, pp. 457-58.

[41]For example the Episcopal General Convention of 1898 adopted a constitutional provision requiring reports of all missionary receipts, *Annual Report, PEC* (1901), p. 28. See also, "Board, MEC," November 28, 1893, p. 141.

[42]"About Records," 2 (October 1918), 6. See also "Board, PEC," December 1907, p. 184; "Board, SBC," April 24, 1902; and *Annual Report, PEC* (1901), p. 27.

[43]"The Problem of Our Church Benevolences," p. 346.

[44]*Annual Report, PEC* (1895), p. 32.

[45]*Journal, MEC* (1916), p. 85.

[46]"Board, MEC," July 20, 1880, p. 189.

[47]"Board, MEC," September 16, 1913, pp. 378-79.

[48]Douglass and Brunner, p. 95. See also Harlan P. Douglass, *1000 City Churches: Phases of Adaptation to Urban Environment* (New York: George H. Doran, 1926), p. xx.

[49]Hallenbeck, *Urban Organization of Protestantism,* p. 191.

[50]"Board, UCMS," November 13, 1923, p. 178.

[51]"Board, PEC," April 14, 1896, p. 205, Rule #17.

[52]"Board, MEC," June 18, 1912, p. 354 and February 20, 1894, p. 199.   See also "Board, MEC," June 15, 1895, pp. 361-362; "Board, PEC," February 14, 1912, p. 146.

[53]"Consecration and Common Sense in Mission Work," *The Churchman*, 84 (July 27, 1901), 101.   See also "Board, PEC," December 19, 1900, p. 90.

[54]Charles Graves, "Are the Churches Declining?," *World's Work*, 4 (May 1902), 2076.

[55]"Board, MEC," February 17, 1914, p. 108.   See also *Annual, SBC* (1922), p. 178.

[56]Educational Secretary Sturgis, "Board, PEC," February 12, 1919, p. 17.   See also report of Board member Hanford Crawford, "Board, MEC," September 16, 1913, p. 380.

[57]"Board, PEC," January 1901, p. 391.

[58]*Annual Report, PEC* (1896), p. 10; (1901), pp. 27-28.

[59]"The Policy of Our Sunday School Board," *Maryland Baptist Church Life*, 3 (April 1919), 3.   See also the statements on the "equality" of all Baptist bodies from Southern Baptist Conventions in the 1920's in Barnes, *Southern Baptist Convention*, pp. 259-261.

[60]"Significance of the Baptist 75 Million Campaign", *Maryland Baptist Church Life*, 4 (January 1920), 3 & 6.   The appearance of democracy is true even today; when the head of the BSSB learned of my research topic, he called me to his penthouse office in a building that covers several city blocks in Nashville to assure me that the SBC differed from other denominations in that all decisions came up from the grassroots.

[61]Bert Young, "Board, UCMS," November 13, 1923, p. 175.

[62]"Board, UCMS," January 19, 1922, p. 511.

[63]"Address to the Board of Managers," January 18, 1922.

[64]Emile L. Patterson, "How to Promote Generous Systematic Giving," 44 (January 4, 1908), 6.

[65]"Organization," *Christian Standard*, 44 (May 30, 1908), 925.

[66]*Proceedings, SBC* (1901), p. 154; "Board, ACMS," June 8, 1906, p. 88; Ford-Porter Controversy File in Frost MSS.; George H. McKnight, *The Churchman*, 34 (July 22, 1876), 684-85.

[67]Letter of November 8, 1900 in Frost MSS., Box 12.   In the same box see the letter of T. P. Bell to Frost, November 5, 1900.

[68]"Board, PEC," June 12, 1900, pp. 502, 507.

[69]I am indebted to Edith Clysdale Magruder, *A Historical Study of the Educational Agencies of the Southern Baptist Convention, 1845-1945* (New York: Columbia University Bureau of Publications, 1951), pp. 52-65, for this idea.   See also Commission on Efficiency Report, *Annual, SBC* (1914), pp. 77-78.

[70]*Annual, SBC,* pp. 77-78.

[71]S. S. Lappin, "A Better System of Offerings," *Christian Standard,* 41 (October 13, 1906), 731.

[72] "Board, UCMS," November 13, 1923, p. 177.

[73]See the *Religious Herald* (a Virginia Baptist paper), May 20, 1909, p. 10; *The Churchman,* 82 (November 17, 1900), 581; and *Annual Report, PEC* (1894), p. 14.

[74]"Board, ACMS," October 30, 1908, p. 499.

[75]"Board, PEC," October 6, 1916, p. 531.

[76]The only example I noted was at the 1907 ACMS Convention when a rival board complained about ACMS truculence, "Convention, ACMS," November 8, 1907.

[77]Memo to F. M. North, April 21, 1919, North File, Methodist MSS.

[78]Lloyd to Wood, September 7, 1906, Lloyd MSS.

[79]"Board, PEC," May 10, 1916, p. 95.

[80]"Board, MEC," July 16, 1912, p. 405.   My own experience in religious archives confirms this penchant for secrecy.   The MEC has a fifty-year seal on all its documents.   At the BSSB in Nashville I was informed by the President, who must approve all access to Baptist files, that since I was a "reputable scholar and not a journalist," I would be permitted to see their files.   Max Weber, *Theory of Social and Economic Organization,* pp. 139-43, noted this tendency on the part of rational organizations for secrecy.

[81]North to Harry Farmer, February 22, 1923, North File, Methodist MSS.

[82]"Board, MEC," February 18, 1913, p. 160.

[83]Webb, "History of the Independent Mission Movement," p. 36.

[84]"Board, ACMS," November 10, 1899, p. 348; December 28, 1903, p. 501.

[85]Letter to Arthur S. Lloyd, June 25, 1907, Lloyd MSS.

[86]"Board, ACMS," June 8, 1906, p. 98.

[87]Letter of Bishop W. F. Oldham to North, September 1919, North File, Methodist MSS.

[88]"An Approach to a Theory of Bureaucracy," *American Sociological Review,* 8 (February 1943), 47-54.

[89]See George Fowles' study on the "Commission Form of Administration for Our Benevolences," c. April 1923, pp. 2-3, in Fowles File, Methodist MSS.

[90]*Annual, SBC* (1934), p. 98.

[91]James Kenna Brett, *Harpers,* 157 (June 1928), 38-44. Murray A. Leiffer's study of *The Role of the District Superintendent in the Methodist Church* (Evanston, Illinois: Bureau of Social and Religious Research, 1960) confirms the view that local executives faced an "increasing amount of administrative and promotional work" in these years, pp. 12, 161-62.

[92]Hammond, "The Economic Struggle Within the Ministerial Profession," p. 520.

[93]Charles Fiske, *Confessions of a Puzzled Parson, and Other Pleas for Reality* (New York: Scribners, 1928), pp. 15-16, 92.

[94]"Practical Theology and Ministerial Efficiency," *American Journal of Theology,* 16 (July 1912), 433-34.

[95]"What is the Matter with Preaching?," *Harpers,* 157 (June 1928), 141.

[96]Bishop Nelson of Albany in "Board, PEC," May 14, 1919, p. 293.

[97]Letter of W. B. Crumpton to Frost, Frost MSS., Box 13.

[98]Hallenbeck, *Urban Organization of Protestantism,* p. 118.

[99]Letter to Frost, September 25, 1914, Frost MSS., Box 29.

[100]R. E. Elmore, "Should the UCMS Be Dissolved?" c. 1926, pp. 8-10.

[101]John T. Brown, *An Experiment that Has Failed,* (Cincinnati: Standard Publishing Company, 1924). Brown was a member of the UCMS' Executive Committee. See also Fred W. Smith, "A History of the Development of and Opposition to Organized Missionary Work Among the Disciples of Christ," unpublished B. D. thesis, Butler University 1940, p. 83.

[102]W. M. Jones to Frost, September 25, 1914, Frost MSS., Box 29.

[103]"Board, PEC," May 13, 1915, p. 584.

[104]Walt N. Johnson, *Spinal Adjustment in Southern Baptist Life* (Mars Hill, N. C.: Mars Hill Press, 1931), p. 50.

[105]"Is It a Groundless Fear?," 46 (July 23, 1910), 1174.

[106]Brown, "An Experiment That Has Failed," p. 15.

[107]Elmore, "Should the UCMS Be Dissolved?," pp. 11, 15.

[108]*Journal, MEC* (1912), p. 197.

[109]*What Is Christian Education?* (New York: Scribners, 1929), pp. 240-41.

[110]*Confessions of a Puzzled Parson,* p. 16.

[111]"Secretarial Domination," *Christian Standard,* 45 (September 18, 1909), 1639.

[112]Jones to J. M. Frost, September 25, 1914, Frost MSS., Box 29.

[113]"For Correction and Instruction," editorial in the *Christian Standard,* 46 (March 12, 1910), 443; Otto Liebner, quoted in an interoffice memo of Harry Farmer to George Sutherland, June 25, 1920, Sutherland File, Methodist MSS.

[114]"Board, PEC," May 10, 1916, pp. 18-19.

[115]Bishop Graves, "Board, PEC," October 25, 1916, pp. 570, 572.

[116]"Board, PEC," October 25, 1916, pp. 568-75. Similar complaints about increasing central controls from bishops in domestic dioceses may be found in "Board, PEC," February 12, 1919, pp. 205-206.

[117]Rev. Clarence O. Kimball, quoted in Reisner, *Church Publicity,* p. 29.

[118]Rev. L. F. Bausman in *ibid.*

[119]*Journal, MEC* (1912), pp. 167-68; (1916), pp. 1328-29.

[120]Johnson, *Spinal Adjustment in Southern Baptist Life,* pp. 7-12, 45.

[121]John T. Brown, *The U.C.M.S. Self-Impeached,* (Cincinnati: Standard Publishing Co., c. 1924).

[122]"Board, PEC," May 1915, p. 586.

[123]Sam H. Campbell to Frost, October 6, 1914, Frost MSS., Box 29.

[124]"Board, UCMS," May 23, 1922, p. 155. See also the similar statement in "Board, MEC," July 16, 1912, p. 413.

[125]Bert Foster, "Withdrawal of Aid from Organized Dioceses," *The Churchman,* 82 (October 13, 1900), 447.

[126]*Confessions of a Puzzled Parson,* p. 14.

[127]*Journal, MEC* (1912), p. 173.

[128]*Protestant Church as a Social Institution,* p. 4.

[129]*Urban Organization of Protestantism,* p. 234.

[130]Gray to Samuel Thorne, Jr., October 22, 1913, Gray File, Methodist MSS. Similar sentiments by the D&FMS toward the Home Missions Council and the Foreign Missions Conference may be found in "Board, PEC," February 14, 1912, p. 146; May 8, 1912, p. 233; September 25, 1912, pp. 67-68; February 12, 1913, p. 52.

[131]North to Taylor, May 4, 1914, Taylor File, Methodist MSS.; "Board, PEC," May 14, 1913, pp. 99-100, 196-97.

[132]North to Taylor, September 8, 1919, Taylor File, Methodist MSS.

[133]Robert S. and Helen Merrell Lynd (New York: Harcourt Brace, 1929), p. 333.

[134]Charles Otis Gill and Gifford Pinchot, pp. 54-57.   Contemporary studies in Church sociology also find that ecumenicalism is at best ritualized. The obstacles to church unity stem not from theology but from questions of authority and polity. See David O. Moberg, *The Church as a Social Institution: The Sociology of American Religion* (Englewood Cliffs, N.J.:   Prentice Hall, 1962), pp. 245, 258-59, but cf. pp. 59-60.

[135]"Report of the Business Methods of the Church Mission House," December 1, 1915, pp. 1, 4-5.

[136]See Ford-Porter Controversy file in Frost MSS.

[137]*Journal, MEC* (1912), p. 171.

[138]"Board, PEC," May 3, 1911, p. 575.

[139]*Protestant Church as a Social Institution,* p. 33.

[140]*The Dilemma of American Protestantism,* pp. 50-53, 60-61, 105-06.   See also Hammond's article on "The Economic Struggle Within the Ministerial Profession," pp. 515-19.

[141]Quoted in Cochran and White, *Captives of the Word,* p. 243.   Welshimer later led "independent" Disciples churches in the formation of the North American Christian Convention.

[142]"The Machinery of Mission Government," *Christian Standard,* 46 (March 12, 1910), 438.

[143]*A Preface to Morals* (New York: Macmillan, 1929), p. 31. Joel Carpenter's study on "Fundamentalist Institutions and the Growth of Conservative Protestantism, 1929-1942," unpublished paper in The American Seminar, Johns Hopkins, 1975, suggests the extent to which these conservative religious leaders also turned to organization.

CHAPTER 9

CONCLUSIONS

Religious bureaucracies have come to exercise enormous influence in the life of American Churches in the twentieth century. In 1977, for instance, the Baptist General Convention of Texas closed out a month-long, $1.5 million campaign called "Good News Texas." The crusade was frankly evangelistic, but it consisted of far more than the simple gospel. To conduct the campaign, a BGCT steering committee—much like one that Proctor and Gamble or Exxon might form—considered a variety of approaches devised by a number of leading advertising firms and finally hired Bloom Advertising Agency of Dallas, a large and successful Jewish-owned firm. When asked about the incongruity of a Jewish firm engaging in Christian evangelism, Baptist executive James Landes answered that "Bob Bloom is a good salesman." A Baptist preacher from conservative East Texas added, "The man knows where he is going." The Bloom Agency produced the attractive logos and catchy mottos associated with this (or any) modern advertising campaign; various radio and television spots were test-marketed to find which would appeal to the target group—the non-Christian. Baptists planned to advertise their wares on such programs as *Mary Hartman, Mary Hartman* and *All in the Family*. This might seem to be an odd place for Christian advertising, but Landes had an answer for this too; he said "public relations" was, after all, "the name of the game."

The most striking observation about the Baptist campaign came, however, from Bob Bloom. Bloom said he had expected a sharp drop-off in intelligence between the Baptist executives and "the men in lower positions," as was common in his experience with businesses. Instead, he found local pastors both "sharp" and "flexible," willing to marry the advertising "craft with their pulpit responsibilities." The pastors, according to Bloom, had "smart, agile minds and they really embraced what we were trying to do." Local pastors responded favorably to the campaign, and adopted the BGCT plans for extensive personal visitations, follow-up work, local advertising, and revivals.[1]

Campaigns like "Good News Texas" point up the importance of studying the origins of the bureaucracies that have acquired so great an influence on contemporary religion in the United States. I have argued in this dissertation for an effort to strike out in new directions in our search for better understanding of American religion between 1876 and 1929. For too long, I think, religious historians have debated the rise and fall of the Social Gospel, modernism versus fundamentalism, and the so-called two party system in American religion; in doing so they have largely overlooked one of the major forces that shaped modern American religion: bureaucracy. The rise of modern, large-scale organization in the Church was less noticed, and some might argue less interesting than these other subjects, but bureaucracy's impact, as we have seen, was prodigious. Indeed, I would argue that nothing so shapes the lives of modern Churches as the agency structure. Its planners decide where churches should be built; its architectual specialists offer guidelines for use of space; its agents train local leaders; its publications determine the direction of Christian education and social action.

This is not to say that the agencies have been unchallenged. The agency structure has frequently been in conflict with a traditional pastoral structure that sought to sustain older geographical and cultural interests. The whole debate over authority shows the persistence of traditional ways. An organizational context does, however, help us see these and other conflicts in American religion in new ways. For too long now historians have, for instance, assumed that Southern Churches were out of the mainstream of American religious life because they refused to adopt the tenets of the Social Gospel, of liberal theology or of church unity in this period; this viewpoint seems now to merit reconsideration.[2] If organization provided one of the primary meanings for the twentieth-century Churches, then Southern Churches—as the SBC clearly shows—were just as much a part of the mainstream as their Northern counterparts. Nor can we any longer see fundamentalist groups as rural bumpkins who sought to hold on to old ways.[3] They too turned to new organizations and techniques in these years; they established Bible colleges and independent mission movements and made impressive use of the new medium of radio.[4]

Viewing American religion from an organizational context also allows us to draw some new—admittedly tentative—conclusions about the relationships between structures and ideas in American Churches. In many ways bureaucratic organization kept American Churches alive and active in these years; meanwhile their European counterparts were empty and dying. Of course this leaves us to ponder whether all the activity in America was not mere spinning of organizational wheels. Were American Churches only secular ghosts of their former selves? There is no easy answer to this question. The recent literature on the concept of secularization has enormously complicated our understanding of what this process means.[5] Research that defined secularization as a decline in the influence of religious symbols and institutions[6] or as the conformity of religious institutions to this world[7] or as the limitation of the religious role to the private sphere[8] have all been attacked for a variety of reasons. These definitions seemed to embody a utopian view of the pre-secular worlds that had supposedly been lost. The measures of religious decline or conformity were ambiguous at best. Did falling Church attendance imply less religiosity or merely less hypocrisy? Secularization can be a very slippery and subjective term; one scholar's subversion of faith is another's reinvigoration. Liberal theology that questioned supernaturalism might well be removing from religion the intellectual problems that kept men away from the gospel rather than perverting the historical faith. Indeed, some have argued that secularization is meaningless in that religiosity is universal—although its forms might vary.[9]

What this literature suggests, I think, is that one must be very careful when calling any phenomenon secularization. My research demonstrates, I believe, that the reigious institutions of 1930 were remarkably different from their predecessors of a half century before; but were they more secular? Bureaucratization of the Churches did not necessarily imply religious declension; efficient religion, as such, was not contrary to traditional faith.

A clear definition of secularization seems called for, and my own is as follows: secularization is the substitution of a rational (in the Weberian sense of quantitatively calculating) world view for a sacred one in understandings of men and society. Such rational thought processes are especially (but not exclusively) associated with large-scale institutions in modern society. Frequently in American Churches, more rational techniques were adopted without affecting sacred viewpoints—especially at first. But we can see the process of secularization clearly in the organizations studied here when institutional demands impinged on Christian ideals; rational choices often had un-Christian and hence, I would argue, secular meanings.

Religious leaders did not intend, of course, to create a more secular institution. The structural adjustments of the late nineteenth century—elaboration and growth of the agency structure—were designed primarily to facilitate the Church's accomplishment of its traditional goal of taking the faith to all the world.[10] Organizations proliferated in these years but did not significantly impinge on the local churches. There remained a sense of a common task at all levels. With the coming of the efficiency craze and the era of scientific management, however, the understanding of the role these agencies should play began to change rapidly. The intent was still to maintain a Church that was alive to its mission to minister to man. But increasingly the agencies adopted bureaucratic forms and these in turn began to shape the mode of operations and values of the Churches. Power shifted to the center as agencies sought to direct the course of religious finance and Church organization from on high. Organizational hierarchies demanded conformity to new sets of regulations in order to govern the Church.

Hierarchies also called forth religious specialists who could exercise rational-legal authority. The new structure succeeded admirably in filling Church coffers, in bringing order to Church affairs, in leading men to Christ and in breathing new life into the old institution.

Along with bureaucratic structures, however, came numerous changes that I believe undermined the historical role of the Church. Business models might achieve order and efficiency, but they did so at an enormous price. Large-scale organization demanded, of necessity, that significant amounts of time and energy be expended by leaders on maintance of appropriate patterns of behavior, on the management of internal tensions, and on adaptation to changes in external environments. When these tasks became primary, as they sometimes did in these years, Church leaders were deflected from concern about religious ends to concentration on structural means. Organizational survival gradually seems to have become the agencies' primary task. Leaders were all too often preoccupied with organization and administration.

This type of goal alienation[11] can be seen in several aspects of the Church during these years. The quantification of the norms of religious success—especially the concern about the number and vitality of religious organizations—suggests where the central emphasis of many religious leaders was.[12] Organizational activity became for many executives a sign of God's activity in the world. The fact that many local pastors believed that a good statistical showing was the significant measure of their work indicates, I think, the degree to which the organization was functioning for its own ends. Rational ways of thinking demanded measurable results.

The agencies' preoccupation with public relations also indicates their interest in organizational maintenance. Often the first question asked of any plan was what will the people think; will the idea play in Peoria, as it were?[13] For these Christians, Madison Avenue salesmanship had replaced the gospel. To the extent that religious leaders opted to define their goals by what would be acceptable, they relied on rational calculation rather than God's direction.[14] To the degree that they sought to remold Church opinion to accept their plans, moreover, Church bureaucrats chose to play God.

This tendency of religious executives to regard themselves as a special elite chosen by God to shape denominational ideas and institutions suggests another of the structural dysfunctions brought on by modern organizations and bureaucratic methods. The denominational structures which needed specialized performances and expertise in order to function properly tended to downplay the qualities of piety and personal inspiration that had marked nineteenth-century leaders in American Churches. These religious qualities were still desirable in agency leaders, but they were often considered to be of secondary importance in choosing new executives. Personality tests began to replace the will of God; organizations sought the services of team players who would work together effectively—and not rock the boat. Denominational executives tried to limit criticism of their agencies as far as possible.[15]

The organization's belief in its own superiority also had the effect of inhibiting local initiative. The preachers who felt they were cogs in machines were a measure of the extent of this problem. The local minister's role frequently became one of conforming to denominational expectations; his professional future was too often shaped by the agency structure. Laymen on denominational boards of managers tended to defer to denominational leadership. Everything seemed to be organized from above. Churches became increasingly dependent on denominational literature, guidance, and planning. Churchmen lost, as a result, a sense of personal involvement in the lives of their denominations. The systematization of finance made men little more than numbers in the next church canvass. Joining the church became more and more like joining any other secular organization; for all the initiative it demanded from local members, going to church was like a visit to the doctor.[16]

Philip Selznick's discussion of bureaucracy is especially instructive as to what, exactly, was happening in the Church in the United States as a result of these changes.[17] Selznick points out that the problems which lead men to organize are different from those which result from operating the organization. While "'ultimate' issues and highly abstract ideas" may play leading roles in the formation of organizations, they have less important effects on the day-to-day behavior of the participants. They may set the context and define certain limits for organizations, but they have little direct influence on human activities. Selznick points out that this is true "not because men are evil or unintelligent," but because such ultimate formulations are seldom useful in achieving solutions to the specific problems of maintaining the organization. In addition, Selznick says that when professed goals conflict with the ordinary business of running an organization, the former tend to yield to the latter (usually by being ignored). Again there is not evil intent in this choice; it is a simple product of organizational imperatives.

In adopting bureaucratic styles of organization, then, denominational leaders set out in a direction that ultimately created a more secular Church. They did not intend for this to happen—indeed they constructed their organizational dominions in order to facilitate the sharing of the gospel. But a hard look at the shape of the Church in

1930 leads me to the conclusion that while bureaucratic organizations and values ably served modern business enterprises, they were less than desirable in our religious denominations. Mechanical images and rigid structures were simply not compatible with the organic image of the Church in Scripture as the body of Christ in which all men are of equal worth. The organizational demand for trained leadership was in a sense a threat to the Biblical picture of God's gifts. Religious hierarchies expected obdience, not creative initiatives from local churches. If public relations and business methods did not seem entirely consistent with the Christ who drove money changers from the Temple, that fact was conveniently ignored (as Selznick's analysis would predict).[18]

The willingness of many religious leaders to use bureaucratic institutions and values in pursuit of more traditional goals also offers some fresh insights on the Progressive period and in particular on the "emerging organizational synthesis in American history." The adoption of bureaucratic values among Church leaders came at a later date and at a slower pace than the leading synthesis in this field, Wiebe's *The Search for Order*, would suggest. The shift to new organizational processes within religious institutions, moreover, seems to me as much a search for modernity as a search for order. Church leaders, concerned by what seemed a declining role for religion in society, chose methods and rhetoric that reinvigorated, at least for a time, an old institution.

This integration of modern rationality with older ideological systems of belief confirms what several scholars have recently said about the Progressive period. John Higham, for instance, argues that "the old ideological framework was temporarily revitalized."[19] Wiebe's more recent work, *The Segmented Society*, also suggests that Progressives attempted to achieve both efficiency and virtue in these years.[20] It was the amalgamation of older ideals and modern techniques that made the Progressive period distinctive. The religious crusades of the first two decades of the century suggest that American Protestantism was deeply involved in this particular process of change. If after World War I the hope of combining the two elements gradually vanished as technical systems triumphed, we should not underestimate the sincerity of those who sought to bring Christianity to the world in their generation.

Indeed my study points to the persistence of nineteenth-century institutions and ideas (as Wiebe argues in *The Segmented Society*). An older network of values based largely on geographical and traditional cultural elements, continued to play important, albeit weakened, roles in the lives of many Americans; they did so even while the newer functional and more economically-oriented institutions were growing.[21] In terms of the Churches, the older pastoral structure continued to define religion in the lives of many Churchmen, quite apart from the organizational hierarchies. The newer structures had the advantages of program and persuasion, and could use the ritual of democracy; but, as Wiebe suggests, relations between the two networks often constituted "a begrudging truce with endless little grabbing maneuvers for advantage."[22] My study of authority suggests that the continuing struggle between these elements has been an important aspect of the Church in this century.

A final word is in order for those who share more than a scholar's interest in the Church. To argue, as I have, that American denominations are more secular today is to overlook the roads not taken. To isolate themselves from the world in order to maintain the purity of the faith would doubtless have left the Churches with even less influence over the lives of Americans in the twentieth century. Religious organizations today have tremendous potential that is not realized, due largely to their self-preoccupation. More careful attention to other types of organization besides the hierarchical one adopted from business—such as the abortive Disciple committee system—might have produced structures more consistent with the faith, even though less efficient in terms of dollars and cents. Until efficiency ceases to be a major end of Christian endeavor, however, modern Churches will continue to find it difficult to convince men of the need for repentence and conversion.

NOTES

[1]William C. Martin, "The Baptists Want You!," *Texas Monthly*, 5 (February 1977), 82-87, 149-57.

[2]For example see C. Vann Woodward, *The Origins of the New South, 1877-1913* (Baton Rouge: LSU Press, 1951), p. 450 and Samuel S. Hill, Jr., *Southern Churches in Crisis* (New York: Holt, Rinehart and Winston, 1967), p. 207.

[3]Such is the general drift of most early histories of the movement. See Stewart G. Cole, *A History of Fundamentalism* (New York: 1931) and Furniss, *The Fundamentalist Controversy.*

[4]See Ferenc M. Szasz, "Protestantism and the Search for Stability: Liberal and Conservative Quests for a Christian America, 1875-1925," *Building the Organizational Society,* pp. 88-102 and Joel Carpenter, "Fundamentalist Institutions."

[5]Larry E. Shiner defines six types in current use in "The Concept of Secularization in Empirical Research," *The Social Meanings of Religion: An Integrated Anthology,* ed. William M. Newman (Chicago: Rand McNally, 1974). The relation of religious sociology to history is discussed in Robert W. Doherty, "Sociology, Religion and Historians," *Historical Methods Newsletter,* 6 (September 1973), 161-69.

[6]Examples of secularization as religious decline are J. Milton Yinger, *Religion, Society and the Individual* (New York: Macmillan, 1957); Charles Y. Glock and Rodney Stark, *Religion and Society in Tension* (Chicago: Rank McNally, 1965); and David O. Moberg, *The Church as a Social Institution: The Sociology of American Religion* (Englewood Cliffs, N. J.: Prentice Hall, 1962).

[7]Studies of American secularization frequently stress religious conformity. See Will Herberg, *Protestant—Catholic—Jew: An Essay in American Religious Sociology* (New York: Anchor Boods, 1960) and "The New Shape of American Religion: Some Aspects of America's Three-Religion Pluralism," *Review of Religious Research,* 4 (1962-63), 39; Martin E. Marty, *The Modern Schism: Three Paths to the Secular* (New York: Harper and Row, 1969), pp. 95-142. Marty's work suggests that the secularization of American religion came in the mid-nineteenth century. My own reading of these years is that the "summit of complacency" came later with the structural changes of the twentieth century.

[8]See Berger, *The Sacred Canopy* and *The Noise of Solemn Assemblies.*

[9]See Thomas Luckmann, *The Invisible Religion: The Problem of Religion in Modern Society* (New York: Macmillan, 1967) and David Martin, *The Religious and the Secular: Studies in Secularization* (London: Routledge and Kegan Paul, 1969).

[10]See John R. Scotfield, "The Perils of Ecclesiastical Bigness," *Christian Century*, 76 (November 4, 1959), 1276-77.

[11]This phenomenon is mentioned in many current sociological studies. See Moberg, *The Church as a Social Institution,* pp. 96-97, 182; Muelder, *Methodism and Society in the Twentieth Century,* p. 391; James M. Gustafson, "An Analysis of the Problem of the

Minister," *Journal of Religion*, 34 (July 1954), 190; and Gibson Winter, "Religious Organizations," p. 440 and *The Suburban Captivity of the Churches* (Garden City, N. Y.: Doubleday, 1961), p. 86.

[12]For example, see Gustafson, pp. 190-91; Moberg, pp. 170, 219; and Muelder, p. 392.

[13]Robert W. Spike, *In But Not of the World* (New York: Association Press, 1957), p. 74; Moberg, p. 176; Muelder, p. 392; Winter, "Religious Organizations," pp. 438, 484.

[14]David O. Moberg, for instance, has suggested that structural imperatives limited reform efforts like the Social Gospel to passing resolutions at Church assemblies. Concrete actions threatened institutional stability and hence were seldom taken, pp. 147-48. See also Lee, "The Organizational Dilemma in American Protestantism," pp. 208-10, on ministers during the civil rights crisis in Little Rock.

[15]See Lee, "Organizational Dilemma," pp. 210-11; Moberg, p. 224; Muelder, p. 392; Scotfield, p. 1277.

[16]See Gustafson, p. 188; Paul Harrison, "Church and Laity Among Protestants," *Annals of the American Academy of Political and Social Science*, 332 (November 1960), 37-40, 45; H. Richard Niebuhr, *The Purpose of the Church and its Ministry* (New York: Harper, 1956), p. 90; Lee, "Organizational Dilemma," pp. 210-11; "Lutherans Centralize," *Christian Century*, 71 (November 27, 1954), 1296; Winter, "Religious Organizations," p. 438; Scotfield, p. 1237.

[17]"An Approach to a Theory of Bureaucracy," pp. 47-54.

[18]See John Hendrix, "Toward a Theology of Organization," unpublished paper by a BSSB executive, 1971.

[19]"Hanging Together: Divergent Unities in American History," pp. 24-25.

[20]p. 64.

[21]Wiebe, *Segmented Society*, pp. 130-31.

[22]*Ibid*, p. 131.

BIBLIOGRAPHY

PRIMARY SOURCES:

A.   Disciples of Christ.

Brown, John T.   *An Experiment that Has Failed.*   Cincinnati: Standard Publishing Company,   1924.

_____.   *The U.C.M.S., Self- Impeached.*   Cincinnati: Standard Publishing Company, c. 1924.

Burnham, F. W.   *Address to the Board of Managers.*   Indianapolis   (?),   1922.

_____.   *Unification.*   St. Louis: UCMS,   1927.

Christian Standard.   Volumes 31-46, 1895-1910.

Elmore, R. E.   *Should the United Christian Missionary Society Be Dissolved?.* Cincinnati: c. 1926.

Garrison, J. H., ed.   *Our First Congress.*   St. Louis: Christian Publishing Co., 1900.

"Minutes of the Annual Convention of the American Christian Missionary Society," 1891-1917. (The Convention was known as the General Christian Missionary Convention from 1891-1895).

"Minutes of the Board of Managers of the American Christian Missionary Society," 1893-1910.   These minutes have apparently been lost after 1910.

"Minutes of the Board of Managers of the United Christian Missionary Society," 1920-1926.

"Minutes of the Committee on Cooperation and Unification," 1917-1920.

Murch, James DeForest.   *Christian Ministers' Manual.*   Cincinnati: Standard Publishing Co., 1937.

"Report of the Committee on Reconstruction and Unification of our Missionary and Philanthropic Interests."   Typescript available in the Disciples of Christ Historical Society, c. 1919.

A Voice Out of the Night [pseud. used the UCMS].   "To All Disciples of Christ Everywhere."   N.p., n.d.

Welshimer, P. H.   *The Dissolution of the United Christian Missionary Society.*   N.p., c. 1929.

Yearbook of the Churches of Christ (Disciples).   1912-1929.

B.   Southern Baptist Convention

Burroughs, P. E. *Fifty Fruitful Years.* Nashville: BSSB, 1941.

————.   *The Story of the Sunday School Board of the Southern Baptist Convention.*
Nashville: BSSB, 1931.

Financial ledgers, Baptist Sunday School Board. 1913-1929.   Found on microfilm,
Dargan-Carver Library.

Frost, J. M. *The Sunday School Board, Southern Baptist Convention: Its History and
Work.* Nashville: BSSB, 1914.

Frost MSS. The manuscript records of the administration of Corresponding Secretary J.
M. Frost of the BSSB.   1891-1916.   Dargan-Carver Library.

Held, John A. *The Organized Class.* Nashville: BSSB, 1915.

Johnson, Walt N. *Spinal Adjustment in Southern Baptist Life.* Mars Hill, N.C.:   Mars
Hill Press, 1931.

Maryland Baptist Church Life. Volumes 1-4, 1917-1920.

"Minutes of the Board of Managers of the Sunday School Board of the Southern Baptist
Convention."   1891-1935.

"Minutes of the Executive Committee of the Southern Baptist Convention."   1919-1934.

The Proceedings [later the *Annual*] *of the Southern Baptist Convention.*   1867-1927.

"Report of the Corresponding Secretary to the Annual Meeting of the Baptist Sunday
School Board."   1917-1932.

Scarboro, J. A. *The Bible, The Baptists, and The Board System: An Appeal for Biblical
Missions.* Chicago: Regan Printing House, 1904.

The Sunday School Builder. House organ of the BSSB.   December 1927 issue describing
church organization.

Tull, Selsus E., et. al. *Church Organization and Methods: A Manual for Baptist
Churches.* Nashville: BSSB, 1917.

Van Ness MSS. The manuscript records of the administration of Corresponding
Secretary I. J. Van Ness of the BSSB.   1916-1932.

C.   Protestant Episcopal Church

Addison, Daniel Dulany. "A Retrospect of the General Convention." *The Independent,*
53 (October 31, 1901), 2573-76.

*Annual Report of the Domestic and Foreign Missionary Society of the Protestant
Episcopal Church in the United States of America.* 1891-1919.   This report is variously

titled before 1900:   *Annual Report on Domestic Missions; Report of the Committee on the Report of the Board of Managers of the Missionary Society.*

Annual Report of the National Council of the Protestant Episcopal Church.   1920-1926.

The Church Almanac and Yearbook.   1880-1920.

The Churchman.   Volumes 33-108, 1876-1913.

Journal of the General Convention of the PEC.   1880-1922.

Living Church Annual.   Chicago: Living Church Press, 1882-1925.

Lloyd MSS.   A small collection of the letters of Arthur S. Lloyd, General Secretary of the D&FMS, primarily from the 1906-1907 mission tour.

"Minutes of the Board of Managers of the Domestic and Foreign Missionary Society." (After 1910, "Minutes of the Board of Missions").   1889-1919.

Nicholson, Meredith.   "Should Smith Go to Church?"   *Atlantic,* 109 (June 1916), 721-733.

Pamphlet Boxes.   Two boxes of miscellaneous pamphlets prepared by the D&FMS between about 1905 and 1920.   Episcopal Archives.

The Protestant Episcopal Almanac and Parochial List.   New York, 1895-1900.

"Report on the Business Methods of the Church Mission House."   Price-Waterhouse, 1915.   Episcopal Archives.

The Spirit of Missions.   Vol. 66, 1901; vol. 75, 1910; vol. 78, 1913.

D.   Methodist Episcopal Church

Baltimore and Richmond Christian Advocate.   Vols. 16-18, 1881-1883; vol. 26, 1891; vol. 29, 1894; vols. 36-42, 1901-1907.

Christian Advocate (New York).   Vol. 51, 1876; vol. 60, 1885; vols. 65-68, 1890-1893.

"General Ledgers of the Board of Missions, MEC."   1890-1910.   Methodist Archives.

Handbook of the General Conference of the Methodist Episcopal Church (also known as the *Manual*).   New York, 1868-1936.

Journal of the Board of Foreign Missions, an annual report of missionary work.   New York, 1916-1925.

Journal of the General Conference of the Methodist Episcopal Church.   1880-1932.

Journal of the General Conference of the Methodist Episcopal Church, South.   Nashville, 1886-1922.

Methodist MSS. Manuscript records of the Methodist Missionary Society. 1890-1924. Methodist Archives.

Methodist Review. Volumes 58-98, 1876-1916.

Methodist Yearbook. New York, 1880-1931.

"Minutes of the Board of Managers of the Missionary Society of the Methodist Episcopal Church." 1880-1919. Central Records Division of the Methodist Board of Global Ministries, New York.

"Minutes of the Staff Conferences" (also known as the "Foreign Department Staff Council Minutes").

"The Office Builder." Interoffice publication of the Methodist Board of Missions. Nos. 1-37, 1919-1926.

Quarterly Review of the Methodist Episcopal Church, South. Volumes 30-69, 1889-1920.

E.   Other Books and Pamphlets

Abbott, Lyman. *The Industrial Problem.* Philadelphia: G. W. Jacobs, 1905.

Andrews, F. Emerson. *Attitudes Toward Giving.* New York: Russell Sage Foundation, 1953.

Andrews, George Arthur. *Efficient Religion.* New York: George H. Doran, 1912.

_____. *A Soldier in Two Armies.* Chicago: Pilgrim Press, 1901.

_____. *What Is Essential?* New York: Thomas Y. Crowell, 1910.

Anthony, Alfred Williams. *Changing Conditions in Public Giving.* New York: FCC, 1929.

_____. *New Wine Skins: Present-Day Problems.* Boston: Morningstar Publishing House, 1901.

_____. *Safeguardings Funds: Financial and Fiduciary Matters.* New York: J. E. Stohlman, 1925.

Ashley, W. B., ed. *Church Advertising: Its Why and How.* Philadelphia: Lippincott, 1917.

Babson, Roger W. *The Future of the Churches: History and Economic Facts.* New York: Fleming H. Revell, 1921.

_____. *New Tasks for Old Churches.* New York: Fleming H. Revell, 1922.

_____. *Religion and Business.* New York: Macmillan, 1920.

Baldwin, Stephen L. *Foreign Missions of the Protestant Churches.* New York: Eaton and Mains, 1900.

Barbour, Clarence A., ed. *Making Religion Efficient.* New York: Association Press, 1912.

Brace, Charles Loring. *The Dangerous Classes of New York and Twenty Years Work Among Them.* New York: Wynkoop and Hollenbeck, 1872.

Cope, Henry Frederick. *Efficiency in the Sunday School.* New York: George H. Doran, 1912.

_____. *The Efficient Layman, or The Religious Training of Men.* Philadelphia: Griffith & Rowland, 1911.

Davis, Jerome, ed. *Business and the Church: A Symposium.* New York: The Century Co., 1926.

Dixon, Thomas, Jr. *The Failure of Protestantism in New York and its Causes.* New York: V.O.A. Strauss, 1896.

Doney, Carl Gregg. *An Efficient Church.* New York: Fleming H. Revell, 1907.

Douglass, Paul. *1000 City Churches: Phases of Adaptation to Urban Environment.* New York: George H. Doran, 1926.

_____ and Edmund deS. Brunner. *The Protestant Church as a Social Institution.* New York: Harper, 1935.

Ely, Richard T. *Ground Under Our Feet.* New York: Macmillan, 1938.

Evangelical Alliance. *National Needs and Remedies.* New York: Baker & Taylor, 1890.

_____. *National Perils and Opportunities.* New York: Baker & Taylor, 1887.

Fahs, Charles A. *Trends in Protestant Giving: A Study of Church Finance in the United States.* New York: Institute of Social and Religious Research, 1929.

Fiske, Charles. *Confessions of a Puzzled Parson, and Other Pleas for Reality.* New York: Scribners, 1928.

Fry, C. Luther. *Diagnosing the Rural Church.* New York: Institute of Social and Religious Research, 1924.

_____. *The U. S. Looks at Its Churches.* New York: Institute of Social and Religious Research, 1930.

Giersbach, Walter Charles. *Protestant Finance in Metropolitan Chicago as Revealed by a Study of Four Denominations.* Chicago: University of Chicago Libraries, 1936.

Gill, Charles Otis and Gifford Pinchot. *The Country Church: The Decline of its Influence and The Remedy.* New York: Macmillan, 1913.

Gill, Charles Otis. *Six Thousand Country Churches.* New York: Macmillan, 1919.

Hallenbeck, Wilbur C. *The Urban Organization of Protestantism.* New York: Harper, 1934.

Hammond, William E. *The Dilemma of American Protestantism.* New York: Harper, 1929.

Harris, George. *A Century's Change in Religion.* Boston: Houghton-Mifflin, 1914.

Henderson, Charles Richmond. *Modern Methods of Charity.* New York: Macmillan, 1904.

Hough, Lynn Harold. *The Man of Power: A Series of Studies in Christian Efficiency.* New York: Abingdon, 1916.

Hurlbut, Jesse L. *Organizing and Building Up the Sunday School.* New York: Eaton & Mains, 1910.

Leach, William H. *Toward a More Efficient Church.* New York: Fleming H. Revell, 1948.

Loomis, Samuel L. *Modern Cities and Their Religious Problems.* New York: Baker & Taylor, 1887.

Lowrie, Walter. *The Church and Its Organization—In Primitive and Catholic Times.* London: Longmans Green, 1904.

Mathews, Shailer. *Scientific Management in the Churches.* Chicago: University of Chicago Press, 1912.

Mills, Samuel J. and Daniel Smith. *Report of a Missionary Tour through that Part of the United States which Lies West of the Allegany Mountains; Performed under the Direction of the Massachusetts Missionary Society.* Andover, Massachusetts, 1815.

Pierson, Arthur T. *Evangelistic Work in Principle and Practice.* New York: Baker & Taylor, 1887.

Rauschenbusch, Walter. *Christianity and the Social Crisis.* New York: Macmillan, 1907.

_____. *Christianizing the Social Order.* New York: Macmillan, 1912.

_____. *The Social Principles of Jesus.* New York: Macmillan, 1917.

Reisner, Christian F. *Church Methods for the Day.* Denver (?), 1904.

_____. *Church Publicity: The Modern Way to Compel Them To Come In.* New York: Methodist Book Concern, 1913.

Shotwell, James T. *The Religious Revolution of Today.* New York: Houghton-Mifflin, 1913.

Stelzle, Charles. *A Son of the Bowery: The Life Story of an East Side American.* New York: George H. Doran, 1926.

Strong, Josiah.   *The New Era.*   New York: Baker & Taylor, 1893.

_____. *Our Country.*   New York: Baker & Taylor, 1885.

_____. *Social Progress.* New York: Young People's Missionary Movement, 1906.

_____. *The Twentieth Century City.*   New York: Baker & Taylor, 1898.

Transactions of the Efficiency Society.   Volume 1, 1912.

Turner, Fennell P. and Frank Knight Saunders, eds. *The Foreign Missions Convention at Washington.*   New York: Fleming H. Revell, 1925.

United States Bureau of the Census. *Census of Religious Bodies: 1890, 1906, 1916, 1926, 1936.*

Weber, H. C. *The Every-Member Canvass: People or Pocket Books.* New York: Fleming H. Revell, 1932.

_____. *Presbyterian Statistics through 100 Years.* Philadelphia: General Council of the Presbyterian Church, USA, 1927.

F.   Articles

Allen, William H. "Efficiency in Religious Work." *Annals of the American Academy of Political and Social Science,* 30 (November 1907), 539-544.

_____. "The 'Goodness' Fallacy." *World's Work,* 13 (November 1906), 8186-89.

Anthony, Alfred Williams. "The New Interdenominationalism." *American Journal of Theology,* 20 (October 1916), 494-516.

"A Billion Dollars for World-Evangelization." *Literary Digest,* 65 (April 17, 1920), 56-57.

Bushnell, Charles J. "The Place of Religion in Modern Life." *American Journal of Theology,* 17 (October 1913), 520-40.

"The Campaign for Church Advertising and Publicity." *Current Opinion,* 61 (September 1916),   184-85.

"Campaigning with the Men and Religion Teams." *The Survey,* 27 (December 23, 1911),   1393-96.

"Church Going a Business Asset."   *Literary Digest,* 50 (June 26, 1915), 1540.

"A Church on Business Principles."   *Literary Digest,* 48 (March 28, 1914), 704.

"The Church's Need of the Efficiency Engineer." *Review of Reviews*, 45 (March 12, 1912), 350-51.

"Combined Church Advertising." *Literary Digest*, 53 (November 25, 1916), 1411-12.

Conwell, Russell H. "How to Make a Church Pay." *Independent*, 54 (March 27, 1902), 730-33.

Dana, Malcolm McG. "Centralization in Congregationalism." *Andover Review*, 12 (September 1889), 255-61.

Dennett, Tyler. "The Interchurch World Movement." *World's Work*, 39 (April 1920), 569-77.

Dike, Samuel W. "Shall the Churches Increase their Efficiency by Scientific Methods." *American Journal of Theology*, 16 (January 1912), 20-30.

"Does the American Board Propose to Continue its Proscriptive Policy?" *Andover Review*, 12 (August 1889), 214-17.

Duffy, P. Gavan. "Is Modern Organized Christianity a Failure?" *The Arena*, 41 (February 1909), 170-76.

Egan, Maurice Francis. "The Decline of Religion: A Catholic View." *The Forum*, 65 (May 1921), 537-49.

Ellis, William T. "A Movement: A Message: A Method." *Independent*, 72 (May 9, 1912), 984-88.

"Embarrassment of the Interchurch Movement." *Literary Digest*, 65 (June 12, 1920), 42-43.

England, George Allan. "The Ebb of Ecclesiasticism." *The Arena*, 39 (February 1908), 176-84.

"Experiments in Advertising the American Church." *Current Opinion*, 57 (September 1914), 188-89.

Fosdick, Harry Emerson. "What Is the Matter with Preaching?" *Harpers*, 157 (June 1928), 133-41.

Fry, C. Luther. "Changes in Religious Organizations." *Recent Social Trends in the United States*. (2 vols.; New York: McGraw Hill, 1933), II, 1009-1060.

Garfield, H. A. "The Limits of Organization." *Hartford Seminary Review*, 18 (July 1908), 210-20.

Gould, E. P. "The Congregational Polity." *Andover Review*, 12 (September 1889), 245-55.

Gruel, Frederick B. "Organizing the Church for Efficient Economic Service a Present Day Necessity." *Journal of the Efficiency Society*, 3 (December 1913), 65-68.

Hamlin, Teunis S.   "Business Principles in the Administration of Churches."
Independent, 53 (September 19, 1901), 2229-32.

Hammond, William E. "The Economic Struggle Within the Ministerial Profession."
Journal of Religion, 1 (September 1921), 513-27.

Holmes, John Haynes. "The Function of the Church—The Function of the State." *The
Survey*, 22 (September 11, 1909), 800-02.

"How Far Scientific Management Can Be Applied to Religion." *Current Literature*, 51
(November 1911), 533-35.

"How to Advertise Religion." *Literary Digest*, 65 (November 20, 1920), 37-38.

"How to Apply Efficiency Tests to a Church." *Current Literature*, 53 (December 1912),
675-76.

"A Huge Drive for Missions." *Literary Digest*, 60 (February 15, 1915), 34.

Kenna, James Brett. "Minister or Business Executive?" *Harpers*, 157 (June 1928), 38-44.

"'The Lord's Press-Agent' and His Church Advertising." *Literary Digest*, 65 (April 17,
1920), 73-74.

McQuaid, B. J. "The Decay of Protestantism." *North American Review*, 136 (February
1883), 135-52.

Martyn, Carlos. "Churchianity Versus Christianity." *The Arena*, 2 (July 1890), 149-58.

"Men and Religion Forward Movement." *The Survey*, 26 (May 6, 1911), 205-06.

Mode, Peter G. "Aims and Methods of Contemporary Church-Union Movements in
America." *American Journal of Theology*, 24 (April 1920), 224-25.

Ordway, Clyde Elbert. "Will the Churches Survive?" *The Arena*, 29 (June 1903), 593-
600.

"Organization by Self-Governing Churches for Mission Work." *Andover Review*, 12
(September 1889), 303-09.

Phillips, David Graham. "This Business Organization of a Church." *Harpers*, 107 (July
1903), 207-213.

Price, Theodore H. "The Economic Value of Religion and the Interchurch Movement."
Outlook, 124 (March 3, 1920), 369-71.

"Religious Advertising." *Current Literature*, 29 (August 1900), 184.

"'Selling' Religion." *Literary Digest*, 70 (August 20, 1921), 28-29.

Smith, Fred B. "The 'Forward Movement.'" *The Survey*, 28 (April 6, 1912), 33.

Smith, George Burman. "The Contribution of Critical Scholarship to Ministerial Efficiency." *American Journal of Theology*, 20 (April 1916), 161-78.

Soares, Theodore G. "Practical Theology and Ministerial Efficiency." *American Journal of Theology*, 16 (July 1912), 426-43.

Sprague, Jesse Rainsford. "Religion in Business." *Harpers*, 155 (September 1927), 431-39.

Stelzle, Charles. "Efficiency in Church Work." *Journal of the Efficiency Society*, 3 (December 1913), 58-64.

Taylor Graham. "Advertising Religion." *The Survey*, 30 (June 21, 1913), 408-10.

Tomlinson, Everett T. "Too Many Churches." *World's Work*, 26 (August 1913), 475-78.

"Two Great Conventions." *Outlook*, 69 (October 19, 1901), 404-06.

Wakeman, Thaddeus B. "Our Unchurched Millions." *The Arena*, 2 (October 1890), 604-13.

Yeomans, Alfred. "The Reorganization of Church Giving." *Presbyterian Review*, 7 (April 1886), 270-76.

SECONDARY SOURCES:

A.   Disciples of Christ.

Cochran, Louis and Bess White. *Captives of the Word.* Garden City, N.Y.: Doubleday, 1969.

Evans, Clyde Harold. "A History of the United Christian Missionary Society to 1926." Unpublished M.A. Thesis, Phillips University, 1944.

Garrison, Winfred Ernest and Alfred T. DeGroot. *The Disciples of Christ: A History.* St. Louis: Bethany Press, 1958.

Harrell, David Edwin, Jr. *A Social History of the Disciples of Christ.* 2 vols. Nashville: Disciples of Christ Historical Society, 1966-73.

Harrison, Ida Withers. *History of the Christian Woman's Board of Missions.* N.p., 1920.

Lair, Loren E. *The Christian Churches and their Work.* St. Louis: Bethany Press, 1963.

Lewis, Grant K. *The American Christian Missionary Society and the Disciples of Christ.* St. Louis: Christian Board of Publications, 1937.

McLean, Archibald. *The History of the Foreign Christian Missionary Society.* New York: Fleming H. Revell, 1919.

Reed, Forrest F.   "Background of Division—Disciples of Christ and Churches of Christ."   Nashville: Disciples of Christ Historical Society, 1968.

Webb, Henry E.   "A History of the Independent Mission Movement of the Disciples of Christ."   Unpublished ThD dissertation, Southern Baptist Theological Seminary, 1954.

B.   Southern Baptist Convention

Allison, William Henry.   *Baptist Councils in America: A History of their Origin and the Principles of their Development.*   Chicago: George K. Hazlitt, 1906.

Baker, Robert A., ed.   *A Baptist Source Book.*   Nashville: Broadman Press, 1966.

_____.   *The Southern Baptist Covention and its People, 1607-1972.*   Nashville: Broadman Press, 1974.

_____.   *The Story of the Sunday School Board.*   Nashville: Convention Press, 1966.

Barnes, William Wright.   *The Southern Baptist Convention, 1845-1953.*   Nashville: Broadman Press, 1954.

Encyclopedia of Southern Baptists.   2 vols.   Nashville: Broadman Press, 1958.

Green, C. Sylvester.   *B. W. Spilman: The Sunday School Man.*   Nashville: Broadman Press, 1953.

Magruder, Edith Clysdale.   *A History of the Educational Agencies of the Southern Baptist Convention 1845-1945.*   New York: Columbia University Bureau of Publications, 1951.

May, Lynn E., Jr.   "A Brief History of Southern Baptist Sunday School Work." Unpublished paper, Nashville, Tennessee: Dargan-Carver Library, 1964.

Moore, David O.   "The Landmark Baptists and their Attack upon the Southern Baptist Convention Historically Analyzed."   Unpublished ThD dissertation, Southern Baptist Theological Seminary, 1949.

Torbet, Robert G.   *A History of Baptists.*   Valley Forge: Judson Press, 1963.

Sweet, William Warren.   *Religion on the American Frontier: The Baptists.*   New York: Henry Holt & Co., 1931.

C.   Protestant Episcopal Church.

Addison, James Thayer.   *The Episcopal Church in the United States.*   New York: Scribners, 1951.

Allbright, Raymond W.   *A History of the Protestant Episcopal Church.*   New York: Macmillan, 1964.

Barnes, C. Rankin.   "The General Convention of 1919."   *Historical Magazine of the Episcopal Church,* 21 (June 1952), 224-50.

Cushman, Joseph D. *A Goodly Heritage.* Gainesville: University of Florida Press, 1965.

DeMille, George E. *The Episcopal Church Since 1900.* New York: Morehouse-Gorham, 1955.

Dawley, Powell Mills. *The Episcopal Church and Its Work.* Greenwich, CT: Seabury Press, 1955.

McFarland, C. A. "Organizational Analysis of the Development of the Executive Council of the Protestant Episcopal Church in the United States." Unpublished paper, Episcopal Archives.

Manross, William Wilson. *A History of the American Episcopal Church.* New York: Morehouse-Gorham, 1950.

Miller, Spencer, Jr. *The Church and Industry.* New York: 1930.

Tiffany, Charles Comfort. *A History of the Protestant Episcopal Church in the United States of America.* New York: Church Literature Co., 1895.

D.   Methodist Episcopal Church

Barclay, Wade C. and J. Tremayne Copplestone. *A History of Methodist Missions.* 4 vols. New York: Board of Global Ministries of the United Methodist Church, 1949-1973.

Bowne, Borden Parker. *Studies in Christianity.* Boston: Houghton-Mifflin, 1909.

Buckley, J. M. *A History of Methodists in the United States.* New York: Church Literature Co., 1896.

Bucke, Emory S., et. al., eds. *A History of American Methodism.* 3 vols. New York: Abingdon, 1964.

Cameron, Richard M. *Methodism and Society in Historical Perspective.* New York: Abingdon, 1961.

Chiles, Robert E. *Theological Transition in American Methodism, 1790-1935.* New York: Abingdon, 1965.

Curts, Lewis. *The General Conferences of the Methodist Episcopal Church to 1896.* Cincinnati: Curts & Jennings, 1900.

Harmon, Nolan B. *Organization of the Methodist Church: Historical Development and Present Working Structure.* Nashville: Methodist Publishing House, 1962.

_____. *Understanding the Methodist Church.* Nashville: Methodist Publishing House, 1955.

Hofler, Durward. "The Methodist Doctrine of the Church." *Methodist History,* 6 (October 1969), 25-35.

Leiffer, Murray H. *The Role of the District Superintendent in the Methodist Episcopal Church.* New York: Abingdon, 1959.

Luccock, Halford E. and Paul Hutchinson. *The Story of American Methodism.* New York: Methodist Book Concern, 1926.

Muelder, Walter George. *Methodism and Society in the Twentieth Century.* New York: Abingdon, 1961.

Outler, Albert C. "Do Methodists Have a Doctrine of the Church?" *Doctrine of the Church*, ed. Dow Kirkpatrick. New York: Abingdon, 1964.

Sweet, William Warren. *Methodism in American History.* New York: Abingdon, 1954.

E.   General Religious Histories

Abell, Aaron Ignatius. *American Catholic Thought on Social Justice.* New York: Bobbs-Merrill, 1968.

_____. *American Catholicism and Social Action: A Search for Social Justice.* New York: Hanover House, 1960.

_____. *The Urban Impact on American Protestantism, 1865-1900.* Cambridge: Harvard University Press, 1943.

Ahlstrom, Sidney E. *A Religious History of the American People.* New Haven: Yale University Press, 1972.

Atkins, Gaius Glen. "The Crusading Church at Home and Abroad." *Church History*, 1 (September 1932), 131-49.

Bacon, Leonard Woolsey. *A History of American Christianity.* New York: The Church Literature Co., 1897.

Bailey, Kenneth K. *Southern White Protestanism in the Twentieth Century.* New York: Harper & Row, 1964.

Bates, Ernest Sutherland. *American Faith, Its Religious, Political and Economic Foundations.* New York: W. W. Norton, 1940.

Bettenson, Henry Scowcroft, ed. *Documents of the Christian Church.* New York: Oxford University Press, 1967.

Boles, John B. *The Great Revival, 1787-1805: The Origins of the Southern Evangelical Mind.* Lexington: University Press of Kentucky, 1972.

Brauer, Jerald C. *Protestantism in America: A Narrative History.* Philadelphia: Westminster Press, 1965.

_____, ed. *Reinterpretation in American Church History.* Chicago: University of Chicago Press, 1968.

Brown, Arlo Ayres. *A History of Religious Education in Recent Times.* New York: Abingdon, 1923.

Carpenter, Joel. "Fundamentalist Institutions and the Growth of Conservative Protestanism, 1929-1942." Unpublished paper, The American Seminar, Johns Hopkins University, 1975.

Carroll, H. K. *The Religious Forces of the United States.* New York: Church Literature Co., 1896.

Carter, Paul A. *The Decline and Revival of the Social Gospel: Social and Political Liberalism in American Protestant Churches, 1920-1940.* rev. ed. Hampden, CT: Archon Books, 1971.

_____. *The Spiritual Crisis of the Gilded Age.* De Kalb: Northern Illinois University Press, 1971.

Cavert, Samuel McCrea. *The American Churches in the Ecumenical Movement, 1900-1968.* New York: Association Press, 1968.

Clark, Elmer T. *The Small Sects in America.* New York: Abingdon-Cokesbury, 1949.

Clebsch, William A. *From Sacred to Profane America: The Role of Religion in American History.* New York: Harper & Row, 1968.

Cole, Stewart G. *History of Fundamentalism.* New York, 1931.

Cross, Robert D., ed. *Church and City, 1865-1910.* Indianapolis: Bobbs-Merrill, 1967.

_____. *The Emergence of Liberal Catholicism in America.* Cambridge: Harvard University Press, 1958.

Cross, Whitney R. *The Burned-Over District: The Social and Intellectual History of Enthusiastic Religion in Western New York, 1800-1850.* Ithaca: Cornell University Press, 1950.

Drummond, Andrew Landale. *The Story of American Protestantism.* Boston: Beacon Press, 1951.

Ellis, John Tracy. *American Catholicism.* Chicago: University of Chicago Press, 1969.

Elsbree, Oliver Wendell. *The Rise of the Missionary Spirit in America, 1790-1815.* Williamsport, Pa.: Williamsport Printing and Binding, 1928.

Ferm, Vergilius, ed. *The American Church of the Protestant Heritage.* New York: Philosophical Library, 1953.

Fineshriber, William H. "Functions of the Church." *Annals of the American Academy of Political and Social Science,* 165 (January 1933), 64-71.

Foster, Charles I. *An Errand of Mercy: The Evangelical United Front, 1790-1837.* Chapel Hill: University of North Carolina Press, 1960.

Furniss, Norman F. *The Fundamentalist Controversy, 1918-1931.* New Haven: Yale University Press, 1954.

Gaustad, Edwin S. *Historical Atlas of Religion in America.* New York: Harper & Row, 1962.

————. *A Religious History of America.* New York: Harper & Row, 1966.

Gleason, Philip. *Catholicism in America.* New York: Harper & Row, 1970.

————. *The Conservative Reformers: German-American Catholics and the Social Order.* Notre Dame: University of Notre Dame Press, 1968.

Goodykoontz, Colin Brummitt. *Home Missions on the American Frontier, With Particular Reference to the American Home Missionary Society.* Caldwell, Idaho: Caxton Printers, 1939.

Greeley, Andrew M. *The Hesitant Pilgrim: American Catholicism after the Council.* New York: Sheed & Ward, 1966.

Griffin, Clifford S. *Their Brothers' Keepers: Moral Stewardship in the United States, 1800-1865.* New Brunswick, N.J.: Rutgers University Press, 1960.

Handy, Robert T. "The American Religious Depression, 1925-1935." *Church History,* 29 (March 1960), 3-16.

————. *A Christian America: Protestant Hopes and Historical Realities.* New York: Oxford, 1971.

————., ed. *The Social Gospel in America, 1870-1920.* New York: Oxford, 1966.

Hill, Samuel S. *Southern Churches in Crisis.* New York: Holt, Rinehart & Winston, 1967.

Hopkins, Charles Howard. *The Rise of the Social Gospel in American Protestantism, 1865-1915.* New Haven: Yale University Press, 1940.

Hudson, Winthrop S. *American Protestantism.* Chicago: University of Chicago Press, 1961.

————. *The Great Tradition of the American Churches.* New York: Harper & Row, 1953.

————. *Religion in America: An Historical Account of the Development of American Religious Life.* New York: Scribners, 1965.

King, William R. *History of the Home Missions Council.* New York: Home Missions Council, 1930

Koch, G. Adolph. *Republican Religion: The American Revolution and the Cult of Reason.* New York: Henry Holt, 1933.

Landis, Benson Y. "A Guide to the Literature on Statistics of Religious Affiliation with References to Related Social Studies." *Journal of the American Statistical Association,* 54 (June 1959), 335-57.

Marty, Martin E. *Righteous Empire: The Protestant Experience in America.* New York: Dial Press, 1970.

May, Henry F. *Protestant Churches and Industrial America.* New York: Harper, 1949.

McAvoy, Thomas T. *A History of the Catholic Church in the United States.* Notre Dame: University of Notre Dame Press, 1969.

McLoughlin, William G. *Modern Revivalism: Charles Grandison Finney to Billy Graham.* New York: Ronald Press, 1959.

Mead, Sidney E. *The Lively Experiment: The Shape of Christianity in America.* New York: Harper & Row, 1963.

Meyer, Donald B. *The Protestant Search for Political Realism, 1919-1941.* Berkeley: University of California Press, 1960.

Miller, Robert Moats. *American Protestantism and Social Issues, 1919-1939.* Chapel Hill: University of North Carolina Press, 1958.

Nash, George H., III. "Charles Stelzle: Social Gospel Pioneer." *Journal of Presbyterian History,* 50 (Fall, 1972), 206-28.

Olmstead, Clifton E. *History of Religion in the United States.* Englewood Cliffs, N.J.: Prentice-Hall, 1961.

Rice, Edwin Wilbur. *The Sunday-School Movement and the American Sunday-School Union.* Philadelphia: American Sunday-School Union, 1917.

Roberts, Windsor H. *The Reaction of American Protestant Churches to the Darwinian Philosophy, 1860-1900.* Chicago: University of Chicago Libraries, 1938.

Sandeen, Ernest R. *The Roots of Fundamentalism: British and American Millenarianism, 1800-1930.* Chicago: University of Chicago Press, 1970.

_____. "Toward a Historical Interpretation of the Origins of Fundamentalism." *Church History,* 36 (March 1967), 66-83.

Sanford, Elias Benjamin. *Origin and History of the Federal Council of the Churches of Christ in America.* Hartford, CT: S. S. Scranton Co., 1916.

Schlesinger, Arthur Meier, Sr. "A Critical Period in American Protestantism, 1875-1900." *Massachusetts Historical Society Proceedings,* 64 (June 1932), 523-47.

Semmel, Bernard. *The Methodist Revolution.* New York: Basic Books, 1973.

Slosser, Gaius Glenn, ed. *They Seek a Country: The American Presbyterians.* New York: Macmillan, 1955.

Smith, Elwyn A. "The Formation of a Modern American Denomination." *Church History*, 31 (March 1962), 74-99.

Smith, James Ward and A. Leland Jamison, eds. *The Shaping of American Religion.* Princeton, N.J.: Princeton University Press, 1961.

Smith, John Abernathy. "National Christianity: The Search for Unity Among American Protestants, 1880-1920. Unpublished PhD thesis, Johns Hopkins, 1971.

Smith, Timothy L. *Called Unto Holiness, The Story of the Nazarenes: The Frontier Years.* Kansas City: Nazarene Publishing House, 1962.

_____. *Revivalism and Social Reform in Mid-Nineteenth Century America: American Protestantism on the Eve of the Civil War.* New York: Abingdon, 1957.

Spain, Rufus B. *At Ease in Zion: A Social History of Southern Baptists, 1865-1900.* Nashville: Vanderbilt University Press, 1967.

Spike, Robert W. *In But Not Of the World.* New York: Association Press, 1957.

Sweet, William Warren. *The American Churches.* New York: Abingdon-Cokesbury, 1948.

_____. *Religion in the Development of American Culture, 1765-1840.* Gloucester, Mass.: Peter, Smith, 1963.

_____. *Religion on the American Frontier.* 4 vols. New York: Harper, 1931-1946.

_____. *The Story of Religion in America.* New York: Harper, 1939.

Thompson, Ernest Trice. *Presbyterians in the South.* 3 vols. Richmond: John Knox Press, 1973.

Wentz, Abdel Ross. *A Basic History of Lutheranism in North America.* Philadelphia: Fortress Press, 1955.

F.   Religious Sociology and Secularization

Berger, Peter. *The Noise of Solemn Assemblies: Christian Commitment and the Religious Establishment in America.* Garden City, N.Y.: Doubleday, 1961.

_____. *The Sacred Canopy: Elements of a Sociological Theory of Religion.* Garden City, N.Y.: Doubleday, 1967.

_____. "The Sociological Study of Sectarianism." *Social Research*, 21 (Winter 1954), 467-85.

Cox, Harvey. *The Secular City: Secularization and Urbanization in Theological Perspective.* New York: Macmillan, 1965.

Doherty, Robert W. "Sociology, Religion and Historians." *Historical Methods Newsletter*, 6 (September 1973), 161-69.

Doherty, William T. "The Impact of Business on Protestantism, 1900-1929." *Business History Review*, 28 (June 1954), 141-53.

Fichter, Joseph Henry. *Religion as an Occupation: A Study in the Sociology of Professions.* South Bend: University of Notre Dame Press, 1961.

Glock, Charles Y. and Rodney Stark. *Religion and Society in Tension.* Chicago: Rand McNally, 1965.

Gustafson, James M. "An Analysis of the Problem of the Minister." *Journal of Religion*, 34 (July 1954), 187-91.

Harrison, Paul M. *Authority and Power in the Free Church Tradition: A Social Case Study of the American Baptist Convention.* Princeton, N.J.: Princeton University Press, 1959.

_____. "Church and Laity Among Protestants." *Annals of the American Academy of Political and Social Science*, 332 (November 1960), 37-49.

Hendrix, John. "Toward a Theology of Organization." Unpublished paper, Baptist Sunday School Board, 1971.

Herberg, Will. *Protestant—Catholic—Jew: An Essay in American Religious Sociology.* New York: Anchor Books, 1960.

Johnson, Roy Harold. "American Baptists in the Age of Big Business." *Journal of Religion*, 11 (January 1931), 63-85.

Leach, William H. "Financing the Local Church." *Annals of the American Academy of Political and Social Science*, 332 (November 1960), 70-79.

Lee, Robert. "The Organizational Dilemma in American Protestantism." *Ethics and Bigness: Scientific, Academic, Religious, Political, and Military*, ed. Harlan Cleveland and Harold D. Lasswell. New York: Conference on Science, Philosophy and Religion in their Relation to the Democratic Way of Life, Inc., 1962.

Lenski, Gerhard. *The Religious Factor: A Sociological Study of Religion's Impact on Politics, Economics, and Family Life.* Garden City, N.Y.: Doubleday, 1961.

Luckmann, Thomas. *The Invisible Religion: The Problem of Religion in Modern Society.* New York: Macmillan, 1967.

"Lutherans Centralize." *Christian Century*, 71 (November 27, 1954), 1295-97.

Martin, David. *The Religious and the Secular.* London: Routledge and Kegan Paul, 1969.

Martin, William C. "The Baptists Want You!" *Texas Monthly*, 5 (February 1977), 82-87, 149-57.

Marty, Martin E. *The Modern Schism: Three Paths to the Secular.* New York: Harper & Row, 1969.

Moberg, David O. *The Church as a Social Institution: The Sociology of American Religion.* Englewood Cliffs, N.J.: Prentice Hall, 1962.

Niebuhr, H. Richard. *The Purpose of the Church and Its Ministry.* New York: Harper, 1956.

_____. *The Social Sources of Denominationalism.* New York: World Publishing Co., 1929.

Pearson, Samuel C. "From Church to Denomination: American Congregationalism in the Nineteenth Century." *Church History,* 38 (March 1969), 67-87.

Scotfield, John R. "The Perils of Ecclesiastical Bigness." *Christian Century,* 76 (November 4, 1959), 1276-78.

Shiner, Larry E. "The Concept of Secularization in Empirical Research." *The Social Meanings of Religion,* ed. William M. Newman. Chicago: Rand McNally, 1974.

Szasz, Ferenc M. "Protestantism and the Search for Stability: Liberal and Conservative Quests for a Christian America, 1875-1925." *Building the Organizational Society: Essays on Associational Activities in Modern America,* ed. Jerry Israel. New York: Free Press, 1972.

Weber, Max. *The Protestant Ethic and the Spirit of Capitalism.* New York: Scribners, 1958.

_____. *The Sociology of Religion.* Boston: Beacon Press, 1963.

Winter, Gibson. "Religious Organization." *The Emergent American Society: Large-Scale Organization,* ed. W. Lloyd Warner. New Haven: Yale University Press, 1967.

_____. *The Suburban Captivity of the Churches.* Garden City, N.J.: Doubleday, 1961.

Yinger, J. Milton. *Religion, Society and the Individual.* New York: Macmillan, 1957.

G. General American History

Allen, Frederick Lewis. *The Big Change: America Transforms Itself, 1900-1950.* New York: Harper, 1952.

Blum, John Morton. *The Republican Roosevelt.* New York: Atheneum, 1971.

Boorstin, Daniel J. *The Americans.* 3 vols. New York: Random House, 1958-1973.

_____. *The Genius of American Politics.* Chicago: University of Chicago Press, 1953.

Bruchey, Stuart. *The Roots of American Economic Growth, 1607-1861: An Essay in Social Causation.* New York: Harper & Row, 1965

Chandler, Alfred D., Jr. and Louis Galambos. "The Development of Large-Scale Economic Organizations in Modern America." *Journal of Economic History*, 30 (March 1970), 201-17.

_____. "Origins of Progressive Leadership" *Letters of Theodore Roosevelt* ed. Elting G. Morison. VIII, Appendix III.

_____. *Strategy and Structure: Chapters in the History of the Industrial Enterprise.* Cambridge: MIT Press, 1962.

Cochran, Thomas C. and William Miller. *The Age of Enterprise: A Social History of Industrial America.* New York: Harper and Row, 1961.

_____. *Business in American Life: A History.* New York: McGraw-Hill, 1972

Commager, Henry Steele. *The American Mind: An Interpretation of American Thought and Character Since the 1880s.* New Haven: Yale University Press, 1954.

Croly, Herbert. *The Promise of American Life.* Cambridge: Belknap Press, 1965.

Cuff, Robert D. "American Historians and the Organizational Factor." *Canadian Review of American Studies.* 4 (Spring 1973), 19-23.

Curti, Merle. *The Growth of American Thought.* New York: Harper, 1943.

_____. *The Social Ideals of American Educators.* New York: Scribners, 1935.

Dangerfield, George. *The Awakening of American Nationalism, 1818-1828.* New York: Harper, 1965.

Faulkner, Harold U. *The Quest for Social Justice.* New York: Macmillan, 1931.

Freidel, Frank. *America in the Twentieth Century.* New York: Knopf, 1960.

Gabriel, Ralph H. *The Course of American Democratic Thought: An Intellectual History Since 1815.* New York: Ronald Press, 1940.

Galambos, Louis. "The Emerging Organizational Synthesis in Modern American History." *Business History Review,* 44 (Autumn 1970), 279-90.

Galbraith, John Kenneth. *American Capitalism: The Countervailing Power.* Boston: Houghton-Mifflin, 1952.

Goldman, Eric. *Rendezvous with Destiny: A History of Modern American Reform.* New York: Knopf, 1952.

Greene, Theodore P. *America's Heroes: The Changing Models of Success in American Magazines.* New York: Oxford, 1970.

Grob, Gerald N. *Workers and Utopia: A Study of Ideological Conflict in the American Labor Movement.* Evanston, Ill.: Northwestern University Press, 1961.

Gusfield, Joseph R. *Symbolic Crusade: Social Politics and the American Temperance Movement.* Urbana: University of Illinois Press, 1963.

Hall, Tom G. "Agricultural History and the 'Organizational Synthesis': A Review Essay." *Agricultural History,* 48 (April 1974), 313-25.

Hays, Samuel P. *Conservation and the Gospel of Efficiency: The Progressive Conservation Movement, 1890-1920.* Cambridge: Harvard University Press, 1959.

_____. *The Response to Industrialism, 1885-1914.* Chicago: University of Chicago Press, 1957.

Haber, Samuel. *Efficiency and Uplift: Scientific Management in the Progressive Era, 1890-1920.* Chicago: University of Chicago Press, 1964.

Higham, John "Hanging Together: Divergent Unities in American History." *Journal of American History,* 61 (June 1974), 5-28.

Hobsbawm, Eric. J. *Labouring Men: Studies in the History of Labour.* New York: Basic Books, 1964.

Hofstadter, Richard. *The Age of Reform: From Bryan to F. D. R.* New York: Vintage, 1955.

Israel, Jerry, ed. *Building the Organizational Society: Essays on Associational Activities in Modern America.* New York: Free Press, 1972.

Johnson, Arthur M. "Theodore Roosevelt and the Bureau of Corporations." *Mississippi Valley Historical Review,* 45 (March 1959), 571-90.

Karl, Barry Dean. *Executive Reorganization and Reform in the New Deal: The Genesis of Administrative Management, 1900-1939.* Cambridge: Harvard University Press, 1963.

Kolko, Gabriel. *Railroads and Regulation, 1877-1916.* Princeton: Princeton University Press, 1965.

_____. *The Triumph of Conservatism: A Reinterpretation of American History, 1900-1916.* New York: Free Press, 1963.

Kuznets, Simon. "Notes on the Patterns of U. S. Economic Growth." *The Nation's Economic Objectives,* ed. Edgar O. Edwards. Chicago: University of Chicago Press, 1964.

Lippmann, Walter. *A Preface to Morals.* New York: Macmillan, 1929.

Lipset, Seymour M. *First New Nation: The United States in Historical and Comparative Perspective.* New York: Basic Books, 1963.

Lubove, Roy. *The Professional Altruist: The Emergence of Social Work as a Career, 1880-1930.* Cambridge: Harvard University Press, 1965.

_____. *The Progressives and the Slums: Tenement House Reform in New York City, 1890-1917.* Pittsburgh: University of Pittsburgh Press, 1962.

Lynd, Robert S. and Helen Merrell. *Middletown, A Study in American Culture.* New York: Harcourt Brace, 1929.

Mills, C. Wright. *White Collar: The American Middle Classes.* New York: Oxford, 1956.

Morison, Samuel Eliot and Henry Steele Commager. *The Growth of the American Republic.* 2 vols. New York: Oxford, 1962.

Mowry, George. "The California Progressive and His Rationale: A Study in Middle Class Politics." *Mississippi Valley Historical Review,* 36 (September 1949), 239-50.

_____. *The Era of Theodore Roosevelt, and the Birth of Modern America, 1900-1912.* New York: Harper & Row, 1958.

Nadworny, Milton J. *Scientific Management and the Unions, 1900-1932.* Cambridge: Harvard University Press, 1955.

North, Douglass C. *The Economic Growth of the United States, 1790-1860.* Englewood Cliffs, N.J.: Prentice Hall, 1961.

Pinkett, Harold T. "The Keep Commission, 1905-1909: A Rooseveltian Effort for Administrative Reform." *Journal of American History,* 52 (September 1965), 297-312.

Raucher, Alan R. *Public Relations and Business, 1900-1929.* Baltimore: Johns Hopkins University Press, 1968.

Riesman, David, et. al. *The Lonely Crowd: A Study of the Changing American Character.* New Haven: Yale University Press, 1950.

Spring, David. "The Clapham Sect: Some Social and Political Aspects." *Victorian Studies,* 5 (September 1961), 35-48.

_____. "Aristocracy, Religion and Social Structure in Early Victorian England." *Victorian Studies,* 6 (March 1963), 263-80.

Taylor, George Rogers. *The Transportation Revolution, 1815-1860.* New York: Holt, Rinehart and Winston, 1951.

Thompson, Edward P. *The Making of the English Working Classes.* New York: Pantheon Books, 1964.

Timberlake, James H. *Prohibition and the Progressive Movement, 1900-1920.* Cambridge: Harvard University Press, 1963.

Turner, Frederick Jackson. *The Rise of the New West, 1819-1927.* New York: Collier, 1962.

United States Bureau of the Census. *Historical Statistics of the United States: Colonial Times to 1970.* Washington: Bureau of the Census, 1975.

Vatter, Harold G. *The Drive to Industrial Maturity: The United States Economy, 1860-1914.* Westport, CT: Greenwood Press, 1975.

Weinstein, James. *The Corporate Ideal in the Liberal State: 1900-1918.* Boston: Beacon Press, 1968.

Whyte, William H., Jr. *The Organization Man.* Garden City, N. Y.: Doubleday, 1956.

Wiebe, Robert M. *Businessmen and Reform: A Study of the Progressive Movement.* Cambridge: Harvard University Press, 1962.

_____. *The Search for Order, 1877-1920.* New York: Hill & Wang, 1967.

_____. *The Segmented Society: An Introduction to the Meaning of America.* New York: Oxford, 1975.

Woodward, C. Vann. *Origins of the New South, 1877-1913.* Baton Rouge: LSU Press, 1951.

H.   Organizational Theory

Barber, Bernard. "Some Problems in the Sociology of the Professions." *Daedelus,* 92 (Fall 1963), 669-88.

Barnard, Chester I. *The Functions of the Executive.* Cambridge: Harvard University Press, 1938.

Blau, Peter M. *Bureaucracy in Modern Society.* New York Random House, 1956.

_____., and William G. Scott. *Formal Organizations: A Comparative Approach.* San Francisco: Chandler, 1962.

Boulding, Kenneth E. *The Organizational Revolution: A Study in the Ethics of Economic Organization.* Chicago: Quadrangle Books, 1968.

Caplow, Theodore. "Organizational Size." *Administrative Science Quarterly,* 1 (March 1957) 484-505.

Constas, Helen. "Max Weber's Two Conceptions of Bureaucracy." *American Journal of Sociology,* 63 (January 1958), 400-49.

Eisenstadt, S. N. "Bureaucracy, Bureaucratization, and Debureaucratization." *Administrative Science Quarterly,* 4 (December 1959), 302-320.

Etzioni, Amitai. *A Comparative Analysis of Complex Organization: On Power, Involvement and their Correlates.* New York: Free Press, 1961.

Gouldner, Alvin W. "Metaphysical Pathos and the Theory of Democracy." *American Political Science Review,* 49 (June 1955), 496-507.

Hall, Richard H., ed. *The Formal Organization.* New York: Basic Books, 1972.

_____ . "Professionalization and Bureaucratization." *American Sociological Review,* 33 (February 1968), 92-104.

Hughes, Everett C. "Professions." *Daedelus,* 92 (Fall 1963), 655-668.

Reissman, Leonard. "A Study of Role Concepts in a Bureaucracy." *Social Forces,* 27 (March 1949), 305-10.

Scott, William G. and Terence R. Mitchell. *Organization Theory: A Structural and Behavioral Analysis.* Homewood, IL: Irwin-Dorsey, 1972.

Selznick, Philip. "An Approach to a Theory of Bureaucracy." *American Sociological Review,* 8 (February 1943), 47-54.

Wardwell, Walter I. "Social Integration, Bureaucratization, and the Professions." *Social Forces,* 33 (May 1955), 356-59.

Weber, Max. *The Theory of Social and Economic Organization.* New York: Oxford, 1947.

INDEX

Addams, Jane, 97
Administration, agency: centralization of,
135-43; departmentalization of, 127-
34; diversification of, 52-53; growth
of, 142; problems of, 52-55; solutions
to problems of, 55-56
African Jubilee Campaign, 98
Agency structure: administrative problems
of, 52-56; adoption of bureaucratic
administration by, 127-48; adoption
of ideology of organization by, 68-82;
adoption of systematic finance by,
93-120; attacks on, 167-75; causes of
development of, 17-19; defined, 13;
denomination differences in, 37-38,
155, 160-63; in 1876, 35-37; finance
of, 36-37; financial problems of, 46-
52; growth of, 44-45; internal
coordination of, 133-34, 157-58,
160-62; internal resistance to change
in, 55-56; legitimation of, 155-67;
over-organization of, 168; unrespon-
siveness of, 169; preconditions for
development of, 14-16; use of by
denominations, 20-23, 25n, 38-39;
use of by Evangelical United Front,
19-22. See also Administration,
agency; Interagency competition
Allan, Ethan, 17
American Christian Missionary Society:
administrative problems of, 52-56;
centralization of, 135-37, 140-41;
departmentalization of, 130-34;
desire for centralized organization,
78-80; desire for efficiency, 74-76;
desire for publicity, 77-78; desire for
specialization, 76-77; desire for
system, 70-74; financial problems of,
46-52; formation of, 34; growth of,
44-45; legitimation of, 158-67;
problems of authority, 155-58; use of
fundraising drives, 94-101; use of
specialists, 143-48; use of systematic
finance, 101-13.
Andrews, George Arthur, 97
Annual Collections, 36; efforts to intensify,
47; problems of, 47-50; replacement
of with systematic finance, 101-02.
Annuities and Legacies, 36, 104
Apportionment Plan, 48, 52, 60n. See also
Finance
Arminian theology: as a precondition of
agency structure, 16
Arnold, H. W., 96

Authority, bureaucratic: problems of, 155-
58; response to problems of
(legitimation), 158-67
Authority, individual (leadership): replacement of charismatic by bureaucratic,
143-48, 168

Babson, Roger, 97, 115, 119
Baptist Sunday School Board: administrative
problems of, 52-56; centralization of,
135-37, 139-40; departmentalization
of, 130-34; desire for centralized
organization, 78-80; desire for
efficiency, 74-76; desire for publicity,
77-78; desire for specialization, 76-77;
desire for system, 70-74; financial
problems of, 46-52; formation of, 32;
growth of, 45; legitimation of, 158-
67; problems of authority, 155-58;
use of fund raising drives, 94-101;
use of specialists, 143-48; use of
systematic finance, 101-13
Baptists. See Landmark Baptists
Barlow, Joel, 15, 17
Barton, Bruce, 97, 119
Beard, William S., 120
Beatty, Admiral David, 99
Beauchamp, Harvey (Field Secretary,
BSSB), 53
Beecher, Lyman, 17
Berger, Peter L., 8-9
Bloom, Bob, 185
Boorstin, Daniel J., 16
Boudinot, Elias, 19
Brunner, Edmund deS., 173, 174
Bryan, William Jennings, 97
Bureaucratization: defined, 1-2; and
impersonality, 1-2, 161. See also
Administration, agency; Agency
structure; Authority, bureaucratic
Bureaucratization of the church: causes of,
1, 4, 7; effects on American Protes-
tantism, 1, 4, 7, 185-90; nature of,
1, 13
Burleson, Hugh (Assistant Secretary,
D&FMS), 134
Burnham, Frederick W. (President, UCMS),
142, 163
Bushnell, Horace, 17
Business: role in shaping ideology of organi-
zation, 65; role in forming agency
structure, 19-20
Business methods: in church administration,